I0819303

THE

SCONE QUEEN

BAKES

SconeQueen

THE SCONE QUEEN BAKES

100 Recipes for Scones, Muffins, Cookies, and Cakes from the Founder of The Hungry Gnome

DANIELLE SEPSY

PHOTOGRAPHS BY NICO SCHINCO

Alfred A. Knopf
New York
2026

A BORZOI BOOK
FIRST HARDCOVER EDITION
PUBLISHED BY ALFRED A. KNOPF 2026

Published by Alfred A. Knopf, a division of Penguin Random House LLC, 1745 Broadway, New York, NY 10019.

Knopf, Borzoi Books, and the colophon are registered trademarks of Penguin Random House LLC.

Library of Congress Cataloging-in-Publication Data
Names: Sepsy, Danielle, author. | Schinco, Nico, photographer.
Title: The Scone Queen bakes : 100 recipes for scones, muffins, cookies, and cakes from the founder of the hungry gnome / Danielle Sepsy; photographs by Nico Schinco.
Description: First edition. | New York: Alfred A. Knopf, 2026. | Includes index.
Identifiers: LCCN 2025002896 | ISBN 9780593801642 (hardcover) | ISBN 9780593801659 (epub)
Subjects: LCSH: Baking. | Scones. | Muffins. | Cake. | Bread. | Desserts. | Pastry. | LCGFT: Cookbooks.
Classification: LCC TX763.S399 2026 | DDC 641.7/1—dc23/eng/20250208
LC record available at https://lccn.loc.gov/2025002896

Book design by Deb Wood

penguinrandomhouse.com | aaknopf.com

Printed in China
10 9 8 7 6 5 4 3 2

Some of the recipes in this book may include raw eggs, meat, or fish. When these foods are consumed raw, there is always the risk that bacteria, which is killed by proper cooking, may be present. For this reason, when serving these foods raw, always buy certified salmonella-free eggs and the freshest meat and fish available from a reliable grocer, storing them in the refrigerator until they are served. Because of the health risks associated with the consumption of bacteria that can be present in raw eggs, meat, and fish, these foods should not be consumed by infants, small children, pregnant women, the elderly, or any persons who may be immunocompromised. The author and publisher expressly disclaim responsibility for any adverse effects that may result from the use or application of the recipes and information contained in this book.

The authorized representative in the EU for product safety and compliance is Penguin Random House Ireland, Morrison Chambers, 32 Nassau Street, Dublin D02 YH68, Ireland, https://eu-contact.penguin.ie.

Lincoln

To my **HUNGRY GNOME** team,
who work tirelessly each and every day and with so much passion
and care: I couldn't do it without you.

To my **PARENTS**,
who taught me that success is no
accident: You showed me what it
means to work hard,
to be committed, loyal, and selfless,
both personally and professionally.

To my sister **CHRISTIANA**,
for putting my head between
my legs on the school bus when
my anxiety was too hard to bear:
You will forever be the breath
that fills my lungs.

To my sister **JULIA**,
for always reminding me that
blood is thicker than water.

To my husband, **DAN**,
who went out in the middle of
the night to buy eggs and delivered
scones on a bike without question:
You keep me grounded.

To **GRANDMA ANITA**,
for always telling me to
"follow my dreams."

To **GRANDPA JIM**,
who fed me cookies for lunch
and helped me discover
my sweet tooth.

To **GRANDPA CARMINE**,
for showing us what true love
and commitment really look like.

And to **GRANDMA ROSEMARIE**
in heaven, for being the shining light that guides me
both in and out of the kitchen:
This book is for you.

INTRODUCTION xi

THE ROYAL PANTRY xxii

CHAPTER 1
Scones 1

CHAPTER 2
Muffins 41

CHAPTER 3
Cookies 62

CHAPTER 4
Brownies & Bars 121

CHAPTER 5
Rolls & Breads 139

CHAPTER 6
Quick Breads & Snacking Cakes 192

ACKNOWLEDGMENTS 243

INDEX 245

INTRODUCTION

My parents knew I was different when I begged for a KitchenAid stand mixer for Christmas at the age of eight. Most kids that young would cry at the sight of anything other than a toy or game when opening a holiday gift—but for me, receiving this shiny blue machine was a joyous event. This whirring kitchen appliance was like some kind of fantastic magic set that would allow me to transform simple substances into wondrous confectionary delights. I carefully tied on my new "Chef Danielle" apron as if it were a magician's cape, and, after a few waves of my rubber spatula wand, a cake eventually appeared from my oven like a rabbit from the proverbial hat. With deftness and sleight of hand, I learned to shuffle spices, flour, and flavorings in ways that went on to surprise and thrill friends and family.

My passion for food and cooking was passed down to me through three generations of my Italian family. I loved to watch my mother and grandmothers work their own magic in the kitchen, as they formed perfect meatballs in the palms of their hands, chopped fresh herbs on a large wooden cutting board, created delicate pastry leaves to top a perfect apple pie, and turned my Sunday morning pancakes into perfect silhouettes of Mickey and Minnie. Food has always been an integral part of who we are as a family. Good food nurtures the soul. It can inspire a conversation with a stranger in line at the market and reunite distant friends and relatives. It's that glimmer in a toddler's eye when she blows out the candles on a pink birthday cake adorned with images of her favorite princess. Food is the centerpiece of togetherness and fond memories.

My discovery of media personalities like Martha Stewart only increased my enthusiasm for all things cooking and baking. I can still remember flipping through my first issue of *Martha Stewart Living* magazine at age eight and grinning from ear to ear. If there was a snow day, you'd better believe I was in front of the TV watching Martha, along with *Lidia's Italian Table* and *Ciao Italia* with Mary Ann Esposito. To this day I still have the tiny scraps of loose-leaf paper on which I frantically jotted down all those recipes, pre-internet. While other kids wore T-shirts with the images of the Backstreet Boys or 'NSYNC, I could be seen roaming the halls of junior high wearing a shirt with a photo of Martha Stewart above the words "*Martha is my Homegirl.*" I realize this wasn't the trendiest wardrobe choice for a teen, but I didn't care—I was not afraid to show everyone my "pop stars."

Every free moment I had—between going to school, taking dance lessons, and hanging out with friends—was spent in the kitchen. The large wooden island was my stage and I danced around it, creating brownies, cookies, cakes, roasted chickens, potatoes—you name it. The possibilities are endless when it comes to food, which was (and is) part of the thrill. I thank my mother for trusting me to experiment in the kitchen on my own from a very young age—despite the obvious dangers presented by sharp knives, spinning mixer blades, and hot ovens. Somehow, I survived with all my fingers and only a few minor burns!

When I was thirteen years old, I created my now-famous scone recipe. One night, after a lot of experimentation, I presented ten different varieties of scones to my family on a wooden board, as if I was on some kind of television cooking competition. Their reactions proved that I had found something special. The next day I created business cards on my computer and, armed with a batch of freshly baked scones in a linen-lined basket, this thirteen-year-old girl (with often debilitating anxiety) marched into local bagel shops, farm stands, and cafés to hand out samples to skeptical owners. By the time I returned home, there were already voicemail messages begging for what they said were "the best scones" they had ever had. I was in business. That summer, I woke up hours before the sun rose to make the scones and write down orders, inventory, and supplies in a black-and-white-marbled notebook (which my mom still has). I was still too young to drive, so on their way to work, my parents delivered the hot scones in disposable pans covered in paper towels and foil. Eventually, I was forced to put the business on hiatus when I went off to college—but I always hoped I would come back to it.

> "Armed with a batch of freshly baked scones in a linen-lined basket, this thirteen-year-old girl . . . marched into local bagel shops, farm stands, and cafés."

I received my degree in Hospitality Management at Penn State University and then went on to graduate with distinction from the International Culinary Center. After graduation, I worked for several years as a food and beverage manager at three of the most prestigious hotels in New York City—the Waldorf Astoria, the Plaza, and the Peninsula—where I managed events for the rich and famous, including US presidents,

foreign royalty, fashion icons, and the Hollywood elite. Catering (literally) to the tastes (and egos) of such distinguished clientele was often a fun and exciting learning experience, but it didn't give me the same satisfaction that I got from serving up my own creations in my little home business. After all, I was peddling someone else's food, and I longed for the chance to show what I could do. Like many people, however, I was afraid to leave the security of a good job in order to take on the risks of starting my own business. Soon, however, that tough decision was made for me.

> "I was afraid to leave the security of a good job. . . . Soon, however, that tough decision was made for me."

In 2020, after leaving the hotel industry to work at a high-end corporate event company in New York City, I suddenly and unexpectedly found myself unemployed due to "corporate restructuring," and it was unknowingly on the eve of the COVID-19 pandemic. Unprepared for the layoff, I went home and tearfully wallowed in self-pity—that is, until my husband and my family reminded me that this was finally the opportunity to start my own baked goods business. After all, I had nothing to lose! Soon The Hungry Gnome was born. For those of you wondering where the name came from, I was inspired by my older sister, Christiana, who secretly had a gnome collection when we were growing up. Gnomes and the world that surrounds them felt rustic yet elegant, classic yet whimsical, all things I envisioned for my baked goods and their branding. The very same night that I lost my job, with tears streaming down my face, I began my mission. I stalked LinkedIn and found the contact information for Jonathan Rubinstein, the founder of Joe Coffee, one of the most popular coffee chains in the city, and told him about my baked goods, offering to bring him some samples. After some hesitation he agreed, and three days later I was in their corporate office with boxes of pastries I had made in my one-bedroom apartment, in a tabletop convection oven (the gas in my apartment had been out for two years, so this toaster-size oven was all I had, but that's another story). That evening I received an email from Jonathan that changed my life forever:

> *Good afternoon. I finally got to the office about an hour ago. First of all, I cannot believe how generous you were. I expected a total of six scones, not six boxes. More importantly, a number of us tested through what you sent and I heard everything from "This is the best thing I've ever eaten" to "This is the best scone I have ever had." Everything was truly amazing. I'm going to talk further with my team today or tomorrow to see how to pilot this and to talk about operations. Thanks! —Jonathan*

I was on my way! Suddenly, I had a customer with twenty cafés, but no infrastructure or systems in place in order to supply him with my products. Due to the pandemic, however, Joe Coffee and other café chains had temporarily closed locations, which was somewhat of a blessing for me because it bought me time to get my wholesale operation set up and to save some money before I had some major overhead costs.

In the interim, I was selling direct to consumer via my website, baking dozens of orders per day in my apartment and then enlisting my husband and neighbors to help me walk the boxes over to the nearest FedEx. In the evenings I was also meeting local customers on street corners, at subway entrances, and even at their front doors to drop off orders, and my husband was zipping down (a very quiet, pandemic version of) Park Avenue on a bike to do more drop-offs. I'll never forget the time when he hit a pothole and went flying over the handlebars, causing the freshly baked scones to catapult out of their boxes and shatter all over the street. Dan still jokes that I first asked if the scones were okay before asking if *he* was okay—whoops! These were truly "interesting" times, living in a scone factory barely fit for a couple to live in, especially when my poor husband was simultaneously trying to focus on his work. Scone-making wasn't his job, after all, he's a landscape architect, and this was not what he signed up for.

We now look back on these "dark times" and laugh, but we can also now appreciate that this enabled me to keep up with the demand until I had the means to rent space in a shared commercial kitchen. By July of 2020 I found a shared kitchen in Long Island City and was able to hire a team of skilled employees who had lost their jobs due to the pandemic, some of whom had been laid off from that very company who let me go a few months prior. I leased my first car and slapped a Hungry Gnome logo magnet proudly on the passenger door, only for the magnet to be stolen about four hours later. But hey, at least I knew my logo was cute?!

> "Suddenly, I had a customer with twenty cafés, but no infrastructure or systems in place in order to supply him with my products."

The first night in the commercial kitchen still haunts me today. It may have been one of the worst nights of my life. I had two wonderful skilled and positive bakers with me ready to take on the challenge of baking for twenty coffee shops. That night we left at 3 a.m. and I sobbed, because there was no way this pace would be sustainable or profitable! Twenty coffee shops seemed like an impossible feat, and to be honest, I almost gave up. To my surprise, the next evening it took four hours less! The moral of this story is, give yourself some damn grace! It takes time to get organized, come up with

a system, and get into a groove. It wasn't easy, as it took some patience, more labor, and up-front costs, but in no time we were bumpin' out hundreds, and then thousands, of baked goods daily. Through word of mouth and the support of our distribution partners, within a couple years' time, The Hungry Gnome quickly grew into one of the most popular and well-respected wholesale bakeries in the city.

> "I longed for recognition for my craft and some reassurance that I was on the right path."

In November of 2021, I saw the opportunity to share my love of all things baking when I responded to a casting call for a new cooking competition show created and hosted by the beloved *Schitt's Creek* star Dan Levy. After a four-month casting process, I was selected from thousands of talented chefs across the United States to compete with nine other contestants in *The Big Brunch,* which would be broadcast on HBO Max. On March 5, 2022, just three days before my thirty-second birthday, I anxiously made my way to Hollywood. As someone whose anxiety stems from a feeling of lack of control, or fearing the unknown, I felt extremely uneasy getting on that plane. It was my dream to be on a show like this, so why did I feel so sick? I think it just felt so "major," and that so much was on the line here. I wasn't seeking fame, but I longed for recognition for my craft and some reassurance that I was on the right path with The Hungry Gnome. I thought that if I got far enough in the competition, perhaps my life and the course of the business could change overnight . . . and it did.

The show proved to be unique among American cooking competition programs. Rather than the contrived backstabbing "drama" of typical reality shows, the vibe was respectful, inclusive, celebratory, and downright beautiful. We taped eight episodes over the course of a demanding four-week period—and I made nine new best friends *and* showcased my baking skills to a national audience. Needless to say, hearing culinary icon Sohla El-Waylly and renowned restaurateur Will Guidara crown me as "The Scone Queen" on national television—and hearing a tearful Dan Levy proclaim my Peanut Butter and Jelly Cinnamon Bun as "the best thing I have ever eaten in *my life*!"—was a true validation of my hard work and dedication. These were judges whom I respected and idolized! To think that four weeks prior I was just hoping to make it past the first episode and then to my surprise I came in second place in a very tight race. It still blows my mind. Every few months I put on the show just to prove to myself that it really did happen.

With this newfound confidence that I gained from the show, in 2023 I built a 5,000-square-foot commercial kitchen in Long Island City for The Hungry Gnome and expanded my team of "Gnomies." This new chapter of my career has been the most rewarding part of this journey.

I have achieved my goal of feeding my scones and baked goods to thousands of people each day. But there was another thing I wanted to do. I had always dreamed the day would come when I could share my love for baking with an even wider audience through a cookbook. Now I sit here, writing in my home in Garden City, New York, the very home that once belonged to my Grandma Rosemarie. The very home where I held my first whisk, rolled my first cookie dough, and heard the unmistakable howl of Julia Child's voice project through the television set. Although Grandma Rosemarie and Julia Child are no longer with us, I felt their spirits come through me as I concocted each recipe and as I signed on the dotted line to be published by *the* Alfred A. Knopf, who published Julia's *Mastering the Art of French Cooking* in 1961.

Here is my book, from my kitchen to yours: a compilation of my greatest hits, many containing secrets I once thought I would take to the grave. I bake because it brings me peace and joy, while simultaneously allowing me to express myself in a creative way that brings me closer to the ones I love. I want to share those feelings—and the baked results—with all of you.

I now officially invite you to the royal court of the Scone Queen! I hope you and your family find these bakes and the stories that go along with them as nostalgic and comforting as I do.

"I had always dreamed the day would come when I would share my love for baking with an even wider audience through a cookbook."

THE ROYAL PANTRY

Here are the staple ingredients I always have on hand in my baking pantry. Stocking these ingredients and preferred brands will ensure you are successful when baking from this book.

Flours & Powders

- All-purpose flour
- Bread flour
- Cake flour (not self-rising; I recommend Swans Down)
- Fine cornmeal
- Blanched almond flour
- Cornstarch
- Baking soda (I use Arm & Hammer)
- Baking powder (I highly recommend Davis)
- Dark Dutch-process cocoa powder, preferably Hershey's Special Dark (using something different can cause discrepancies)
- Jell-O instant vanilla pudding mix
- Jell-O instant chocolate fudge pudding mix

Sugars & Sweeteners

- Granulated sugar (I use Domino)
- Dark brown sugar (I use Domino)
- Powdered sugar
- Raw or turbinado sugar (I like Sugar in the Raw)
- Pure maple syrup
- Molasses (I use Grandma's)
- Clover honey

 SCONE QUEEN TIP 

This does not list every single ingredient in this book, but these are the most commonly used items.

Oils & Fats

- Canola or vegetable oil
- Vegetable shortening (I use Crisco sticks)
- Butter (see Refrigerated)

Chocolate & Mix-Ins

- Semisweet chocolate chips (I use Nestlé Toll House)
- Mini semisweet chocolate chips (I use Nestlé Toll House)
- Bittersweet chocolate chips (I use Ghirardelli)
- Peanut butter chips (I use Reese's)
- White chocolate chips (I use Nestlé Toll House)
- Unsweetened chocolate (I use Baker's)
- Shelled walnuts
- Shelled pecans
- Shelled lightly salted roasted pistachios (I use Kirkland)
- Almonds: slivered, whole, and sliced
- Sweetened coconut flakes (I use Baker's)
- Rainbow sprinkles and nonpareils
- Food coloring (primary colors: red, blue, yellow, and green)
- Canned pumpkin puree (I use Libby's always!)
- Canned crushed pineapple (I use Dole)
- Whole rolled oats
- Raisins
- Dried Zante currants

Extracts & Spices

- Pure vanilla extract (I use Kirkland)
- Vanilla bean paste (I use Nielsen-Massey)
- Pure almond extract
- Pure lemon extract
- Coconut extract (I use McCormick)
- Ground cinnamon
- Ground nutmeg
- Ground ginger
- Ground allspice
- Ground cloves
- Fine table salt (Red Cross iodized salt is my favorite)
- Poppy seeds

Refrigerated

- Unsalted butter (Plugra, Kirkland, or Land O'Lakes are some of my favorites)
- Heavy cream
- Whole milk
- Large eggs
- Full-fat sour cream (I prefer Daisy or Fage)
- Active dry yeast: I keep the envelopes in my pantry at room temperature, but for the yeast in a jar, once opened I keep it in the fridge (I highly recommend Fleischmann's)

Spreads & Preserves

- Nutella
- Creamy peanut butter (I like Skippy or Reese's)
- Lotus Biscoff spread, speculoos butter, or other cookie butter
- Strawberry preserves (I like Smucker's)
- Raspberry preserves (I like Smucker's or Bonne Maman)
- Apricot preserves (I like Smucker's)
- Applesauce (I use Mott's Original)

CHAPTER 1

SCONES

THE ART OF THE SCONE . . . 3

12 MONTHS OF SCONES . . . 6

- January: Classic Vanilla Bean Scones . . . 8
  - Vanilla Bean Glaze . . . 9
- February: Red Bean Scones with a Sesame Crust . . . 12
- March: Danielle's Birthday Confetti Scones . . . 14
- April: Coconut Chocolate Chunk Scones . . . 17
- May: Lavender Lemon Scones . . . 18
- June: Strawberry Cornmeal Scones . . . 20
- July: Blueberry White Chocolate Scones . . . 23
- August: Peach Almond Scones . . . 24
- September: Apple Walnut Scones . . . 27
- October: Butter Pecan Scones . . . 28
- November: Cranberry Orange Scones . . . 31
- December: THE Chocolate Chip Scones . . . 32

SPREADS & ACCOMPANIMENTS . . . 34

- Honey Butter . . . 35
- Lemon Curd . . . 36
- Raspberry Rose Jam . . . 36
- Easy Clotted Cream . . . 36
- Puppy Scones . . . 39

THE ART OF THE SCONE

5 TIPS TO MASTERING THE ART

It is less about the recipe itself and more about understanding the touch and feel of the dough. You can use my step-by-step process photos for a visual of the dough texture at each stage, but here are some important things to always remember . . .

1 Make sure your dry ingredients are whisked thoroughly to ensure the baking powder is properly distributed before adding the butter.

2 Cold! Cold! COLD! Your butter chunks should be very cold (they don't have to be frozen but just cold, right out of the fridge) when you cut them into the dry ingredients with the pastry cutter. Your heavy cream should also be super cold to keep the dough and butter pieces as cold and present in the dough as possible. After you form your dough into a disc, rule of thumb should be to always pop it into the fridge or freezer for 15 to 20 minutes just to resolidify the butter before you bake the scones.

3 When cutting the butter into the dry ingredients, you want to keep going until the butter is just slightly smaller than pea size. You want to see flecks of butter scattered throughout the dough, because when the dough hits the heat of the oven, the cold butter will melt, creating steam pockets within the scones, creating a moister, more buttery texture. Leaving too large butter pieces in the dough will result in flat or misshaped scones and improper distribution of butter flavor and moisture throughout the dough.

4 Your environment can affect the dough! Depending on the humidity or altitude, you may need to add a touch more heavy cream. If you find when you are incorporating the wet ingredients into the dry that the dough is not coming together into one mass and there appears to be a lot of floury mix at the bottom of the bowl, you may need to add a splash or two of heavy cream to help it come together. The dough should be moist but *not* wet enough that it is really sticking to your hands. This is *not* a "drop" style scone, so the dough does need to be dry enough to form into a disc and slice easily.

5 When gathering the dough together, treat it like it's your fragile, newborn baby. You want to use your hands to gently gather the dough together, but you are never kneading the dough. Kneading the dough will make the butter pieces in the dough melt prematurely, and it will cause the glutens in the dough to develop too much, making a tough, dense, or dry scone.

PREPPING DOUGH IN ADVANCE

All of the scone dough can be made ahead of time and refrigerated for up to 3 days or frozen for up to about 2 months. I like to prep my dough, cut it, and then place the scones in a plastic bag or sealed container in my freezer so I can take individual pieces out and bake as needed. You can bake the scones from frozen by simply egg washing and topping right before baking and then increasing the bake time by 2 to 4 minutes.

Storing and Reheating

Store baked scones in sealed glass or tin containers at room temperature or wrapped in parchment paper and then aluminum foil or plastic wrap and kept at room temperature. I do not like to use plastic Tupperware or plastic bags as they tend to change the taste of the baked goods.

To reheat scones: Preheat the oven to 350°F, place the scone(s) on a baking sheet, and reheat in the oven for 5 to 7 minutes, until they are warmed through.

A Note on Baking

When I'm baking, I always use the convection setting, so I have both convection and bake temperatures listed for each recipe, but it is important to remember that every oven is different and that even the weather can cause discrepancies in your baking from day to day. Here is something to always keep in mind: If your scones or cookies are spreading too much, *raise* your temperature initially. If they are spreading too much on 350°F, try 375°F. Think of it like searing a meatball: The higher temperature will lock in the shape of the scone or cookie earlier on in the baking process, whereas a lower temperature may cause an item to "melt" before it fully bakes, losing its ideal form.

A Note on Baking Trays

I call them "cookie sheets" and "baking sheets," but technically what I use to bake with is a half-sheet pan (roughly 18 × 13 inches), unless otherwise specified.

12 MONTHS OF SCONES

Scone dough is a beautiful blank canvas that can take on all different flavors and aesthetics. I love to celebrate the ingredients and flavors of each season by incorporating them into delicious fresh-baked scones. Follow my Scone Calendar, and you and your loved ones will surely look forward to each delicious treat the next month has in store.

JANUARY

Classic Vanilla Scones & Currant Scones

FEBRUARY

Red Bean Scones with a Sesame Crust

MARCH

Danielle's Birthday Confetti Scones

Coconut Chocolate Chunk Scones

MAY

Lavender Lemon Scones

JUNE

Strawberry Cornmeal Scones

JULY

Blueberry White Chocolate Scones

Peach Almond Scones

SEPTEMBER

Apple Walnut Scones

OCTOBER

Butter Pecan Scones

Cranberry Orange Scones

DECEMBER

THE Chocolate Chip Scones

ILLUSTRATIONS BY DANIELLE AND DAN SEPSY

classic vanilla bean scones

There is no better way to start than with a classic vanilla bean scone and another afternoon tea staple, the currant scone (see Variation on page 9). Sometimes simplicity is best, especially if there are delicious butters and spreads on the table. I prefer currants over raisins here as they are smaller and more delicate, and they scatter beautifully throughout the dough, giving you the perfect pop of natural sweetness in every bite. Master this scone base and then get creative by customizing with different extracts and mix-ins!

MAKES 8 SCONES

2 cups all-purpose flour, plus more for dusting

⅓ cup granulated sugar

1½ teaspoons baking powder

½ teaspoon fine table salt

6 tablespoons (3 ounces) very cold unsalted butter, cut into small cubes

¾ cup cold heavy cream

2 large egg yolks

2 teaspoons vanilla bean paste (see Tip), ½ vanilla bean split lengthwise, or 2 teaspoons pure vanilla extract

Egg wash: 1 egg beaten with 1 tablespoon milk or cream

2 tablespoons raw or turbinado sugar, for sprinkling

Vanilla Bean Glaze (optional; recipe follows)

1 Preheat the oven to 400°F (or 375°F on the convection setting). Line a sheet pan with parchment paper.

2 In a bowl, whisk together the flour, granulated sugar, baking powder, and salt.

3 Using a pastry cutter, cut the cold cubes of butter into the flour mixture until you have pea-size crumbs.

4 In a glass measuring cup (which I prefer, as it has a spout for pouring) or a small bowl, combine the heavy cream, egg yolks, and vanilla bean paste (if using a vanilla bean, scrape in the seeds) and whisk together (with a fork or whisk) until just combined.

5 Using a fork, make a well in the center of the dry ingredients. Pour the cream mixture into the center of the well and stir with the fork from the outside inward, gently, just until the dough comes together. Use your hands to gently gather the dough into a shaggy ball.

6 Dump the dough ball onto a lightly floured surface or piece of parchment paper and use floured hands to flatten the dough ball into a disc 6½ inches in diameter. Wrap the disc in parchment paper or plastic wrap and refrigerate for 20 to 30 minutes, until nice and cold.

7 Remove the dough from the fridge and use a large chef's knife to cut the dough into 8 equal triangular wedges (like a pizza).

8 With a pastry brush, lightly coat the tops of the scones with the egg wash. Generously sprinkle the tops with the raw sugar.

9 Arrange the scones on the lined pan about 1½ inches apart. Transfer to the oven.

10 Bake for 12 minutes. Quickly rotate the pan front to back, reduce the oven temperature to 375°F (or 350°F on the convection setting), and bake for 7 to 9 minutes, until the scones are golden brown on the edges and cooked through.

11 Remove from the oven and let them cool on the pan for 5 minutes before serving.

12 Optional glaze: When the scones are cool, dip the tops of the scones in the glaze and let the excess run off. Place the scones on a wire rack and allow the glaze to dry.

13 Scones are best served warm! To reheat, place in a 350°F oven for 5 to 7 minutes, or until warmed through.

VANILLA BEAN GLAZE (OPTIONAL)

1 cup powdered sugar, sifted

Pinch of fine table salt

¼ teaspoon vanilla bean paste

2 to 3 tablespoons heavy cream or milk

In a small bowl, whisk together the powdered sugar, salt, and vanilla bean paste. Add the cream 1 tablespoon at a time, until the glaze is loose but still fairly opaque.

STORAGE: **Store in an airtight container or wrapped in parchment paper and then aluminum foil at room temperature for up to 3 days. Store any extra glaze in a sealed container in the fridge for up to a week. Add more water as needed.**

VARIATION: **Stir ⅔ cup dried Zante currants (preferably Sunmaid) into the flour/butter mixture in step 3, tossing to coat well. The rest of the recipe is the same.**

SCONE QUEEN TIP

Vanilla bean paste has a more robust vanilla flavor than vanilla extract, and the specks of seeds enhance the overall look of the scones when you break into them.

PYREX

red bean scones with a sesame crust

My hometown, Saint James, New York, had a surprisingly decent amount of tasty fast-casual and quick-service Chinese restaurants. I always loved the rich, umami flavors of Asian cuisine, especially because it was so different from the tomato sauce–clad dishes that frequented our dining room table. My father is a lawyer and worked in Manhattan for a good chunk of his career, giving him a more dynamic palate than some of my other family members. I will never forget when he took me to my first Japanese restaurant and ordered a "sushi boat." My mother often fears the unfamiliar when it comes to food and requires a bit of coercing, but even eight-year-old me was able to defy this trait and found trying new foods thrilling. I immediately fell in love with sushi, and to this day, I still can't get enough. When it was time for dessert, my dad ordered two scoops of green tea ice cream and two scoops of red bean ice cream. When it came to the table I was shocked to see that the red bean ice cream was not white with black flecks like "vanilla bean," but was light purple/mauve and had flecks of what looked like red kidney beans. It had the subtle essence of vanilla but with a nutty finish, and the starchy, slightly mealy texture of the beans was surprisingly pleasant.

As an ode to one of my favorite treats and in celebration of Lunar New Year, which often falls in February, I give you the red bean scone. The sweetened adzuki bean paste gives these a buttery, crumbly texture and combined with the sesame seed crust the flavor reminds me of reginelle, the Italian seeded cookies that my grandma always had readily available on her countertop. Enjoy these beside a cup of hot green or jasmine tea and perhaps a spread of clotted cream or softened butter for the perfect afternoon.

MAKES 8 SCONES

- **2 cups all-purpose flour, plus more for dusting**
- **⅓ cup plus 2 teaspoons sugar**
- **1½ teaspoons baking powder**
- **½ teaspoon fine table salt**
- **6 tablespoons (3 ounces) very cold unsalted butter, cut into small cubes**
- **3 tablespoons sweet red bean paste (I prefer Morinaga)**
- **¾ cup cold heavy cream**
- **2 large egg yolks**
- **½ teaspoon pure vanilla extract**
- **Egg wash: 1 egg beaten with 1 tablespoon milk or cream**
- **2 to 3 tablespoons sesame seeds (white, black, or a mix)**

1. Preheat the oven to 400°F (or 375°F on the convection setting). Line a sheet pan with parchment paper.
2. In a bowl, whisk together the flour, ⅓ cup of the sugar, the baking powder, and salt.
3. Using a pastry cutter, cut the cold cubes of butter into the flour mixture until you have pea-size crumbs.
4. In a glass measuring cup or a small bowl, whisk together (with a fork or whisk) the red bean paste, heavy cream, egg yolks, and vanilla until just combined.
5. Using a fork, make a well in the center of the dry ingredients. Pour the cream mixture into the center of the well and stir with the fork from the outside inward, gently, just until the dough comes together. (If it's too dry, add a splash of heavy cream.) Use your hands to gently gather the dough into a shaggy ball.
6. Dump the dough ball onto a lightly floured surface or piece of parchment paper and use floured hands to flatten the dough ball into a disc 6½ inches in diameter. Wrap the disc in parchment or plastic wrap and refrigerate for 20 to 30 minutes, until nice and cold.
7. Remove the dough from the fridge and use a large chef's knife to cut the dough into 8 equal triangular wedges (like a pizza).
8. Using a pastry brush, lightly coat the tops of the scones with the egg wash. Sprinkle the tops with the sesame seeds, followed by the remaining 2 teaspoons of sugar.
9. Arrange the scones on the lined pan about 1½ inches apart. Transfer to the oven.

10 Bake for 12 minutes. Quickly rotate the pan front to back, reduce the oven temperature to 375°F (or 350°F on the convection setting), and bake 6 to 8 minutes, until the scones are golden brown on the edges and cooked through.

11 Remove from the oven and let cool for 5 minutes before serving. Scones are best served warm! To reheat, place in a 350°F oven for 5 to 7 minutes, or until warmed through.

STORAGE: **Store in an airtight container or wrapped in parchment paper and then aluminum foil at room temperature for up to 3 days.**

danielle's birthday confetti scones

It's March 8 and we are celebrating my birthday with the most adorable and festive scone! At The Hungry Gnome, we try to stay away from anything too gimmicky, but *everyone* loves "birthday cake" flavoring, which we obtain here by using almond and vanilla extract, as well as sprinkles and white chocolate.

MAKES 8 SCONES

- 2 cups all-purpose flour, plus more for dusting
- ⅓ cup plus 2 tablespoons granulated sugar
- 1½ teaspoons baking powder
- ½ teaspoon fine table salt
- 6 tablespoons (3 ounces) very cold unsalted butter, cut into small cubes
- ⅓ cup rainbow sprinkles
- ⅓ cup white chocolate chips
- ¾ cup cold heavy cream
- 2 large egg yolks
- 2 teaspoons pure vanilla extract or vanilla bean paste
- ¼ teaspoon pure almond extract
- Egg wash: 1 egg beaten with 1 tablespoon milk or cream
- 2 tablespoons raw or turbinado sugar, for sprinkling

GLAZE

- 1 cup powdered sugar
- Pinch of fine table salt
- ¼ teaspoon pure vanilla extract or vanilla bean paste
- ⅛ teaspoon pure almond extract
- A few drops of pink or red food coloring
- 2 to 3 tablespoons heavy cream
- Rainbow sprinkles, for decorating

STORAGE: **Store in an airtight container or wrapped in parchment paper and then aluminum foil at room temperature for up to 3 days.**

1. Preheat the oven to 400°F (or 375°F on the convection setting). Line a sheet pan with parchment paper.
2. In a bowl, whisk together the flour, granulated sugar, baking powder, and salt.
3. Using a pastry cutter, cut the cold cubes of butter into the flour mixture until you have pea-size crumbs. With a fork, stir in the sprinkles and white chocolate chips.
4. In a glass measuring cup or a small bowl, whisk together (with a fork or whisk) the heavy cream, egg yolks, vanilla, and almond extract until just combined.
5. Using a fork, make a well in the center of the dry ingredients. Pour the cream mixture into the center of the well and stir with the fork from the outside inward, gently, just until the dough comes together. Use your hands to gently gather the dough into a shaggy ball.
6. Dump the dough ball onto a lightly floured surface or piece of parchment paper and use floured hands to flatten the dough ball into a disc 6½ inches in diameter. Wrap the disc in parchment or plastic wrap and refrigerate for 20 to 30 minutes, until nice and cold.
7. Remove the dough from the fridge and use a large chef's knife to cut the dough into 8 equal triangular wedges (like a pizza).
8. Use a pastry brush to lightly coat the tops of the scones with the egg wash. Generously sprinkle the tops with the raw sugar.
9. Arrange the scones on the lined pan about 1½ inches apart. Transfer to the oven.
10. Bake for 12 minutes. Quickly rotate the pan front to back, reduce the oven temperature to 375°F (or 350°F on the convection setting), and bake for 7 to 9 minutes, until the scones are golden brown on the edges and cooked through.
11. Remove the scones from the oven and let them cool completely on a wire rack.
12. Meanwhile, make the glaze: In a bowl, whisk together the powdered sugar, salt, vanilla, and almond extract. Add the food coloring and then add the heavy cream 1 tablespoon at a time, until the glaze is loose but fairly opaque.
13. When the scones are cool, dip the tops of the scones in the glaze and let the excess run off. Scatter the tops with sprinkles and allow the glaze to dry.

SCONE QUEEN TIP

To toast the coconut, preheat the oven to 350°F. Spread the coconut evenly over an ungreased baking sheet and place it in the preheated oven for 4 minutes. Remove from the oven and use a spatula to toss or flip the coconut for even browning. Return the pan to the oven and bake for another 4 to 5 minutes, until golden. Remove the coconut from the pan and place in a bowl to avoid overtoasting. Cool completely before using.

coconut chocolate chunk scones

These scones are inspired by my incredible mommy and her favorite candy in the whole world, Mounds. The nutty flavor of the toasted coconut combined with the slightly bitter chocolate and the sweet vanilla bean paste are the perfect combination. Enjoy these warm out of the oven for perfect pools of melty chocolate throughout. For a slightly sweeter variation, use half bittersweet chocolate and half white chocolate or you can even use ¾ cup milk chocolate chips and ¼ cup lightly toasted chopped almonds because . . . "sometimes you feel like a nut and sometimes you don't."

MAKES 8 SCONES

2 cups all-purpose flour, plus more for dusting

⅓ cup granulated sugar

1½ teaspoons baking powder

¾ teaspoon fine table salt

6 tablespoons (3 ounces) very cold unsalted butter, cut into small cubes

¾ cup bittersweet chocolate chunks, preferably hand-chopped, or bittersweet chocolate chips (I like Ghirardelli 60% cacao)

½ cup sweetened coconut flakes, toasted (see Tip)

¾ cup cold heavy cream

2 large egg yolks

1½ teaspoons vanilla bean paste or pure vanilla extract

½ teaspoon coconut extract

Egg wash: 1 egg beaten with 1 tablespoon milk or cream

1½ tablespoons raw, turbinado, or regular granulated sugar, for sprinkling

1. Preheat the oven to 400°F (or 375°F on the convection setting). Line a sheet pan with parchment paper.
2. In a bowl, whisk together the flour, granulated sugar, baking powder, and salt.
3. Using a pastry cutter, cut the cold cubes of butter into the flour mixture until you have pea-size crumbs.
4. Using a fork, stir in the chocolate chips and toasted coconut flakes.
5. In a glass measuring cup or a small bowl, whisk together (with a fork or whisk) ¾ cup of the heavy cream, the egg yolks, vanilla bean paste, and coconut extract until just combined.
6. Using a fork, make a well in the center of the dry ingredients. Pour the cream mixture into the center of the well and stir with the fork from the outside inward, gently, just until the dough comes together. (If it's too dry, add a splash of heavy cream.) Use your hands to gently gather the dough into a shaggy ball.
7. Dump the dough ball onto a lightly floured surface or piece of parchment paper and use floured hands to flatten the dough ball into a disc 6½ inches in diameter. Wrap the disc in parchment or plastic wrap and refrigerate for 20 to 30 minutes, until nice and cold.
8. Remove the dough from the fridge and use a large chef's knife to cut the dough into 8 equal triangular wedges (like a pizza).
9. Use a pastry brush to lightly coat the tops of the scones with the egg wash. Generously sprinkle the tops of the scones with the raw sugar.
10. Arrange the scones on the lined pan about 1½ inches apart. Transfer to the oven.
11. Bake for 12 minutes. Quickly rotate the pan front to back, reduce the oven temperature to 375°F (or 350°F on the convection setting) and bake for 7 to 9 minutes, until the scones are golden brown on the edges and cooked through.
12. Remove from the oven and let them cool on the pan for 5 minutes before serving. Scones are best served warm! To reheat, place in a 350°F oven for 5 to 7 minutes, or until warmed through.

STORAGE: **Store airtight at room temperature for up to 3 days.**

lavender lemon scones

One summer I was lucky enough to spend a couple of weeks in the South of France with my husband, Dan. It was everything I hoped it would be and more, from its gorgeous landscapes to its quaint villages and bountiful outdoor markets. One of my favorite days (of all time) was my morning at the Bédoin market outside the spectacular medieval-town-turned-hotel Crillon-le-Brave. This market was bustling with locals and travelers and had all sorts of treats and treasures, from handwoven baskets to artisanal cheeses, locally made kitchen tools to beautiful linen clothing. One of the most widely featured ingredients in the Provence region is lavender, as it grows in abundance in the early summer months. The Bédoin market had handmade lavender soaps, sachets of herbes de Provence with lavender, and the most incredible marmalades you've ever tasted, made from fruits like clementine and apricot and flavored with a hint of lavender. Although some people see lavender only as a fragrance rather than an edible ingredient due to its perfumy scent, in the right amount and with the right blend of ingredients, it is bright and luxurious, especially in a baked good. These scones are perfect for a Mother's Day afternoon tea spread, accompanied by tea, homemade lemon curd, and perhaps some small sandwiches or petits fours.

MAKES 8 SCONES

⅓ cup plus 2 teaspoons granulated sugar

1½ teaspoons finely grated lemon zest

2 cups all-purpose flour, plus more for dusting

1½ teaspoons baking powder

½ teaspoon fine table salt

1 teaspoon food-grade dried lavender (grind it with a mortar and pestle or with your fingers the best you can)

6 tablespoons (3 ounces) very cold unsalted butter, cut into small cubes

¾ cup cold heavy cream

2 large egg yolks

1 teaspoon vanilla bean paste or pure vanilla extract

Egg wash: 1 egg beaten with 1 tablespoon milk or cream

1 Preheat the oven to 400°F (or 375°F on the convection setting). Line a sheet pan with parchment paper.

2 In a bowl, combine ⅓ cup of the granulated sugar and the lemon zest. Use your hands to massage the lemon zest into the sugar to better release the oils and lemon flavor. Whisk in the flour, baking powder, salt, and lavender.

3 Using a pastry cutter, cut the cold cubes of butter into the flour mixture until you have pea-size crumbs.

4 In a glass measuring cup or a small bowl, whisk together (with a fork or whisk) the heavy cream, egg yolks, and vanilla bean paste until just combined.

5 Using a fork, make a well in the center of the dry ingredients. Pour the cream mixture into the center of the well and stir with the fork from the outside inward, gently, just until the dough comes together. Use your hands to gently gather the dough into a shaggy ball.

6 Dump the dough ball onto a very lightly floured surface or a piece of parchment paper and use floured hands to flatten the dough ball into a disc 6½ inches in diameter. Wrap the disc in parchment or plastic wrap and refrigerate for 20 to 30 minutes, until nice and cold.

7 Remove the dough from the fridge and use a large chef's knife to cut the dough into 8 equal triangular wedges (like a pizza).

8 Use a pastry brush to lightly coat the tops of the scones with the egg wash. Generously sprinkle the tops with the remaining 2 teaspoons of granulated sugar.

9 Arrange the scones on the lined pan about 1½ inches apart. Transfer to the oven.

GLAZE

⅔ cup powdered sugar

Pinch of fine table salt

1½ tablespoons freshly squeezed lemon juice

Purple food coloring (optional)

Lavender buds (optional), for decorating

10 Bake for 12 minutes. Quickly rotate the pan front to back, reduce the oven temperature to 375°F (or 350°F on the convection setting), and bake for 6 to 8 minutes, until the scones are golden brown on the edges and cooked through.

11 Remove the scones from the oven and let cool for 15 minutes before glazing.

12 Meanwhile, make the glaze: In a small bowl, whisk together the powdered sugar, salt, and lemon juice. Add a few drops at a time of water (and the food coloring, if using) until the glaze is a pourable consistency.

13 Carefully dunk the tops of the scones in the glaze allowing the excess to run off. If desired, sprinkle a few buds of lavender on the top and then allow the glaze to set.

STORAGE: Store airtight at room temperature for up to 3 days.

strawberry cornmeal scones

Like a cross between a corn muffin and a scone, these have a crisp edge, a tender center, and a jammy strawberry glaze that tastes like summer on Long Island. Sweet corn and berries bring the farm stand vibes in every bite.

MAKES 8 SCONES

1⅓ cups all-purpose flour, plus more for dusting

⅔ cup fine cornmeal

¾ teaspoon fine table salt

1¾ teaspoons baking powder

⅓ cup plus 2 teaspoons granulated sugar

8 tablespoons (4 ounces/1 stick) very cold unsalted butter, cut into cubes

1 cup diced (½ inch) hulled fresh strawberries

1 cup cold heavy cream, plus more as needed

2 large egg yolks

½ teaspoon pure vanilla extract

Egg wash: 1 egg beaten with 1 tablespoon milk or cream

GLAZE

⅔ cup powdered sugar

Pinch of fine table salt

2 tablespoons strawberry preserves or jelly

STORAGE: These scones are best the same day you make them due to the moisture in the berries, but you can keep them in an airtight container for up to 2 days.

1 Preheat the oven to 400°F (or 375°F on the convection setting). Line a sheet pan with parchment paper.

2 In a large bowl, stir together the flour, cornmeal, salt, baking powder, and ⅓ cup of the granulated sugar.

3 Using a pastry cutter, cut the cold cubes of butter into the flour mixture until you have pea-size crumbs. Add the diced strawberries and gently toss them in the mix to coat.

4 In a glass measuring cup or small bowl, whisk together (with a fork or whisk) the heavy cream, egg yolks, and vanilla until just combined.

5 Using a fork, make a well in the center of the dry ingredients. Pour the cream mixture into the center of the well and stir with the fork from the outside inward, gently, just until the dough comes together. Use your hands to gently gather the dough into a shaggy ball. If it appears too dry and will not come together, add another 1 or 2 tablespoons heavy cream.

6 Dump the dough ball onto a very lightly floured surface or a piece of parchment paper and use floured hands to flatten the dough ball into a disc 6½ inches in diameter. Wrap the disc in parchment or plastic wrap and refrigerate for 20 to 30 minutes, until nice and cold.

7 Remove the dough from the fridge and use a large chef's knife to cut the dough into 8 equal triangular wedges (like a pizza).

8 Use a pastry brush to lightly coat the tops of the scones with the egg wash. Sprinkle the tops with the remaining 2 teaspoons of granulated sugar.

9 Arrange the scones on the lined pan about 1½ inches apart. Transfer to the oven.

10 Bake for 12 minutes. Quickly rotate the pan front to back, reduce the oven temperature to 375°F (or 350°F on the convection setting) and bake another 6 to 8 minutes or until the scones are golden brown on the edges and cooked through.

11 Remove the scones from the oven and let them cool on the pan for 15 to 20 minutes before glazing.

12 Meanwhile, make the glaze: In a small bowl, whisk together the powdered sugar, salt, and strawberry preserves. Add a few drops of water at a time until the glaze is a pourable consistency, but still thick.

13 Drizzle the tops of the scones generously with the glaze and then allow it to set.

"Signora" caffettiera
made in italy

blueberry white chocolate scones

These are one of The Hungry Gnome's greatest hits. The combination of blueberries and white chocolate is the perfect match. White chocolate, which can sometimes be too sweet, balances the tartness of the blueberries in the perfect way, so much so that people like my sister who typically don't like white chocolate still claim these as their favorite flavor. In true Scone Queen fashion these are perfectly crisp on the outside with a pleasant crunch from the turbinado sugar and are super fluffy and moist on the inside, from the butter and the added moisture from the bursting blueberries.

MAKES 8 SCONES

2 cups all-purpose flour, plus more for dusting

⅓ cup granulated sugar

1½ teaspoons baking powder

½ teaspoon fine table salt

1 cup frozen blueberries, preferably wild blueberries or other small varieties (no need to thaw)

6 tablespoons (3 ounces) very cold unsalted butter, cut into small cubes

¾ cup cold heavy cream

2 large egg yolks

1 teaspoon pure vanilla extract

⅓ cup white chocolate chips

Egg wash: 1 egg beaten with 1 tablespoon milk or cream

2 tablespoons raw or turbinado sugar, for sprinkling

STORAGE: **Store in an airtight container or wrapped in parchment paper and then aluminum foil at room temperature for up to 2 days.**

1 Preheat the oven to 400°F (or 375°F on the convection setting). Line a sheet pan with parchment paper.

2 In a bowl, whisk together the flour, granulated sugar, baking powder, and salt. Remove 2 tablespoons of the dry mix and put it in a separate bowl. Add the frozen blueberries and toss them gently to coat (this prevents the color from bleeding too much into the dough). Set the coated blueberries aside.

3 Using a pastry cutter, cut the cold cubes of butter into the flour mixture until you have pea-size crumbs.

4 In a glass measuring cup or a small bowl, whisk together (with a fork or whisk) the heavy cream, egg yolks, and vanilla until just combined.

5 Using a fork or rubber spatula, gently stir in the frozen blueberries and white chocolate chips.

6 Using a fork, make a well in the center of the dry ingredients. Pour the cream mixture into the center of the well and stir with the fork from the outside inward, gently, just until the dough comes together. Use your hands to gently gather the dough into a shaggy ball.

7 Dump the dough ball onto a lightly floured surface or piece of parchment paper and use floured hands to flatten the dough ball into a disc 6½ inches in diameter. Wrap the disc in parchment or plastic wrap and place in the freezer for 15 minutes, or until nice and cold.

8 Remove the dough from the freezer and use a large chef's knife to cut the dough into 8 equal triangular wedges (like a pizza).

9 Use a pastry brush to lightly coat the tops of the scones with the egg wash. Generously sprinkle the tops with the raw sugar.

10 Arrange the scones on the lined pan about 1½ inches apart. Transfer to the oven.

11 Bake for 12 minutes. Quickly rotate the pan front to back, reduce the oven temperature to 375°F (or 350°F on the convection setting), and bake for 6 to 8 minutes, until the scones are golden brown on the edges and cooked through.

12 Remove from the oven and let them cool on the pan for 5 minutes before serving. Scones are best served warm! To reheat, place in a 350°F oven for 5 to 7 minutes, or until warmed through.

peach almond scones

In peak August, there's nothing like a juicy peach! These scones are studded with tender peach and chewy almond paste for a rich texture and flavor. Canned peaches work just as well, like my grandmas always used in their go-to dessert in a pinch, Peach Melba. Serve them with Raspberry Rose Jam (page 36) and Easy Clotted Cream (page 36) for a nod to classic Melba flavors.

MAKES 8 SCONES

2 cups all-purpose flour, plus more for dusting

⅓ cup granulated sugar

1½ teaspoons baking powder

½ teaspoon fine table salt

¼ teaspoon ground cinnamon

6 tablespoons (3 ounces) very cold unsalted butter, cut into small cubes

1 cup ½-inch chunks drained juice-packed canned peaches or peeled fresh yellow peaches

⅓ cup almond paste (I like Solo), cut into ¼-inch chunks

¾ cup cold heavy cream

2 large egg yolks

1 teaspoon pure vanilla extract

Egg wash: 1 egg beaten with 1 tablespoon milk or cream

2 tablespoons raw or turbinado sugar, for sprinkling

¼ cup slivered almonds

STORAGE: **These scones are best the same day you make them due to the fruit, but you can keep them in an airtight container for up to 2 days.**

1. Preheat the oven to 400°F (or 375°F on the convection setting). Line a sheet pan with parchment paper.
2. In a bowl, whisk together the flour, granulated sugar, baking powder, salt, and cinnamon.
3. Using a pastry cutter, cut the cold cubes of butter into the flour mixture until you have pea-size crumbs.
4. Gently pat the diced peaches dry between two paper towels. Using a fork, gently stir in the diced almond paste and peaches into the flour/butter mixture.
5. In a glass measuring cup or a small bowl, whisk together (with a fork or whisk) the heavy cream, egg yolks, and vanilla until just combined.
6. Using a fork, make a well in the center of the dry ingredients. Pour the cream mixture into the center of the well and stir with the fork from the outside inward, gently, just until the dough comes together. Use your hands to gently gather the dough into a shaggy ball. This scone flavor is more fragile and requires a more gentle touch as the peaches are wet and juicy. This dough should be baked right away.
7. Dump the dough onto a lightly floured surface or piece of parchment paper and use floured hands to gather the dough together and flatten it into a disc 6½ inches in diameter.
8. Use a sharp chef's knife to cut down into the dough to divide the dough into 8 equal triangular wedges (like a pizza).
9. Use a pastry brush to lightly coat the tops of the scones with the egg wash. Sprinkle the tops with the raw sugar and the slivered almonds.
10. Arrange the scones on the lined pan about 1½ inches apart. Transfer to the oven.
11. Bake for 12 minutes. Quickly rotate the pan front to back, reduce the oven temperature to 375°F (or 350°F on the convection setting) and bake for 6 to 8 minutes, until the scones are golden brown on the edges and cooked through.
12. Remove from the oven and let them cool on the pan for about 10 minutes before serving. Scones are best served warm! To reheat, place in a 350°F oven for 5 to 7 minutes, or until warmed through.

apple walnut scones

Every September I love to go apple picking with my family on the north shore of Long Island and with my husband's family in Solebury, Pennsylvania. Running through the maze of apple trees and climbing on ladders to score the best varieties just makes you feel like a kid again. I love to munch on an apple while swinging my tote bag, basking in the sweet scents of the orchard and hot apple cider donuts. We go home with overflowing bags of apples and then bake them into desserts like my Grandma Rosemarie's apple pie (which I have yet to master), strudels, fritters, and, of course, now scones. These apple walnut scones are subtly sweet and packed with chunks of tender cooked apple, crunchy walnuts, and warm spices. They are perfect for breakfast and feel like a warm hug, similar to your favorite bowl of morning oatmeal.

MAKES 8 SCONES

2 cups all-purpose flour, plus more for dusting

⅓ cup granulated sugar

1½ teaspoons baking powder

½ teaspoon fine table salt

½ teaspoon ground cinnamon, plus more for dusting

⅛ teaspoon ground allspice

⅛ teaspoon ground nutmeg

6 tablespoons (3 ounces) very cold unsalted butter, cut into small cubes

½ cup chopped lightly toasted walnuts

¾ cup finely diced peeled Honeycrisp apple, tossed in 1 teaspoon lemon juice

¾ cup cold heavy cream

2 large egg yolks

1 teaspoon pure vanilla extract

Egg wash: 1 egg beaten with 1 tablespoon milk or cream

1½ tablespoons raw or turbinado sugar, for sprinkling

1. Preheat the oven to 400°F (or 375°F on the convection setting). Line a sheet pan with parchment paper.
2. In a bowl, whisk together the flour, granulated sugar, baking powder, salt, cinnamon, allspice, and nutmeg.
3. Using a pastry cutter, cut the cold cubes of butter into the flour mixture until you have pea-size crumbs. With a fork, gently stir in the walnuts and apples.
4. In a glass measuring cup or a small bowl, whisk together (with a fork or whisk) the heavy cream, egg yolks, and vanilla until just combined.
5. Using a fork, make a well in the center of the dry ingredients. Pour the cream mixture into the center of the well and stir with the fork from the outside inward, gently, just until the dough comes together. Use your hands to gently gather the dough into a shaggy ball.
6. Dump the dough ball onto a lightly floured surface or piece of parchment paper and use floured hands to flatten the dough ball into a disc 6½ inches in diameter. Wrap the disc in parchment or plastic wrap and freeze for 20 to 30 minutes, until very cold.
7. Remove the dough from the freezer and use a large chef's knife to cut the dough into 8 equal triangular wedges (like a pizza).
8. Use a pastry brush to lightly coat the tops of the scones with the egg wash. Sprinkle the tops with the raw sugar and dust the tops with a little cinnamon.
9. Arrange the scones on the lined pan about 1½ inches apart. Transfer to the oven.
10. Bake for 12 minutes. Quickly rotate the pan front to back, reduce the oven temperature 375°F (or 350°F on the convection setting), and bake for 7 to 9 minutes, until the scones are golden brown on the edges and cooked through.
11. Remove from the oven and let them cool on the pan for 5 minutes before serving. Scones are best served warm! To reheat, place in a 350°F oven for 5 to 7 minutes, or until warmed through.

STORAGE: **Store airtight at room temperature for up to 2 days.**

butter pecan scones

My first "real job" besides slinging scones out of my parents' kitchen, was scooping Italian ices at a local hot spot at age fourteen. I worked there from March to October with all of my closest friends, including Nick, who has been my best buddy since we were ten. We would blast music, scoop hundreds of ices a day, and, in between customers, practice our cheerleading routines. After years of working there, we became a bit clairvoyant and called out people's orders before they even approached the register. I always knew that elderly people would choose Almond Joy or Butter Pecan. Being the old soul that I am, I had to agree, as it was the perfect blend of salty and sweet. This scone has all the same flavors of "your grandma's" favorite ice cream, and let me tell you, baby, the salty maple butter glaze is droolworthy!

MAKES 8 SCONES

2 cups all-purpose flour, plus more for dusting

⅓ cup plus 2 teaspoons granulated sugar

1½ teaspoons baking powder

¾ teaspoon fine table salt

½ teaspoon ground cinnamon

6 tablespoons (3 ounces) very cold unsalted butter, cut into small cubes

1 cup roughly chopped lightly toasted pecans

¾ cup plus 2 tablespoons cold heavy cream

2 large egg yolks

½ teaspoon pure vanilla extract

Egg wash: 1 egg beaten with 1 tablespoon milk or cream

MAPLE BUTTER GLAZE

2 tablespoons (1 ounce) unsalted butter, melted

¼ cup pure maple syrup

⅛ teaspoon fine table salt

¾ cup powdered sugar

8 pecan halves, for decorating

STORAGE: **Store airtight at room temperature for up to 3 days.**

1. Preheat the oven to 400°F (or 375°F on the convection setting). Line a sheet pan with parchment paper.
2. In a bowl, whisk together the flour, ⅓ cup of the granulated sugar, the baking powder, salt, and cinnamon.
3. Using a pastry cutter, cut the cold cubes of butter into the flour mixture until you have pea-size crumbs. With a fork, gently stir in the chopped pecans.
4. In a glass measuring cup or a small bowl, whisk together (with a fork or whisk) the heavy cream, egg yolks, and vanilla until just combined.
5. Using a fork, make a well in the center of the dry ingredients. Pour the cream mixture into the center of the well and stir with the fork from the outside inward, gently, just until the dough comes together. Use your hands to gently gather the dough into a shaggy ball.
6. Dump the dough ball onto a lightly floured surface or piece of parchment paper and use floured hands to flatten the dough ball into a disc 6½ inches in diameter. Wrap the disc in parchment or plastic wrap and freeze for 20 to 30 minutes, until very cold.
7. Remove the dough from the freezer and use a large chef's knife to cut the dough into 8 equal triangular wedges (like a pizza).
8. Use a pastry brush to lightly coat the tops of the scones with the egg wash. Sprinkle the tops with the remaining 2 teaspoons of granulated sugar.
9. Arrange the scones on the lined pan about 1½ inches apart. Transfer to the oven. Bake for 12 minutes. Quickly rotate the pan front to back, reduce the oven temperature to 375°F (or 350°F on the convection setting), and bake for 7 to 9 minutes, until the scones are golden brown on the edges and cooked through. Remove from the oven and let them cool completely on the pan before glazing them.
10. Meanwhile, make the maple butter glaze: In a small bowl, whisk together the melted butter, maple syrup, salt, and powdered sugar. The glaze should be thick and fairly opaque but pourable. Add a few drops of water if you need to thin it out.
11. Once the scones are cooled, use a tablespoon to spoon/spread the glaze on top of each scone, allowing the excess to just slightly drip down the sides. Place a pecan half (or two) centered on the top of each scone and then allow the glaze to set slightly before enjoying.

cranberry orange scones

November on the East Coast means colorful leaves, cozy sweaters, pumpkin spice lattes, fall baking, and one of my favorite holidays: Thanksgiving! My Aunt Christine and Uncle Craig host Thanksgiving each year at their home in Remsenburg, New York, and the spread could be mistaken for a *Martha Stewart Living* cover. My uncle makes not one but two massive turkeys that have been slow-roasted, sometimes smoked, or even basted with a spicy honey. The sides are abundant and consist of both American and Italian favorites, such as mashed potatoes, stuffed artichokes, my grandma's Neapolitan egg stuffing, and, of course, cranberry sauce, just to name a few. These cranberry orange scones have the essence of the season with their warm spices and fresh citrus notes that remind me of my favorite turkey brine. The cranberries are mildly sweet and tart, making them great for breakfast, dessert, or even in a bread basket beside your savory roast.

MAKES 8 SCONES

2 cups all-purpose flour, plus more for dusting

⅓ cup granulated sugar

1½ teaspoons baking powder

½ teaspoon fine table salt

¼ teaspoon ground cinnamon, plus more for dusting

⅛ teaspoon ground nutmeg

Pinch of ground cloves

6 tablespoons (3 ounces) very cold unsalted butter, cut into small cubes

1 cup dried cranberries

2 teaspoons finely grated orange zest (about 1 medium orange)

¾ cup cold heavy cream

2 large egg yolks

1½ teaspoons pure vanilla extract

1 tablespoon freshly squeezed orange juice (use the orange you zested!)

Egg wash: 1 egg beaten with 1 tablespoon milk or cream

1½ tablespoons raw or turbinado sugar, for sprinkling

STORAGE: Store airtight at room temperature for up to 3 days.

1. Preheat the oven to 400°F (or 375°F on the convection setting). Line a sheet pan with parchment paper.
2. In a bowl, whisk together the flour, granulated sugar, baking powder, salt, cinnamon, nutmeg, and the pinch of cloves.
3. Using a pastry cutter, cut the cold cubes of butter into the flour mixture until you have pea-size crumbs. With a fork, stir in the dried cranberries and orange zest.
4. In a glass measuring cup or a small bowl, whisk together (with a fork or whisk) the heavy cream, egg yolks, vanilla, and orange juice until just combined.
5. Using a fork, make a well in the center of the dry ingredients. Pour the cream mixture into the center of the well and stir with the fork from the outside inward, gently, just until the dough comes together. Use your hands to gently gather the dough into a shaggy ball.
6. Dump the dough ball onto a lightly floured surface or piece of parchment paper and use floured hands to flatten the dough ball into a disc 6½ inches in diameter. Wrap the disc in parchment or plastic wrap and refrigerate for 20 to 30 minutes, until nice and cold.
7. Remove the dough from the fridge and use a large chef's knife to cut the dough into 8 equal triangular wedges (like a pizza).
8. Use a pastry brush to lightly coat the tops of the scones with the egg wash. Sprinkle the tops with the raw sugar and a light dusting of cinnamon.
9. Arrange the scones on the lined pan about 1½ inches apart. Transfer to the oven.
10. Bake for 12 minutes. Quickly rotate the pan front to back, reduce the oven temperature to 375°F (or 350°F on the convection setting), and bake for 7 to 9 minutes, until the scones are golden brown on the edges and cooked through.
11. Remove from the oven and let them cool on the pan for 5 minutes before serving. Scones are best served warm! To reheat, place in a 350°F oven for 5 to 7 minutes, or until warmed through.

THE chocolate chip scones

This is where it all began. Every summer, my family took weekend trips to the Hamptons—just ninety minutes away, but it felt like another world. Our mornings started early to claim a spot on Main Beach and, most importantly, to grab a warm chocolate chip scone from the farmers' market in Amagansett. They were crisp on the outside, soft on the inside, and packed with dark and white chocolate. One bite, and I knew—this was what I was meant to do. Years later, when the market closed, I set out to re-create that perfect scone. With the help of my Aunt Christine, who shares my love of baking, we tested recipes from her favorite cookbooks. After dozens of trials and a full tasting spread for my parents, I landed on the winner, my now famous recipe. At thirteen, I launched my first scone business with a homemade business card and my aunt driving me all over town. We handed out samples to local shops and farm stands, and by the time I got home, the voicemail box was full with order inquiries! I was officially in business. I baked every morning before the sun came up, tracking orders and ingredient inventory in a marble notebook. Years passed, life happened, and the business paused. But seventeen years later, after being laid off, I returned to my roots. Same recipe, same passion—now with a commercial kitchen, a team, and thousands of scones a day. This is that original scone. The one that started it all.

MAKES 8 SCONES

2 cups all-purpose flour, plus more for dusting

⅓ cup granulated sugar

1½ teaspoons baking powder

½ teaspoon fine table salt

6 tablespoons (3 ounces) very cold unsalted butter, cut into small cubes

1 cup semisweet chocolate chips

¾ cup cold heavy cream

2 large egg yolks

1½ teaspoons pure vanilla extract

Egg wash: 1 egg beaten with 1 tablespoon milk or cream

2 tablespoons raw or turbinado sugar, for sprinkling

1. Preheat the oven to 400°F (or 375°F on the convection setting). Line a sheet pan with parchment paper.
2. In a bowl, whisk together the flour, granulated sugar, baking powder, and salt.
3. Using a pastry cutter, cut the cold cubes of butter into the flour mixture until you have pea-size crumbs. With a fork, stir in the chocolate chips.
4. In a glass measuring cup or a small bowl, whisk together (with a fork or whisk) the heavy cream, egg yolks, and vanilla until just combined.
5. Using a fork, make a well in the center of the dry ingredients. Pour the cream mixture into the center of the well and stir with the fork from the outside inward, gently, just until the dough comes together. Use your hands to gently gather the dough into a shaggy ball.
6. Dump the dough ball onto a lightly floured surface or piece of parchment paper and use floured hands to flatten the dough ball into a disc 6½ inches in diameter. Wrap the disc in parchment or plastic wrap and refrigerate for 20 to 30 minutes, until nice and cold.
7. Remove the dough from the fridge and use a large chef's knife to cut the dough into 8 equal triangular wedges (like a pizza).
8. Use a pastry brush to lightly coat the tops of the scones with the egg wash. Generously sprinkle the tops with the raw sugar.
9. Arrange the scones on the lined pan about 1½ inches apart. Transfer to the oven.

10 Bake for 12 minutes. Quickly rotate the pan front to back, reduce the oven temperature to 375°F (or 350°F on the convection setting), and bake for 7 to 9 minutes, until the scones are golden brown on the edges and cooked through.

11 Remove from the oven and let them cool on the pan for 5 minutes before serving. Scones are best served warm! To reheat, place in a 350°F oven for 5 to 7 minutes, or until warmed through.

STORAGE: **Store airtight at room temperature for up to 3 days.**

SPREADS & ACCOMPANIMENTS

The only thing better than a fresh, warm homemade scone is one topped with a delicious butter or spread. Honey butter is a must in the Scone Queen household, and it adorns every breakfast and brunch table. The Easy Clotted Cream (page 36) is a lighter version of the UK classic and adds a gorgeous tang and creaminess to each scone bite. The Lemon Curd (page 36) is a bright and tart topping perfect for fruit-based scones, like the Currant Scones (page 9), the Strawberry Cornmeal Scones (page 20), and the Blueberry White Chocolate Scones (page 23). Finally, the Raspberry Rose Jam (page 36) is so delectable you'll be eating it by the spoonful. The slight essence of rose water elevates the raspberry flavor in the most elegant way without being too perfumy or floral. Use the base of this recipe to make all sorts of fruit jams!

honey butter

MAKES ABOUT ¾ CUP, OR 8 TO 12 SERVINGS

8 tablespoons (4 ounces/1 stick) unsalted or salted butter, at room temperature

½ teaspoon fine table salt (use only ¼ teaspoon if using salted butter)

⅓ cup honey, preferably clover honey

1. In a stand mixer fitted with the whisk, beat together the softened butter and salt. Slowly stream in the honey while beating, until the butter is smooth and there are no visible lumps.
2. Serve immediately at room temperature or store in the fridge for later.

STORAGE: Store the honey butter airtight in the refrigerator for up to 2 weeks. Bring back to room temperature before serving, but once at room temperature, use it all or otherwise dispose of it. Do not refrigerate it again.

VARIATION: Add 1 teaspoon finely grated lemon or orange zest for a beautiful citrus-infused honey butter.

lemon curd

MAKES ABOUT 1 CUP, OR 8 SERVINGS

- ⅓ cup sugar
- 2 teaspoons finely grated lemon zest
- ⅓ cup freshly squeezed lemon juice
- 2 large eggs, lightly beaten, at room temperature
- ¼ teaspoon vanilla bean paste
- Dash of fine table salt
- 4 tablespoons (2 ounces / ½ stick) unsalted butter, cut into small cubes

1 In a small saucepan, whisk together the sugar, lemon zest, lemon juice, eggs, vanilla, and salt. Add the butter and cook over low heat, whisking constantly, until the curd is thick enough to hold marks of the whisk, 3 to 4 minutes.

2 Transfer the hot curd to a bowl or jar and immediately cover the surface with plastic wrap while warm. Refrigerate until cold.

STORAGE: Store in a mason jar or sealed container in the fridge for up to 2 weeks or in the freezer for 8 months to a year!

raspberry rose jam

MAKES ¾ CUP, OR 6 TO 8 SERVINGS

- 1½ cups raspberries, fresh or frozen (see Tip)
- ¾ cup granulated sugar
- Dash of fine table salt
- 1 tablespoon freshly squeezed lemon juice
- 1 teaspoon rose water
- 2 teaspoons cornstarch

1 In a small saucepan, combine the raspberries, sugar, salt, lemon juice, rose water, and cornstarch. Cook over low heat, stirring occasionally, until the sugar dissolves, the berries break down, and it reaches a jammy consistency, 7 to 10 minutes.

2 Pour into a glass jar or container, cover, and store in the fridge to chill.

STORAGE: Store in the fridge in a sealed container or jar for up to 2 months.

easy clotted cream

MAKES 1⅓ CUPS, OR 8 TO 12 SERVINGS

- 1 cup heavy cream
- ⅓ cup sour cream
- 1½ tablespoons powdered sugar
- Dash of fine table salt

1 In a stand mixer fitted with the whisk, beat the heavy cream until stiff peaks form.

2 Remove the cream from the mixer and use a hand whisk to add the sour cream, powdered sugar, and salt until just combined.

STORAGE: Store in a sealed container or jar in the fridge for about 1 week.

SCONE QUEEN TIP

You can swap the raspberries for another berry and omit the rose water if you prefer. Try combinations like strawberries with ½ teaspoon vanilla bean paste, or blueberries with 1 teaspoon grated lemon zest, or even blackberries and 1 tablespoon bourbon!

puppy scones

I grew up in a household that only had pets that could fit in a small tank, so I never truly understood the connection between a dog and its owner. But in 2022 Dan and I got Porcini and I was forever changed. Cini is a fifty-five-pound Lagotto Romagnolo (aka an Italian water dog or truffle hunting dog), who looks like a Muppet but has the personality and empathy of a human. He is the sweetest boy with the biggest appetite and so of course he deserves to have a special treat, too!

MAKES 8 DOG TREATS

2 cups whole wheat flour

½ teaspoon fine table salt

½ teaspoon ground cinnamon

2 large eggs, lightly beaten

½ cup canned pumpkin puree (I like Libby's)

3 tablespoons natural peanut butter

1 to 2 tablespoons hulled pumpkin seeds, for garnish

1. Preheat the oven to 375°F (or 350°F on the convection setting). Line a baking sheet with parchment paper.
2. In a large bowl, whisk together the whole wheat flour, salt, and cinnamon.
3. Make a well in the center and add the eggs, pumpkin puree, peanut butter, and 2 tablespoons water. Mix until it comes together into a dough consistency. If it is too dry and crumbly, add more water until it comes together. Gather the dough together with your hands into a ball and then press the ball down gently into a flat disc about ¾ inch thick. Use a sharp knife to cut the disc into 8 equal triangular wedges (like a pizza).
4. Place them on the lined baking sheet at least 1 inch a part. Brush the tops lightly with water and sprinkle a few raw pumpkin seeds on the tops.
5. Bake for 30 to 35 minutes, until golden and dry.
6. Allow to cool completely and then serve to your pup (serving size is 1 per day for medium-large dogs or a half for small dogs)!

STORAGE: **Store in an airtight container or tin at room temperature for up to 1 week or in the freezer for 3 months.**

CHAPTER 2

MUFFINS

BLUEBERRY CRUMB MUFFINS 43

PUMPKIN SPICE MUFFINS 44

RASPBERRY RICOTTA MUFFINS 47

COCOA-SWIRLED COFFEE CAKE MUFFINS 48

DOUBLE-CHOCOLATE MUFFINS/DOUBLE-CHOCOLATE CREAM CHEESE MUFFINS 51

GINGERBREAD MUFFINS 52

CHOCOLATE CHIP PANCAKE MUFFINS 54

LEMON POPPYSEED MUFFINS 56

HONEY CORN MUFFINS 58

HUMMINGBIRD MUFFINS 61

blueberry crumb muffins

Everyone thinks that my best seller at The Hungry Gnome is the Chocolate Chip Scone, but in fact, our top-selling wholesale baked good is the Blueberry Crumb Muffin. When I think of quintessential, classic baked goods, the blueberry muffin is right up there with the chocolate chip cookie. It's the best seller because everyone, young and old, enjoys one—it feels equally pleasurable and nourishing. It is a tried-and-true breakfast (or anytime) treat that will never go out of style, and this recipe right here is the only blueberry muffin recipe you'll ever need. The addition of the buttery, cinnamon crumb topping gives these fluffy, plush muffins the perfect crunchy contrast. I dare you to not eat the whole top first. When you read the ingredient list, you'll see my bestie, sour cream. Sour cream adds the perfect tang, acid, and moisture to so many different baked goods, so I always have a tub on hand. Now go ahead and fold down the corner of this page, because I know this one will be in your regular rotation.

MAKES 10 JUMBO MUFFINS

- 2 cups cake flour (not self-rising), plus 2 teaspoons for the berries
- ½ teaspoon baking powder
- ½ teaspoon baking soda
- ¾ teaspoon fine table salt
- ¼ teaspoon ground cinnamon
- 8 tablespoons (4 ounces/1 stick) unsalted butter, at room temperature
- ⅓ cup canola or other vegetable oil
- 1¼ cups granulated sugar
- 1½ teaspoons pure vanilla extract
- 2 large eggs, at room temperature
- 1 cup sour cream
- 1½ cups blueberries, fresh or frozen

CRUMB TOPPING

- ¼ cup granulated sugar
- 2 tablespoons dark brown sugar
- ⅛ teaspoon fine table salt
- ½ teaspoon ground cinnamon
- 4 tablespoons (2 ounces/½ stick) unsalted butter, melted
- ¾ cup cake flour (not self-rising)

Powdered sugar, for dusting

1. In a medium bowl, stir together the 2 cups of cake flour, the baking powder, baking soda, salt, and cinnamon. Set aside.
2. In a stand mixer fitted with the paddle, beat the butter, canola oil, granulated sugar, and vanilla on medium speed until light and fluffy, about 3 minutes.
3. Add the eggs one at a time, beating to just combine after each addition. Add the flour mixture in two additions, alternating with the sour cream, mixing on low speed until just combined. (Overmixed batter will result in tough muffins!) In a small bowl, toss the blueberries with the 2 teaspoons of flour to coat, then gently fold the blueberries into the batter.
4. Let the batter sit at room temperature for 20 to 30 minutes to allow the flavors to develop further. (You can also cover the batter with plastic wrap and refrigerate overnight or up to 3 days.)
5. Meanwhile, make the crumb topping: In a bowl, stir together the granulated sugar, brown sugar, salt, and cinnamon. Pour in the melted butter and stir to combine. Add in the cake flour and use a fork to toss everything together to create crumbs. It is important to toss rather than whisk or stir, which will create a paste rather than crumbs.
6. When ready to bake, preheat the oven to 425°F (or 400°F on the convection setting). Line 10 cups of two jumbo muffin tins with paper liners.
7. Spoon the batter into the muffin cups to fill them two-thirds of the way to the top. Generously top each muffin with the reserved crumb topping, starting around the perimeter of the muffins first and then making your way to the middle. This helps with weight distribution to ensure the muffins rise properly. Transfer to the oven.
8. Bake for 5 minutes. Then, while keeping the oven closed, reduce the oven temperature to 350°F (or 325°F on the convection setting) and bake for 18 to 22 minutes, until a toothpick inserted in the center of a muffin comes out clean.
9. Allow the muffins to cool for 10 minutes in the pan, then dust them with powdered sugar. I prefer to enjoy these while they're still warm.

STORAGE: **Store in a sealed container or wrapped in parchment paper and then aluminum foil at room temperature for up to 3 days.**

pumpkin spice muffins

Call me basic, but this girl loves fall, especially in the Northeast. Crisp air, colorful leaves, trips out East on Long Island to the apple orchards and pumpkin patches, and all the soups, stews, squash, and warm spices. When I started The Hungry Gnome, my mom hounded me about creating a fluffy and moist pumpkin muffin with the right amount of spice, a crumb topping, and a white icing drizzle just like the one from the national doughnut chain we won't mention, but better. After a few tries, I presented my mom with this muffin, and since that moment it has been one of my most popular seasonal items at The Hungry Gnome. Just wait until you smell these babies baking . . . the candle companies could never!

MAKES 9 JUMBO MUFFINS

8 tablespoons (4 ounces/1 stick) unsalted butter, at room temperature

¾ cup granulated sugar

¾ cup packed dark brown sugar

¼ cup pure maple syrup

¼ cup canola or other vegetable oil

2 large eggs

1¼ cups canned pumpkin puree (I like Libby's)

1½ teaspoons pure vanilla extract

2 cups cake flour (not self-rising)

1 teaspoon baking soda

¾ teaspoon fine table salt

2½ teaspoons ground cinnamon

¼ teaspoon ground cloves

¼ teaspoon ground nutmeg

⅛ teaspoon ground ginger

⅓ cup sour cream

1 In a stand mixer fitted with the paddle, beat the butter until creamy, about 3 minutes.

2 Add the granulated sugar and brown sugar and beat on medium speed until light and fluffy, about 5 minutes.

3 Add the maple syrup and canola oil and mix until combined. Add the eggs one at a time, beating to just combine after each addition. Add the pumpkin puree and vanilla and mix until combined.

4 In a separate bowl, stir together the cake flour, baking soda, salt, cinnamon, cloves, nutmeg, and ginger until combined.

5 Add about one-third of the flour mixture and half of the sour cream to the batter and beat on low speed until combined. Add another one-third of the flour mixture and the rest of the sour cream and continue to beat on low speed. Add the remaining flour mixture and beat on low speed until just combined.

6 Cover the batter with plastic wrap and refrigerate for at least 2 hours, or until the batter is nice and chilled. (You can keep refrigerated for up to 48 hours.)

7 Make the crumbs: In a bowl, stir together the cake flour, granulated sugar, brown sugar, cinnamon, and salt. Pour in the melted butter and use a fork to toss everything together to create crumbs.

8 Preheat the oven to 425°F (or 400°F on the convection setting). Line 9 cups of two jumbo muffin tins with paper liners.

9 Using a 6-ounce ice cream scoop or a spoon, fill the muffin cups three-quarters of the way with batter. Sprinkle about 1 tablespoon of the crumbs over each muffin starting at the perimeter and moving to the center. Transfer to the oven.

10 Bake for 5 minutes. Then, while keeping the oven closed, reduce the oven temperature to 350°F (or 325°F on the convection setting) and bake for 20 to 25 minutes, until a toothpick inserted into the center of a muffin comes out clean.

11 Let the muffins cool in the pans.

CRUMBS

- ¾ cup cake flour (not self-rising)
- ¼ cup granulated sugar
- 3 tablespoons packed dark brown sugar
- ½ teaspoon ground cinnamon
- ⅛ teaspoon fine table salt
- 4 tablespoons (2 ounces/ ½ stick) unsalted butter, melted

GLAZE

- 1 cup powdered sugar
- ⅛ teaspoon pure vanilla extract
- Pinch of fine table salt
- 2 to 4 tablespoons milk or water

12 Make the glaze: In a small bowl, whisk together the powdered sugar, vanilla, and salt. Whisk in enough of the milk until the glaze is smooth and thin enough to drizzle.

13 Drizzle the glaze over the tops of the cooled muffins. Let the icing set before eating.

STORAGE: Store airtight at room temperature for up to 3 to 5 days (if they last that long!).

raspberry ricotta muffins

I love to add sour cream to my muffin and cake batters for added moisture and "fluff," but one day I spotted a container of ricotta cheese in the back of my fridge and wondered, what if . . . ? Well, an absolutely stinkin' delicious muffin was born. The texture is light, the flavor is rich and punchy—but not so decadent that you won't enjoy it for breakfast. I add a touch of lemon zest to better showcase the fruity, sour notes of the raspberries. The brown sugar streusel on top isn't exactly necessary, but why skip it? Feel free to swap out the raspberries for blueberries, blackberries, or hey, even leave them out altogether. It's that good.

MAKES 10 JUMBO MUFFINS

BROWN SUGAR STREUSEL

- ½ cup flour (any type)
- ½ cup packed light brown sugar
- Pinch of fine table salt
- 4 tablespoons (2 ounces / ½ stick) unsalted butter, at room temperature

MUFFINS

- 2 cups cake flour (not self-rising), plus 2 teaspoons for the berries
- 1 teaspoon fine table salt
- ½ teaspoon baking powder
- ½ teaspoon baking soda
- ¼ teaspoon ground cinnamon
- 8 tablespoons (4 ounces/1 stick) unsalted butter, at room temperature
- ½ cup canola oil or other neutral vegetable oil
- 1¼ cups granulated sugar
- 1½ teaspoons pure vanilla extract
- 1 teaspoon grated lemon zest
- 2 large eggs, at room temperature
- 1 cup whole-milk ricotta (I like Galbani)
- 1½ cups raspberries, fresh or frozen, halved if large
- Powdered sugar (optional), for dusting

1. Make the brown sugar streusel: In a small bowl, use your fingers to blend together the flour, brown sugar, and salt. Add the softened butter and use your fingers again to work it into the flour mixture until it looks like damp sand. You want small crumbs that you can sprinkle on top of the muffins. Set aside and start the batter.
2. Make the muffins: In a medium bowl, stir together the 2 cups of cake flour, salt, baking powder, baking soda, and cinnamon. Set aside.
3. In a stand mixer fitted with the paddle, beat the butter, canola oil, granulated sugar, vanilla, and lemon zest on medium speed until light and fluffy, about 3 minutes.
4. Add the eggs one at a time, beating to just combine after each addition. Beat in the ricotta cheese just until blended. It's okay if there are some lumps.
5. With the mixer on low speed, add the flour mixture and mix just until incorporated. Remember, overmixed batter will result in tough muffins. In a small bowl, toss the raspberries with the 2 teaspoons of flour until evenly coated. Gently fold the raspberries into the batter.
6. Let the batter sit at room temperature for 20 to 30 minutes. You can also cover the batter with plastic wrap and refrigerate overnight or up to 3 days. (You can bake the batter right away and it will be great, but for amazing results, allow for a little rest time.)
7. When ready to bake, preheat the oven to 425°F (or 400°F on the convection setting). Line 10 cups of two jumbo muffin tins with paper liners.
8. Fill the muffin cups three-quarters of the way with batter (it should be a rounded, heaping mound). Top each muffin with 1 tablespoon of the streusel topping, starting around the perimeter of the muffins first and then making your way to the middle. This helps with weight distribution to ensure your muffins rise properly. Transfer to the oven.
9. Bake for 5 minutes. Then, while keeping the oven closed, reduce the oven temperature to 350°F (or 325°F on the convection setting) and bake for 18 to 20 minutes, until a toothpick inserted in the center comes out clean. When the muffins are done, dust them lightly with powdered sugar if desired.

STORAGE: **Store airtight at room temperature for up to 3 days.**

cocoa-swirled coffee cake muffins

These muffins have a tangy sour cream base with ribbons of bittersweet cocoa running through their centers and crumbly tops made of nutty, brown butter streusel that melts in your mouth. For an extra decadent treat, melt some salted butter in a skillet, cut a muffin in half, place it cut-side down in the pan, and cook until a golden crust forms.

MAKES 8 JUMBO MUFFINS

STREUSEL TOPPING

1¼ cups all-purpose flour

¼ cup granulated sugar

⅓ cup packed light brown sugar

¼ teaspoon fine table salt

1 teaspoon ground cinnamon

10 tablespoons (5 ounces) unsalted butter

MUFFINS

12 tablespoons (6 ounces/ 1½ sticks) unsalted butter, at room temperature

1½ cups granulated sugar

2 teaspoons pure vanilla extract

3 large eggs

2¼ cups cake flour (not self-rising)

1 teaspoon fine table salt

2½ teaspoons baking powder

⅛ teaspoon ground nutmeg

1 cup sour cream

COCOA SWIRL

½ cup packed light brown sugar

1 tablespoon dark Dutch-process cocoa powder, preferably Hershey's Special Dark, sifted to remove lumps

1 teaspoon ground cinnamon

1. Make the streusel topping: In a bowl stir, together the flour, granulated sugar, brown sugar, salt, and cinnamon. Set aside.
2. In a small skillet or saucepan, melt the butter over medium heat, stirring frequently. (Medium heat ensures the butter cooks evenly, an important factor in making brown butter.) When it starts to foam you will begin to see the milk solids of the butter brown and it will have a nutty aroma. Once the butter has browned, remove from the heat immediately as it can burn quickly, and pour it into the bowl with the flour/sugar mixture. Toss it together with a fork to form the crumbs. Place the bowl in the fridge to chill while you make the muffin batter.
3. Make the muffins: In a stand mixer fitted with the paddle, beat together the butter, granulated sugar, and vanilla until light and fluffy, about 5 minutes.
4. Add the eggs one at a time, beating to just combine after each addition and scraping the bowl with a rubber spatula.
5. In a separate bowl, stir together the cake flour, salt, baking powder, and nutmeg.
6. Add the flour mixture in two additions, alternating with the sour cream, mixing on low speed until just combined.
7. Cover the bowl with plastic wrap and refrigerate for at least 30 minutes or up to overnight.
8. When ready to bake, preheat the oven to 425°F (or 400°F on the convection setting). Line 8 cups of two jumbo muffin tins with paper liners.
9. Make the cocoa swirl: In a small bowl, whisk together the brown sugar, cocoa powder, and cinnamon. Set aside.
10. Using an ice cream scoop or a large spoon, fill the muffin cups only halfway up. Sprinkle 2 teaspoons of the cocoa swirl evenly over the tops all the way to the edges (so you can see it on the outside of the finished muffin), then top each muffin with more batter being sure to cover the swirl. You want the muffin cups three-quarters filled. Next sprinkle about ½ teaspoon more of the cocoa mixture on top before adding the streusel.

11 Take the streusel out of the fridge and sprinkle the crumbs evenly on top of each muffin, starting at the perimeter of the muffin and finishing in the center to ensure proper weight distribution. Transfer to the oven.

12 Bake for 5 minutes. Then, while keeping the oven closed, reduce the oven temperature to 350°F (or 325°F on the convection setting) and bake for 22 to 25 minutes, until a toothpick inserted in the center comes out clean.

13 Serve the muffins warm, at room temperature, or even cut in half and griddled in a frying pan with butter!

STORAGE: **Store in a sealed container or wrapped in parchment paper and then aluminum foil at room temperature for up to 3 days.**

double-chocolate muffins

Maybe it was the hormones or the growth spurts, but when I was in middle school I would repeatedly get hooked on a particular food item and eat it sometimes two or three times a day. There was a flavored oatmeal stint, Pop-Tarts, Eggo waffles with peanut butter, SnackWell's cookies—and the Costco Jumbo Double-Chocolate Muffins. Every morning I would wrap the muffin in a paper towel, microwave it for a few seconds to melt the chocolate, and then devour it on the bus on the way to school. For better or worse, I can still smell the vinyl seats mixed with chocolatey goodness. My homemade version has rich chocolate flavor and a moist, tender crumb, thanks to my favorite secret ingredient, pudding mix. Leave them as is or turn them into a Long Island deli staple and add a cream cheese filling (see Variation) for a tangy, creamy surprise!

MAKES 10 JUMBO MUFFINS

8 tablespoons (4 ounces/1 stick) unsalted butter, at room temperature

1 cup sugar

½ cup canola or other vegetable oil

1 tablespoon pure vanilla extract

3 large eggs

1 (1.4-ounce) box Jell-O instant chocolate pudding mix (I like fudge)

1½ cups cake flour (not self-rising)

½ cup dark Dutch-process cocoa powder, preferably Hershey's Special Dark, sifted to remove lumps

1 teaspoon baking soda

1½ teaspoons baking powder

¾ teaspoon fine table salt

1 cup sour cream, preferably full-fat

⅓ cup milk or buttermilk, preferably whole or 2%

1¾ cups mini semisweet chocolate chips

1 Preheat the oven to 425°F (or 400°F on the convection setting). Line 10 cups of two jumbo muffin tins with paper liners.

2 In a stand mixer fitted with the paddle, beat the butter, sugar, and canola oil until light and creamy, 3 to 4 minutes.

3 Add the vanilla and beat until combined. Add the eggs one at a time, beating to just combine after each addition. Beat in the dry pudding mix until blended.

4 In a separate bowl, sift together the cake flour, cocoa powder, baking soda, baking powder, and salt to ensure there are no lumps.

5 Add the flour mixture to the butter mixture in two additions, alternating with the sour cream, mixing on low speed until just combined and no flour streaks are visible. Beat in the milk until just combined. Fold in 1½ cups of the mini chocolate chips.

6 Scoop the batter into the lined muffin cups about three-quarters of the way to the top. Sprinkle the muffins with the remaining ¼ cup of mini chips. Transfer to the oven.

7 Bake for 5 minutes. Then reduce the temperature to 350°F (or 325°F on the convection setting) and bake for about 20 minutes, or until a toothpick inserted into the center of a muffin comes out clean.

8 Cool in the pan for 10 minutes then enjoy. Cool leftovers completely before wrapping them up.

STORAGE: Store in a sealed container or wrapped in parchment paper and then aluminum foil at room temperature for up to 4 days.

VARIATION: Double-Chocolate Cream Cheese Muffins: In a medium bowl, stir together 6 ounces full-fat cream cheese (preferably Philadelphia), ¼ cup sugar, and ½ teaspoon pure vanilla extract. Make the muffin batter as directed and scoop into the muffin cups three-quarters of the way to the top. Dividing evenly, dollop the cream cheese mixture on the top of the muffin batter in the center, and then sprinkle the ¼ cup mini chocolate chips on top. Bake as directed.

gingerbread muffins

To avoid menu fatigue at The Hungry Gnome, I like to come out with some treats that have all the nostalgic flavors of each season. I have so many fond memories of opening Grandma Rosemarie's door in the fall and winter to find a house filled with the pungent aroma of sweet, warm spices. Sometimes it was her famous apple pie, gingerbread cookies, or even Great-Grandma Lena's Applesauce Cake (page 224). I wanted these muffins to give you this warm, fuzzy feeling as they bake in the oven and bring people undeniable holiday cheer—even if you make them in July (and trust me, you will want them year-round). They have a light, fluffy texture inside and the tops have perfect chew from the brown sugar and molasses. Add the sweet glaze to make them even more reminiscent of a holiday cookie, or leave them plain for a less sweet variation.

MAKES 10 JUMBO MUFFINS

- 8 tablespoons (4 ounces/1 stick) unsalted butter, melted
- ¼ cup canola or other vegetable oil
- ½ cup granulated sugar
- 1 cup packed dark brown sugar
- ¼ cup molasses
- 1 teaspoon pure vanilla extract
- ¼ teaspoon orange extract
- 2 large eggs, at room temperature
- 1¼ cups applesauce (I prefer Mott's)
- 2 cups cake flour (not self-rising)
- 1 teaspoon baking soda
- ¾ teaspoon fine table salt
- 2½ teaspoons ground ginger
- 2 teaspoons ground cinnamon
- ¼ teaspoon ground allspice
- ¼ teaspoon ground cloves
- ⅓ cup full-fat sour cream

GLAZE

- 1½ cups powdered sugar
- ½ teaspoon pure vanilla extract or vanilla bean paste
- 2 to 3 tablespoons milk (any milk will do, dairy or nondairy)
- Nonpareil sprinkles (optional), for decorating

1. In a stand mixer fitted with the paddle, beat together the melted butter, canola oil, granulated sugar, brown sugar, molasses, vanilla, and orange extract until light and creamy in texture, about 5 minutes.
2. Add the eggs one at a time, beating to just combine after each addition. Beat in the applesauce until just combined.
3. In a separate bowl, whisk together the cake flour, baking soda, salt, ginger, cinnamon, allspice, and cloves.
4. On low speed, add the flour mixture to the butter mixture in two additions, alternating with the sour cream and ending with the sour cream. Beat until just combined and no flour streaks are visible.
5. Cover the bowl with plastic wrap and refrigerate for about 1 hour to allow the flavors to develop and the leavening agents to activate. This batter tends to be fairly thin so it also helps thicken it slightly.
6. Meanwhile, preheat the oven to 425°F (or 400°F on the convection setting). Line 10 cups of two jumbo muffin tins with paper liners.
7. Scoop the batter into the lined muffin cups filling three-quarters of the way up. Transfer to the oven.
8. Bake for 5 minutes. Then, while keeping the oven closed, reduce the oven temperature to 350°F (or 325°F on the convection setting) and bake for 20 to 22 minutes, until a toothpick inserted in the center of a muffin comes out clean.
9. Let the muffins cool in the pans for about 10 minutes, then transfer to a wire rack to cool completely.
10. Meanwhile, make the glaze: In a small bowl, whisk together the powdered sugar, vanilla, and 2 tablespoons of milk. Add more milk, splash by splash, if needed. You want the glaze to be thin enough to drizzle, but still fairly opaque so it maintains its shape on the muffins.
11. Using a spoon, drizzle the glaze over the muffins and then sprinkle some nonpareils over the top if you're feeling festive. Let the glaze set for 15 to 30 minutes.

STORAGE: Store in a sealed container or wrapped in parchment paper and then aluminum foil at room temperature for up to 3 to 4 days.

chocolate chip pancake muffins

One of my greatest joys as a chef is to combine everyday favorites into new, delicious hybrids that are better than the originals. Call it selective brunch breeding, if you will! While muffins and pancakes are both very popular breakfast items, pancakes are not suitable for a quick grab-and-go breakfast. That's where this recipe comes in. It's a practical yet delicious breakfast confection that—thanks to real maple syrup, semisweet chocolate chips, and brown butter—has the flavor and aroma of chocolate chip pancakes. The texture inside is moist and fluffy and the tops are crisp from the maple and sugar caramelizing in the oven. Make these for guests on the weekend (your house will smell amazing) and keep extras (if you have any!) for breakfast-on-the-go come Monday morning.

MAKES 8 JUMBO MUFFINS

4 tablespoons (2 ounces/ ½ stick) unsalted butter, cut into pieces

1 cup granulated sugar

½ cup pure maple syrup

⅓ cup canola or other vegetable oil

2 large eggs

2 teaspoons pure vanilla extract

2 cups plus 1 tablespoon cake flour (not self-rising)

½ teaspoon baking powder

½ teaspoon baking soda

1¼ teaspoons fine table salt

Pinch of ground nutmeg

1 cup sour cream

1½ cups semisweet chocolate chips, plus more (optional) for topping

1. In a skillet, melt the butter over medium heat. Stir the butter the entire time to keep it moving. Once melted, the butter will begin to foam and sizzle around the edges. Keep stirring. In 5 to 8 minutes, the butter will turn golden brown. Some foam will subside and the milk solids at the bottom of the pan will be toasty brown. It will smell intensely buttery and nutty. Immediately remove the pan from the heat and pour the butter into a heatproof bowl to stop the cooking process. (If left in the hot pan, the butter will burn.) Set aside to cool.
2. Pour the granulated sugar into the bowl of a stand mixer fitted with the paddle. With the mixer on low speed, slowly add the cooled brown butter. Mix until combined, about 2 minutes. Add the maple syrup and canola oil and mix again, until combined.
3. With the mixer on medium speed, add one egg at a time and beat just until incorporated before adding the next. Stir in the vanilla.
4. In a separate bowl, stir together 2 cups of the cake flour, the baking powder, baking soda, salt, and nutmeg until combined.
5. Add about one-third of the flour mixture and half of the sour cream and beat on low speed until combined. Add another one-third of the flour mixture and the rest of the sour cream and beat on low speed again, until combined. Add the remaining flour mixture and beat on low speed until just combined.
6. In a medium bowl, use a spoon or rubber spatula to toss the chocolate chips with the remaining 1 tablespoon of flour. This will help them not to sink during the baking process. Gently fold the chocolate chips into the batter.
7. Cover the batter with plastic wrap and refrigerate for at least 2 hours, or until it slightly firms up. (Or for up to 48 hours in a sealed container.)
8. When ready to bake, preheat the oven to 375°F (or 350°F on the convection setting). Line 8 cups of two jumbo muffin tins with paper liners.
9. Using a 6-ounce ice cream scoop or a spoon, fill the muffin cups three-quarters of the way each with batter.

GLAZE

1 cup powdered sugar

¼ teaspoon fine table salt

2 tablespoons pure maple syrup

1 tablespoon unsalted butter, melted

¼ teaspoon pure vanilla extract

10 Transfer to the oven and immediately reduce the oven temperature to 350°F (or 325°F on the convection setting). Bake for 25 to 30 minutes, until a toothpick inserted in the center of a muffin comes out clean.

11 Let the muffins cool in the pan.

12 Meanwhile, make the glaze: In a small bowl, whisk together the powdered sugar, salt, maple syrup, melted butter, and vanilla. While whisking, gradually add water 1 teaspoon at a time until the glaze is thin enough to drizzle but still fairly opaque in color.

13 Remove the muffins from the pan. Using a spoon or a pastry bag, drizzle the icing on top of the muffins. Before the icing sets, add more chocolate chips on top for decoration, if you'd like.

STORAGE: **Store in a sealed container or wrapped in parchment paper and then aluminum foil at room temperature for about 5 days.**

lemon poppyseed muffins

At The Hungry Gnome, the best-selling seasonal item is our Lemon Poppy Muffin. For me, when it comes to citrusy confections like this, the more lemon the better. When creating this recipe, I wanted the muffin to be fluffy and moist and to have a perfectly pleasant tang. Beating the lemon zest with the sugar and butter really helps to release the oils in the zest and the addition of the sour cream helps emphasize the natural tang. I had my mom in mind when I created the glaze, because although she doesn't like anything "too sweet," she loves a good chewy powdered sugar glaze with the right amount of lemony "pop." Although these muffins seem like the perfect spring and summer treat, you will find yourself making them year-round.

MAKES 10 JUMBO MUFFINS

2 cups cake flour (not self-rising)

1 teaspoon baking powder

½ teaspoon baking soda

¾ teaspoon fine table salt

2 tablespoons poppyseeds, plus more for garnish

8 tablespoons (4 ounces/1 stick) unsalted butter, at room temperature

⅓ cup canola or other vegetable oil

1¼ cups granulated sugar

2 teaspoons finely grated lemon zest

½ teaspoon pure vanilla extract

2 teaspoons pure lemon extract

2 large eggs, at room temperature

1 cup sour cream

3 tablespoons freshly squeezed lemon juice

GLAZE

1½ cups powdered sugar

⅛ teaspoon pure vanilla extract

1 tablespoon freshly squeezed lemon juice

Pinch of fine table salt

1. In a medium bowl, stir together the cake flour, baking powder, baking soda, salt, and poppyseeds. Set aside.
2. In a stand mixer fitted with the paddle (or in a large bowl using a hand mixer), beat the butter, canola oil, and granulated sugar on medium speed until light and fluffy, about 3 minutes.
3. Add the lemon zest, vanilla, and lemon extract and beat for another minute to release the natural oils of the zest. Add the eggs one at a time, beating to just combine after each addition.
4. Add the flour mixture in two additions, alternating with the sour cream, mixing on low speed until just combined. (Overmixed batter will result in tough muffins!) Beat in the lemon juice until just combined.
5. Let the batter sit at room temperature for 20 to 30 minutes to allow the flavors to develop further and the ingredients to become one.
6. When ready to bake, preheat the oven to 425°F (or 400°F on the convection setting). Line 10 cups of two jumbo muffin tins with paper liners.
7. Spoon the batter into the muffin cups to come about three-quarters of the way to the top. Transfer to the oven.
8. Bake for 5 minutes. Then, while keeping the oven closed, reduce the oven temperature to 325°F and bake for 15 to 18 minutes, until a toothpick inserted in the center of a muffin comes out clean.
9. Meanwhile, make the glaze: In a small bowl, whisk together the powdered sugar, vanilla, lemon juice, and salt. Add a few drops of water at a time until smooth and pourable but still fairly opaque.
10. Let the muffins cool in the pan on a wire rack for about 5 minutes. Then remove the muffins from the pan to the rack to cool completely.
11. When the muffins have cooled completely, carefully dunk the tops into the glaze, allowing the excess to run off. Sprinkle the tops with poppyseeds and let the glaze set at room temperature.

STORAGE: **Store in a sealed container or wrapped in parchment paper and then aluminum foil at room temperature for up to 3 days.**

honey corn muffins

When I think of the foods that truly symbolize growing up on Long Island, one of them has to be the humble corn muffin. Bagel shop (or, as we call it, "bagel place") and deli culture is something we Long Islanders take very seriously. Both establishments require great bagels, buttered kaiser rolls, bacon-egg-and-cheese sandwiches, thin chicken cutlets, massive slabs of crumb cake (see Classic Top-Heavy Deli Crumb Cake, page 197), overly sweetened iced tea lemonades (we call them half and halfs), and cakey corn muffins. No matter what you're ordering, you always ask for the side-car corn muffin, which is cut in half, buttered, and toasted on the griddle. You'll be handed a grease-stained brown paper bag with a massive, yellow corn muffin inside, with a quarter pound of softened margarine plopped in the center. The muffin is somehow moist yet dry. And most of the time only half of it ends up in your mouth because it shatters into a million bits on your lap. (I still think my parents are cleaning crumbs out of their cars from decades ago LOL.) Despite the mess, they are a sweet and savory staple and something I will forever crave. When creating this recipe, I wanted all the flavors of corn muffins past—but with a slightly less crumbly texture for an even more enjoyable eating experience.

MAKES 7 JUMBO MUFFINS

1¼ cups cake flour (not self-rising)

¾ cup fine cornmeal

½ cup sugar

1 teaspoon baking powder

½ teaspoon baking soda

1½ teaspoons fine table salt

¼ cup canola or other vegetable oil

2 large eggs, at room temperature

½ teaspoon pure vanilla extract

¼ cup whole milk

1 cup sour cream

8 tablespoons (4 ounces/1 stick) unsalted butter, melted

Salted butter (optional), for serving

3 tablespoons honey (I prefer clover honey), plus more for serving (optional)

1. In a large bowl, whisk together the cake flour, cornmeal, sugar, baking powder, baking soda, and salt.
2. Create a well in the center and add the canola oil, eggs, vanilla, milk, and sour cream. Whisk until just combined.
3. In a separate bowl, whisk together the melted butter and honey. Slowly pour the mixture into the batter while whisking to ensure it doesn't separate. Just whisk until combined.
4. Cover the batter with plastic wrap and refrigerate for 30 minutes so the dry ingredients can fully absorb the wet ingredients and the cornmeal can soften slightly.
5. When ready to bake, preheat the oven to 425°F (or 400°F on the convection setting). Line 7 cups of two jumbo muffin tins with paper liners.
6. Scoop the batter into the muffins cups, filling them three-quarters of the way to the top. Transfer to the oven.
7. Bake for 5 minutes. Then, while keeping the oven closed, reduce the oven temperature to 350°F (or 325°F on convection setting) and bake for 15 to 18 minutes, until the muffins are lightly golden brown and a toothpick inserted in the center comes out clean. You don't want to overbake these—you want them just set, so they do not dry out.
8. Serve on their own or the real Long Island way: cut in half with a big pat of salted butter. For added sweetness, add a little drizzle of honey with the butter.

STORAGE: **Store in a sealed container or wrapped in parchment paper and then aluminum foil at room temperature for up to 3 days.**

hummingbird muffins

Sometimes I create recipes while I'm dreaming in bed or when I am craving a particular flavor . . . or, in all honesty, because I am cleaning out my fridge and I have a particular ingredient left over that needs to be used up. One day, I had leftover crushed pineapple from a carrot cake, along with a few bunches of browning bananas, so I decided it was the perfect time for a Hummingbird Muffin. These are my take on the classic Southern cake, but they're frosting-free, which makes them more suitable for breakfast. The pineapple is slightly acidic, which really brightens up the batter, and—combined with the banana and coconut—it just feels fun and subtly tropical. I love the fresh and bright flavors combined with warm, buttery notes from the pecans and cinnamon. I knew these were a winner when my husband and I went to a Mets game and he pulled one, wrapped in paper towels, out of his pocket. He said he couldn't stop eating them and needed another for a midgame snack!

MAKES 12 JUMBO MUFFINS

8 tablespoons (4 ounces /1 stick) unsalted butter, at room temperature

¾ cup granulated sugar

¾ cup packed dark brown sugar

⅓ cup canola oil

2 teaspoons pure vanilla extract

2 large eggs

1 cup mashed very ripe banana (about 3 medium)

¾ cup juice-packed canned crushed pineapple (do not drain)

½ cup sweetened coconut flakes

2 cups all-purpose flour

¾ teaspoon ground cinnamon

1 teaspoon baking soda

½ teaspoon baking powder

¾ teaspoon fine table salt

½ cup chopped pecans

½ cup sour cream

1. In a stand mixer fitted with the paddle, beat the butter, granulated sugar, brown sugar, and canola oil until light and creamy, about 3 minutes.
2. Add the vanilla and beat until combined. Add the eggs one at a time, beating to just combine after each addition. Beat in the mashed banana, crushed pineapple, and coconut flakes and mix until combined.
3. In a separate bowl, whisk together the flour, cinnamon, baking soda, baking powder, salt, and pecans.
4. Add the flour mixture to the butter mixture in two additions, alternating with the sour cream, mixing on low speed until just combined and no flour streaks are visible.
5. Cover the bowl with plastic wrap and refrigerate for 30 minutes to allow the flavors to develop and the leavening agents to activate.
6. When ready to bake, preheat the oven to 425°F (or 400°F on the convection setting). Line 12 cups of two jumbo muffin tins with paper liners.
7. Scoop the batter into the muffin cups filling them three-quarters of the way to the top. Transfer to the oven.
8. Bake for 5 minutes. Then reduce the temperature to 350°F (or 325°F on the convection setting) and continue to bake them for about 22 minutes, or until a toothpick inserted into the center of the muffin comes out clean.

STORAGE: **Store in a sealed container or wrapped in parchment paper and then aluminum foil at room temperature for up to 4 days.**

CHAPTER 3

COOKIES

SOFT & CHEWY CHOCOLATE CHIP COOKIES 64

CHOCOLATE PEANUT BUTTER PUDDING COOKIES 67

BETTER BAKERY SPRINKLE COOKIES 68

GRANDMA'S NUT CUPS 71

GRANDMA'S CREAM CHEESE THUMBPRINT COOKIES 72

LUNCH BOX CHOCOLATE CHIP COOKIES 74

GINGER MOLASSES CHEWS 77

JULIA GULIA COOKIES 78

ITALIAN FIG COOKIES 81

ITALIAN RAINBOW COOKIES 84

BBB (BADA$$ BAKING B*TCH) COOKIES 88

ONE TOFF COOKIES 90

Homemade Toffee Chunks 91

CHOCOLATE BAKLAVA 92

VEGAN COOKIE BUTTER CHIP COOKIES 95

STRAWBERRIES & CREAM COOKIES 96
CHOCOLATE MOLASSES COOKIES 99
DOUBLE-CHOCOLATE ESPRESSO NUT COOKIES 100
MOM'S TOFFEE ALMOND BRITTLE 102
CHOCOLATE-DIPPED BUTTER COOKIES 103
GRANDMA'S GINGERBREAD COOKIES 104
Royal Icing 105
ANISETTE TOAST 107
CHOCOLATE-DIPPED PISTACHIO CHERRY BISCOTTI 108
JUMBO CHOCOLATE CRINKLE COOKIES 110
PIGNOLI COOKIES 113
MAPLE PECAN SANDWICH COOKIES 114
THE DANS' COOKIES 117
GNOMMIES (M&M OATMEAL CHIP) COOKIES 118

soft & chewy chocolate chip cookies

People always ask me what my favorite food is, which is a very tough question for a professional chef who pretty much eats everything. I've thought long and hard about this and have come to the conclusion that a good ol' chocolate chip cookie is probably my biggest pleasure in life. Whether crispy, gooey, thick, thin, big, small . . . I LOVE them all. I've noticed that unlike me, most people are rather opinionated about their cookies. Some like them soft and some like crispy crunchy. My best friend, Chris, is one of those people who only likes cookies that are soft and chewy, never crunchy, and when I was invited over to his apartment for dinner I decided I would surprise him with some soft, chewy cookies! After some research I found that there are two things that may help the cookies retain that soft, just-baked feel: pudding mix and cake flour. There is also more brown sugar in this recipe than white sugar, which helps to obtain that perfect chew. The pudding gives the cookies a beautifully sweet and robust vanilla flavor, but its creamy and gelatinous qualities keep these babies soft for the long haul—even days after you bake them, which is often hard to do!

MAKES 12 TO 14 COOKIES

½ cup packed dark brown sugar

2 tablespoons granulated sugar

8 tablespoons (4 ounces / 1 stick) unsalted butter, at room temperature

1¼ cups cake flour (not self-rising)

½ teaspoon baking soda

½ teaspoon fine table salt

⅓ cup dry vanilla instant pudding mix (I prefer Jell-O)

1 large egg

1 teaspoon pure vanilla extract

1 cup semisweet chocolate chips

Flaky sea salt (optional)

STORAGE: **Store in an airtight container or tin or wrapped in parchment paper and then aluminum foil at room temperature for up to 5 days. Cookie dough balls can be stored in a ziplock bag in the freezer for up to 6 months. Thaw slightly at room temperature for 30 minutes before baking.**

1. Preheat the oven to 350°F (or 325°F on the convection setting). Line a cookie sheet with parchment paper.
2. In a stand mixer fitted with the paddle, beat the brown sugar, granulated sugar, and butter until light and creamy, about 3 minutes.
3. In a separate bowl, stir together the cake flour, baking soda, and fine salt. Set aside.
4. Add the dry pudding mix, egg, and vanilla to the butter/sugar mixture and beat until combined. Scrape down the sides of the bowl to ensure everything is incorporated evenly and blend again on high for another 3 minutes.
5. On low speed, gradually beat the flour mixture into the butter mixture until everything comes together. Scrape down the sides of the bowl to make sure it is evenly mixed.
6. On low speed (or by hand with a wooden spoon), mix in the chocolate chips until just combined. Do not overmix.
7. Using a cookie scoop or a spoon, drop 4-tablespoon balls of dough on the prepared cookie sheet, leaving at least 1 inch of space between them in case they spread slightly. Although these can be baked right away, it is always best to chill the cookie dough balls for 1 hour or overnight. This will result in a more flavorful cookie with a more favorable texture. You want the dough to be in a fairly round, high mound before baking to ensure it gets a nice chewy consistency after baking. If you'd like a salty finish you can sprinkle a few flakes of sea salt on top of each ball of dough before baking. Transfer to the oven.
8. Bake for 8 to 10 minutes, until the edges are golden but the cookies are still a bit gooey and soft.
9. Let them cool slightly on the pan before serving. They can be enjoyed warm or cold—they will be soft and chewy regardless!

chocolate peanut butter pudding cookies

As we learned from the previous recipe, if you want an everlasting soft and chewy texture to your cookie, then pudding is the answer. In the first week of COVID quarantine back in March 2020 I created this recipe as a coping mechanism. Like many, my husband and I were stranded in our tiny, one-bedroom apartment in Manhattan, afraid and confused. Dan and I both have a love of chocolate and peanut butter, so I whipped up these cookies with the hope that they would bring us comfort. We held each other close while eating the warm cookies, watching movies and doing jigsaw puzzles. It was truly a time I will never forget and I hope these bring you comfort and joy.

MAKES 12 COOKIES

8 tablespoons (4 ounces/1 stick) unsalted butter, at room temperature

½ cup packed dark brown sugar

2 tablespoons granulated sugar

⅓ cup dry instant pudding mix, either chocolate fudge or chocolate (I prefer Jell-O)

1 large egg, at room temperature

1 teaspoon pure vanilla extract

1 cup cake flour (not self-rising)

¼ cup dark Dutch-process cocoa powder, preferably Hershey's Special Dark, sifted to remove lumps

½ teaspoon fine table salt

½ teaspoon baking soda

1 cup peanut butter chips (or half semisweet chocolate chips and half peanut butter chips for a nice melty texture)

1. Preheat the oven to 375°F (or 350°F on the convection setting). Line a cookie sheet with parchment paper.
2. In a stand mixer fitted with the paddle, beat together the butter, brown sugar, and granulated sugar until light and creamy, about 3 minutes.
3. Add the dry pudding mix, egg, and vanilla and beat until combined. Scrape down the sides of the bowl to ensure everything is incorporated evenly and blend again on high for another 2 to 3 minutes.
4. Meanwhile, in a separate bowl, stir together the cake flour, cocoa powder, salt, and baking soda.
5. On low speed, gradually beat the flour mixture into the butter/sugar mixture just until everything is incorporated. Scrape down the sides of the bowl to make sure it is evenly incorporated.
6. Add the peanut butter chips on low speed until just combined. Do not overmix.
7. Using a cookie scoop or a spoon, drop 4-tablespoon balls of dough onto the lined cookie sheet, leaving at least 1 inch of space around them as they do spread slightly. Transfer to the oven.
8. Bake for about 8 minutes, or until the outside appears dry to the touch but the cookies are still fudgy and soft on the inside.
9. Let them cool slightly on the pan for 10 to 15 minutes before serving. They can be enjoyed warm or cold, they will be soft and chewy regardless!

STORAGE: **Store in an airtight container or tin or wrapped in parchment paper and then aluminum foil at room temperature for up to 5 days. Cookie dough balls can be stored in a ziplock bag in the freezer for up to 6 months. Thaw slightly at room temperature for 30 minutes before baking.**

better bakery sprinkle cookies

I think when I was between the ages of two and five, bakery sprinkle cookies were one of my main food groups. My Grandpa Jim would take me to the bakery with him every morning and I would almost always choose a character-shaped cookie that was encrusted with sprinkles and had a big, round sugar head. These cookies are the slightly more adult version of the bakery classic. They are sweet and colorful and "birthday cakey" in taste, but the texture is pleasantly chewy and rich from the addition of the almond paste. Both children and adults will be fighting over these!

MAKES 14 COOKIES

12 tablespoons (6 ounces / 1½ sticks) unsalted butter, at room temperature

3 tablespoons vegetable shortening, such as Crisco

4 ounces almond paste, broken up into little pieces the best you can

1½ cups sugar

1 teaspoon pure vanilla extract

½ teaspoon pure almond extract

2¾ cups all-purpose flour

½ teaspoon baking soda

½ teaspoon cream of tartar

½ teaspoon fine table salt

2 large eggs, at room temperature

½ to ¾ cup sprinkles, for rolling the cookies in (I like to do some in regular ice cream–style sprinkles and some in nonpareil, as shown in the photo)

1. In a stand mixer fitted with the paddle, beat together the butter, shortening, almond paste, sugar, vanilla, and almond extract until light and fluffy, 3 to 5 minutes.
2. Meanwhile, in a separate bowl, whisk together the flour, baking soda, cream of tartar, and salt. Set aside.
3. Add the eggs to the butter/sugar mixture one at a time, beating to just combine after each addition.
4. On low speed, add the flour mixture to the butter mixture until everything is incorporated. Scrape down the sides of the bowl and mix again to make sure it is evenly incorporated. Do not overmix!
5. Scoop the dough into 3-tablespoon balls and roll them in your hands to round them. Roll them completely in the sprinkles, place them on a tray, and refrigerate for at least 3 hours or overnight.
6. When you're ready to bake, preheat the oven to 350°F (or 325°F on the convection setting). Line two cookie sheets with parchment paper.
7. Place the balls at least 2 inches apart on the lined cookie sheets and transfer to the oven.
8. Bake for 8 minutes. Then, with oven mitts on, carefully rap/bang the cookie sheet on the counter or on the oven rack just to release some air and to encourage spreading/cracking. Rotate the tray front to back and bake for another 3 to 5 minutes, until the cookies begin to crack in the center. The dough will not get much color.
9. Transfer the cookies to wire racks to cool.

STORAGE: **Store in an airtight container at room temperature for up to 5 days.**

grandma's nut cups

These buttery nut cup cookies are another Grandma Rosemarie classic! She always stressed the importance of variety on a holiday cookie tray, whether that be in flavor, texture, or shape and size. You would find these babies next to the crispy gingerbread cookies, the tender jam thumbprints, and the creamy chocolate pudding-filled cream puffs. These were a lovely addition, as they are almost like having a bite-size pecan pie, which is of course fun for kids (and adults). The crust is tender yet flaky and has a subtle tang from the cream cheese, which really makes them special. You can customize these by using whatever nuts and spices you like or even by adding mini chocolate chips to the filling!

MAKES 15 COOKIES

DOUGH

3 ounces cream cheese (I prefer Philadelphia), at room temperature

8 tablespoons (4 ounces/1 stick) unsalted butter, at room temperature

2 tablespoons granulated sugar

¼ teaspoon fine table salt

1 cup all-purpose flour

Cooking spray

NUTTY FILLING

¾ cup packed dark brown sugar

1 large egg

1 teaspoon pure vanilla extract

1½ tablespoons unsalted butter, melted

¼ teaspoon ground cinnamon

¾ cup chopped pecans

Powdered sugar (optional), for dusting

1. Make the dough: In a stand mixer fitted with the paddle, beat together the cream cheese, butter, granulated sugar, and salt until smooth and homogenous, about 3 minutes.
2. On low speed, add the flour and mix until just combined. The dough will be fairly stiff.
3. Roll the dough into 15 small balls and then press the dough balls into the bottom and up the sides of 15 cups of a prepared mini muffin tin (sometimes I help it along with the back of a wooden spoon). Refrigerate the mini muffin tin for 1 hour.
4. When ready to bake, preheat the oven to 350°F (or 325°F on the convection setting).
5. Make the nutty filling: Using the stand mixer again fitted with the paddle (or in a bowl using a hand mixer), beat together the brown sugar, egg, vanilla, melted butter, and cinnamon until smooth and well blended. Stir in the pecans by hand.
6. Fill each shell three-quarters of the way to the top of the crusts. Transfer to the oven.
7. Bake for 20 to 25 minutes, until the crusts are golden brown.
8. Let cool almost completely in the pan and then carefully remove them from the pans. If desired, dust lightly with powdered sugar before serving.

STORAGE: **Store in a sealed container or tin at room temperature for up to 1 week. You can also freeze these wrapped in parchment paper and then plastic wrap for up to 60 days. Thaw at room temperature on wire racks.**

grandma's cream cheese thumbprint cookies

These tender thumbprint cookies, made with a rich cream cheese dough, were always a highlight on my grandma's holiday dessert table. Each bite holds a sweet surprise of jam—apricot and raspberry are my favorites, but this simple and classic dough is a perfect canvas for any flavor you love.

MAKES 18 COOKIES

8 tablespoons (4 ounces/1 stick) unsalted butter, at room temperature

4 ounces cream cheese (I prefer Philadelphia)

½ cup sugar

¼ teaspoon fine table salt

¼ teaspoon pure vanilla extract

1 cup all-purpose flour

⅓ cup ground walnuts (see Tip)

About 5 teaspoons raspberry or apricot jam (or whatever jam you like!)

1. In a stand mixer fitted with the paddle, beat together the butter, cream cheese, sugar, salt, and vanilla until smooth and homogenous, about 3 minutes.
2. Add the flour and ground walnuts and mix until just combined. Cover the bowl with plastic wrap and refrigerate for at least 1 hour as the dough will be too soft and will cause too much spreading.
3. When ready to bake, preheat the oven to 375°F (or 350°F on the convection setting).
4. Roll the chilled dough into 1-tablespoon balls and place them 1 inch apart on two ungreased cookie sheets (about 18 cookies). Use your thumb to press a light indent into the center of each dough ball. Drop ¼ teaspoon of the jam into each indentation. Transfer to the oven.
5. Bake for 15 to 20 minutes, until the edges and bottoms start to brown slightly.
6. Let cool on the pans.

STORAGE: **Store in a sealed container or tin at room temperature for up to 1 week. You can also freeze these wrapped in parchment paper and then plastic wrap for up to 60 days. Thaw at room temperature on wire racks.**

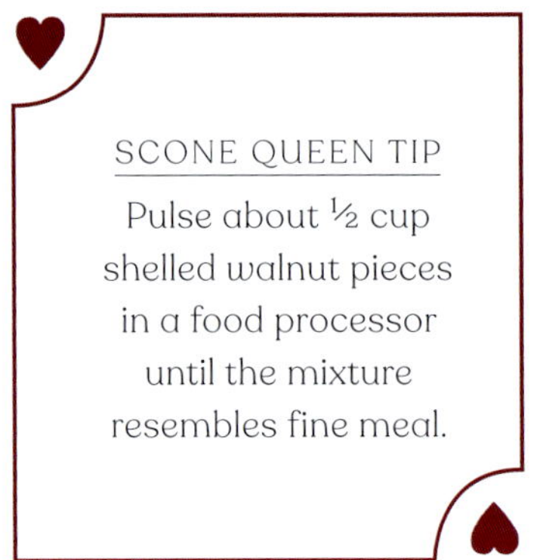

SCONE QUEEN TIP

Pulse about ½ cup shelled walnut pieces in a food processor until the mixture resembles fine meal.

Recipes

lunch box chocolate chip cookies

I may be biased, but I have the best mom in the world. She not only worked full time as a third grade teacher, she also came home and cooked for us, helped us with our schoolwork, took us to after-school activities, and even found the strength to have fun and play games with us. She probably didn't know it at the time, but she did little things throughout my childhood that left a lasting impression on me. There was the homemade bread on snow days (see Mom's Snow Day Bread, page 170), homemade Play-Doh, eating frozen orange juice concentrate out of the can together, always letting me taste the first piece of pasta to let her know if it was done, "Sunday Night Toast," which was leftover Italian bread with butter on Sunday nights when we got hungry (since dinner was at 2 p.m.), and finally "cookie cereal" in the morning when my cousins slept over. Cookie cereal was a big serving bowl filled with crushed-up Chips Ahoy! cookies and topped with cold milk. We would eat it like cereal with big spoons and just laugh because it felt so wrong but so right. These are the little things you never, ever forget. This cookie recipe is inspired by this classic boxed cookie in that it has a sort of buttery, crisp, and crumbly exterior that just screams "dunk me."

MAKES 24 COOKIES

- 18 tablespoons (9 ounces / 2¼ sticks) unsalted butter, melted
- 2 tablespoons vegetable shortening, such as Crisco
- 1 cup packed dark brown sugar
- 1½ cups granulated sugar
- 2 teaspoons pure vanilla extract
- 1 large egg
- 1 large egg yolk
- 1½ cups bread flour
- 1½ cups cake flour (not self-rising)
- 1 teaspoon baking soda
- 1 teaspoon baking powder
- 1½ teaspoons fine table salt
- 1 tablespoon cornstarch
- 2 cups chocolate chips, preferably Ghirardelli bittersweet chips (or a blend of bittersweet and semisweet chips)

1. In a stand mixer fitted with the paddle, beat the melted butter, shortening, brown sugar, granulated sugar, and vanilla until smooth and creamy, about 4 minutes.
2. Add the whole egg and egg yolk and beat until just combined.
3. In a separate bowl, whisk together the bread flour, cake flour, baking soda, baking powder, salt, and cornstarch.
4. On low speed, add the flour mixture to the butter/sugar mixture and mix until just combined. On low speed or by hand with a rubber spatula, stir in the chocolate chips.
5. Scoop the dough into 3-ounce balls (about the size of a golf ball), place them on a parchment-lined sheet pan, cover with plastic wrap, and refrigerate for at least 3 hours or preferably overnight.
6. When ready to bake, preheat the oven to 375°F (or 350°F on the convection setting). Line four sheet pans with parchment paper.
7. Place the dough balls on the lined pans at least 3 inches apart to give them room to spread. Transfer to the oven.
8. Bake for 12 to 15 minutes, until they are golden brown but the centers are still slightly gooey. Remove them from the oven and instantly tap the pans on the counter to help them to spread and crack slightly. This will help expose the little pools of melted chocolate.
9. Let the cookies cool on the pans for 5 to 10 minutes before enjoying. You can enjoy warm or room temperature—whatever you prefer!

STORAGE: **Store in an airtight container or tin or wrapped in parchment paper and then aluminum foil at room temperature for up to 5 days. Cookie dough balls can be stored in a ziplock bag in the freezer for up to 6 months. Thaw slightly at room temperature for 30 minutes before baking.**

ginger molasses chews

If you love the flavors of a classic gingerbread cookie but prefer soft and chewy rather than crisp and snappy, this is for you! When these cookies bake, they spread slightly and the most beautiful cracks form. Serve them as is or with a simple vanilla bean glaze that settles stunningly in every crevice.

MAKES 15 COOKIES

12 tablespoons (6 ounces / 1½ sticks) unsalted butter, at room temperature

½ cup granulated sugar

½ cup packed dark brown sugar

2¾ cups cake flour (not self-rising)

½ teaspoon fine table salt

2 teaspoons baking soda

1½ teaspoons ground cinnamon

1½ teaspoons ground ginger

½ teaspoon ground cloves

⅛ teaspoon ground allspice

1 teaspoon pure vanilla extract

¼ cup molasses

1 large egg

VANILLA GLAZE (OPTIONAL)

1½ cups powdered sugar

¼ teaspoon vanilla bean paste or pure vanilla extract

Pinch of fine table salt

Optional: sprinkles, edible shimmer dust, or colorful sanding sugar

---

STORAGE: Store in an airtight container or tin or wrapped in parchment paper and then aluminum foil at room temperature for up to 1 week. Un-iced cookies can be frozen for up to 60 days wrapped in parchment paper and then aluminum foil and in a ziplock bag. Thaw at room temperature on wire racks and then ice with the icing.

1. In a stand mixer fitted with the paddle, beat together the butter, granulated sugar, and brown sugar until light and creamy, 3 to 5 minutes.
2. Meanwhile, in a separate bowl, whisk together the cake flour, salt, baking soda, cinnamon, ginger, cloves, and allspice. Set aside.
3. Add the vanilla and molasses to the butter/sugar mixture and beat until combined. Add the egg, beating to combine.
4. On low speed, gradually add the flour mixture to the butter mixture and beat until everything is incorporated. Scrape down the sides of the bowl and mix again to make sure it is evenly incorporated. Do not overmix!
5. Using a 2-ounce cookie/ice cream scoop or a spoon, scoop 1½-tablespoon mounds of dough and roll them into balls using the palms of your hands.
6. Place the dough balls on a tray, cover them with plastic wrap. and refrigerate for at least 2 hours or up to overnight so all the flavors can really get to know each other. (You can also freeze the dough balls in a sealed plastic bag or container for about 3 months.)
7. When you're ready to bake, preheat the oven to 350°F (or 325°F on the convection setting). Line a cookie sheet with parchment paper.
8. Place the dough balls on the lined cookie sheet at least 2 inches apart as they will spread a bit. Transfer to the oven.
9. Bake for 10 minutes. Then, with oven mitts on, carefully rap/bang the cookie sheet on the counter or oven rack to help them to spread and crackle. Rotate the pan front to back and continue baking for 2 to 4 minutes, until they have spread out and they have cracked on top. When you remove the baking sheet from the oven rap/bang the tray two or three times again to release any air.
10. Allow the cookies to cool completely on a wire rack before icing.
11. Make the vanilla glaze (if desired): In a small bowl, whisk together the powdered sugar, vanilla, and salt. Add water 1 tablespoon at a time until the icing thins into an opaque white icing that slowly runs off a spoon.
12. Take the cooled cookies and dip the crackled tops into the icing, allowing the excess to run off as you hold them upside down for a moment. Place the cookies on a wire rack and if desired, while the icing is still wet, sprinkle on edible shimmer dust, sprinkles, or sanding sugar. Let the icing set before enjoying.

julia gulia cookies

In February 2024, when I was asked to a Valentine's Day baking segment on *The Drew Barrymore Show,* I knew I had to reference my favorite rom-com and one of Drew's most iconic roles, Julia from *The Wedding Singer.* These rich, dark chocolate cookies have creamy chunks of white chocolate and chewy tart cherries. As I told Drew, the rich chocolate and cherries are both aphrodisiacs, so if you make these, you'll be ready for some romancin'—and hey, maybe you'll meet someone to "grow old with you."

MAKES 12 TO 14 COOKIES

8 tablespoons (4 ounces/1 stick) unsalted butter, at room temperature

¼ cup vegetable shortening, such as Crisco

1 cup packed dark brown sugar

½ cup granulated sugar

1 tablespoon pure vanilla extract

2 cups cake flour (not self-rising)

¾ cup dark Dutch-process cocoa powder, preferably Hershey's Special Dark, sifted to remove lumps

½ teaspoon baking powder

¾ teaspoon fine table salt

2 large eggs, at room temperature

½ cup semisweet chocolate chips

¾ cup white chocolate chunks (I use Ghirardelli or Baker's white chocolate), preferably hand-chopped

¾ cup dried tart cherries, such as Trader Joe's dried Montmorency cherries

Crushed freeze-dried cherries (optional), for garnish

1. In a stand mixer fitted with the paddle, blend together the butter, shortening, brown sugar, granulated sugar, and vanilla until light and creamy, 3 to 5 minutes.
2. Meanwhile, in a separate bowl, stir together the cake flour, cocoa powder, baking powder, and salt. Set aside.
3. Add the eggs to the butter/sugar mixture one at a time, beating to just combine after each addition.
4. On low speed, gradually add the flour mixture to the butter/sugar mixture and beat until just combined. Do not overmix! Scrape down the sides of the bowl to make sure it is evenly incorporated.
5. On low speed (or by hand with a wooden spoon), mix in the chocolate chips, white chocolate chunks, and dried cherries until just combined. Do not overmix.
6. Using a cookie scoop or a spoon, drop 3-tablespoon balls of dough onto a parchment-lined cookie sheet, leaving at least 1½ inches between them to allow them to spread. You want the dough to be in a round, high mound before baking to ensure it gets a nice chewy consistency after baking. Refrigerate the dough balls for at least 1 hour before baking.
7. When ready to bake, preheat the oven to 375°F (or 350°F on the convection setting).
8. Bake for 8 minutes. Then, with oven mitts on, carefully rap/bang the cookie sheet on the counter to release some air and help the cookies to spread a bit. Rotate the sheet front to back and continue baking for 4 to 5 minutes, until the cookies have cracked in the centers and appear drier on the outer edges but still gooey in their centers.
9. As soon as they come out of the oven rap/bang the cookie sheet on the counter again to help them spread further and then, if desired, crumble freeze-dried cherries onto the cookies so they adhere to the melted chocolate. Enjoy warm or cooled on a wire rack!

STORAGE: **Store in an airtight container or tin or wrapped in parchment paper and then aluminum foil at room temperature for up to 5 days. Cookie dough balls can be stored in a ziplock bag in the freezer for up to 6 months. Thaw slightly at room temperature for 30 minutes before baking.**

italian fig cookies

This Sicilian classic is the star of our holiday cookie table and a recipe that has been passed down in my family for over one hundred years. This cookie is an integral part of our Christmas season, so much so that we say the holiday season hasn't begun until we have taken our first bite of that sweet fig filling. Even the sheer smell of these cookies catapults me into holiday mode. For those who have never experienced an Italian fig cookie, it is the firmer, more citrussy cousin of a Fig Newton. Although there are many variations, my family's filling consists of ground-up dried yellow figs, candied orange peel and citron, nuts, warm spices, and sweet honey. Every family and bakery also seem to have their own special way of shaping these, and no recipe is alike. Some people prefer to shape them into a log and then cut them into basic square shapes similar to a Newton, but my grandma's signature shape is reminiscent of a fig leaf and is nothing short of a work of art. Be sure to follow my step-by-step photos to get a clear understanding of how to execute the details, and don't fret, after a few tries you'll be a master in no time.

MAKES ABOUT 60 COOKIES

DOUGH

7 cups all-purpose flour, plus more for dusting

1¼ cups powdered sugar

1 teaspoon fine table salt

8 ounces plus 2 tablespoons vegetable shortening, such as Crisco

¼ cup Marsala wine

1 tablespoon pure vanilla extract

1 large egg

About 1 cup cold water

FILLING

2 pounds dried yellow figs (Smyrna figs work perfectly here), stems cut off and quartered

1 cup walnuts

1 cup pecans

½ cup diced candied orange peel (about 75 grams)

⅓ cup diced candied citron

1 teaspoon ground cinnamon

¼ teaspoon ground nutmeg

⅛ teaspoon ground cloves

1 cup clover honey

ASSEMBLY

Cooking spray

Nonpareil sprinkles

1 Make the dough: In the bowl of a stand mixer, sift together the flour, powdered sugar, and salt.

2 With a pastry cutter or a stand mixer fitted with the paddle, cut in the vegetable shortening until there are small crumbs throughout.

3 In a glass measuring cup or bowl, whisk together the Marsala, vanilla, and egg until combined.

4 Set the bowl on the stand mixer and snap on the dough hook. With the mixer on low speed, add in the egg mixture to the flour mixture. Gradually stream in the water until the dough moistens and comes together. You don't want to add too much, just enough for the dough to form.

5 Dump the dough out onto a very lightly floured surface and knead the dough a few times just until it comes together into a ball. Cut the ball into 4 equal portions and form each piece into a disc. Wrap the dough discs in plastic wrap and place them in the freezer to chill while you make the filling.

6 Make the filling: In a large bowl, mix together the figs, walnuts, pecans, orange peel, citron, cinnamon, nutmeg, and cloves until combined evenly. Divide it into 2 equal portions, as the food processor will not be able to blend it all at once.

7 Working with one portion at a time, in a food processor, combine the fig mixture and half of the honey and blend until the filling is a thick paste. You will still see the seeds of the dried figs and bits of nuts and fruit, however it should be fairly smooth. Remove the paste from the food processor and then repeat with the second half of the fig mixture and honey.

8 Assemble the cookies: Preheat the oven to 375°F (or 350°F on the convection setting). Lightly coat up to four cookie sheets with cooking spray.

♥ *recipe continues*

9 Working with one portion of dough at a time, roll out the dough into a roughly 8 × 16-inch rectangle and use a pizza cutter (or sharp knife) to cut out 16 rectangles measuring 2 × 4 inches. Using a spoon, mound together 2 to 3 teaspoons of filling and then roll it in your hands to create a log. Place the filling log on one of the longer sides of a dough rectangle and fold the other half over to cover it. Seal the seam with your fingers.

10 Once they are folded over and sealed, cut a slit 1½ to 2 inches long down the middle. Then cut 4 slits in the upper right side and 4 slits in the lower left side. Use your hands to bend the top right and bottom left to form an S shape, at the same time splaying open the slits to reveal the filling.

11 Gently dip the tops of the cookies in the sprinkles and place them 1 inch apart on the coated cookie sheets. Transfer to the oven.

12 Bake for 12 to 15 minutes, until slightly golden on the bottoms but still light in color on the tops.

13 Transfer the cookies to wire racks and allow them to cool completely before you eat them.

STORAGE: **Store in an airtight container at room temperature in a cool, dry place for up to 6 weeks or in the freezer for several months (thaw at room temperature).**

italian rainbow cookies

Rainbow cookies are an Italian American classic, especially in the New York tristate area. They are a bit of a labor of love, but man are they worth it! My Grandma Rosemarie made them every Christmas and they were something we always looked forward to. Grandma's were cakier and had a chocolate buttercream frosting on top rather than the traditional hard chocolate shell, which was delicious, but I sometimes longed for a differentiation in texture. When I was writing this book my sister Christiana (the biggest rainbow cookie fan) and I put our heads together to figure out how we could tweak Grandma's recipe to make it even better. After several trial runs and taste tests with my sisters and my employees, I got it. They are super moist but still have that subtle denseness from the almond paste, and there is both apricot and raspberry jam because why choose? The tart and sweet notes of the raspberry and the slightly floral essence of the apricot both complement the almond beautifully. This recipe makes about 35 cookies (though you can cut them to any size you would like), and when sealed in a container you will find that days later they are still perfection . . . maybe even better than the day prior.

MAKES ABOUT 35 COOKIES

1½ cups sugar

8 ounces almond paste (I prefer Solo)

24 tablespoons (12 ounces / 3 sticks) unsalted butter, at room temperature

2 teaspoons pure almond extract

1¼ teaspoons pure vanilla extract

4 large eggs, separated

2 cups all-purpose flour

½ teaspoon baking powder

½ teaspoon fine table salt

½ cup buttermilk, either whole or low-fat work

Red, green, and yellow food coloring (or whatever 3 colors you like!)

Cooking spray

7 ounces seedless raspberry jam

7 ounces apricot jam

1. Position the middle and bottom racks and preheat the oven to 350°F (or 325°F on the convection setting).
2. In a stand mixer fitted with the paddle, beat the sugar and almond paste together for 2 to 3 minutes to break up the almond paste. Add the butter and beat on medium speed until smooth, about 4 minutes.
3. Beat in the almond extract and vanilla. Then beat in the egg yolks one at a time until smooth and combined.
4. In a separate bowl, whisk together the flour, baking powder, and salt.
5. Add the flour mixture to the butter mixture in two additions, alternating with the buttermilk, mixing on low speed until just combined.
6. In a clean stand mixer bowl fitted with the whisk (or in a bowl using a hand mixer), beat the egg whites until stiff peaks form, 4 to 5 minutes.
7. Add half the beaten egg whites to the batter and fold them in. Fold in the remaining beaten egg whites being careful not to overmix.
8. Ideally using a kitchen scale to ensure even baking and even layers, weigh the batter. Once weighed, divide it into 3 equal portions and place each in a separate bowl. (Note, if you don't have a scale, you can also use a cookie scoop to divide the batter the best you can.) Put about ¼ teaspoon food coloring into each bowl of batter: green in one, yellow in the other, and red in the last. Gently stir in the dyes but don't overmix.
9. Coat three 9 × 13-inch quarter-sheet pans with cooking spray and then line them with parchment paper. Spray the top of the parchment paper lightly as well and then spread each color batter evenly onto each separate pan.
10. Bake for 10 minutes, or until just set.
11. Let the cakes cool slightly in the pans, 15 to 20 minutes.

recipe continues on page 86

GANACHE

10 ounces bittersweet chocolate chips, preferably Ghirardelli, or semisweet chips

2 teaspoons vegetable shortening, such as Crisco

12 When the cakes are just slightly warm, spread the raspberry jam evenly over the top of the green cake layer. Carefully place or flip the yellow layer on top of the raspberry jam layer, removing the parchment paper. Top the yellow layer with the apricot jam and then place or flip the pink cake layer on top of the apricot jam, discarding the parchment paper. Cover the top of the cake with plastic wrap and then top it with another sheet pan. Use cans or a carton of broth to weigh down the layers and refrigerate for at least 4 hours or overnight. (The texture gets better with time, so it is best to let these sit overnight.)

13 Make the ganache: In a microwave-safe bowl, combine the chocolate chips and shortening. Microwave for about 1 minute, then in 15-second increments, stirring until melted and smooth.

14 Pour half of the chocolate onto the top of the cake and spread it out evenly. Place it in the fridge for about 20 minutes to set the chocolate.

15 Once the chocolate has set, flip the cake onto a cutting board discarding the bottom layer of parchment. Spread the other half of the chocolate on top and then place it in the fridge again for about 30 minutes to set.

16 Heat a sharp, thin chef's knife or filleting knife under hot water and then wipe off the excess water. Cut the cake into 1½-inch squares (or in larger rectangles if you prefer). Heating the knife with every cut will help get clean cuts through the set chocolate.

17 You can serve the cookies right away or place them in a sealed tin or glass container at room temperature with parchment paper in between to avoid sticking. I like to let the cookies sit overnight at room temperature so the jam can further soften the cakes and the flavors can meld together.

STORAGE: **Store in a sealed container at room temperature for up to 10 days or frozen for up to 3 months. Thaw at room temperature and serve.**

SCONE QUEEN TIP

If you want to make these for the holidays, bake and assemble everything all the way to covering the two sides with chocolate. Then wrap the whole cake in parchment and then plastic wrap and freeze it! The night before you want to serve the cookies you can take the cake out of the freezer to thaw, then slice and serve!

bbb (bada$$ baking b*tch) cookies

This cookie is a spin-off of my Soft & Chewy Chocolate Chip Cookies (page 64), but this time "feminized"! These cookies have all sorts of flavors and textures mixed in, each one bringing something unique and powerful to the table . . . just like women! They also happen to be my absolute PMS dream because they are packed with chocolate (three different kinds, to be exact), they have buttery toffee, chewy coconut flakes, a hint of warm cinnamon, and finally . . . crunchy, salty potato chips! The texture is unlike any other cookie, as each bite will have you experiencing something different, in the best way possible. Be sure to use kettle-cooked chips as they will retain their crunch even if you freeze the cookie dough balls and bake them off another day. Trust me, this is one of those treats you will always want to have on hand for "emergency cravings," so make the dough balls, place them in plastic bags, freeze them, and then bake them off as needed.

MAKES 12 TO 14 COOKIES

- **½ cup packed dark brown sugar**
- **2 tablespoons granulated sugar**
- **8 tablespoons (4 ounces/1 stick) unsalted butter, at room temperature**
- **1¼ cups cake flour (not self-rising)**
- **½ teaspoon baking soda**
- **½ teaspoon fine table salt**
- **¼ teaspoon ground cinnamon**
- **⅓ cup dry vanilla instant pudding mix (I prefer Jell-O)**
- **1 large egg, at room temperature**
- **1 teaspoon pure vanilla extract**
- **¾ cup bittersweet chocolate chips (I like Ghirardelli); see Tip**
- **⅓ cup milk chocolate chips**
- **⅓ cup white chocolate chips**
- **⅓ cup sweetened coconut flakes**
- **Heaping ⅓ cup crushed salted kettle-cooked potato chips**
- **¼ cup toffee bits, such as Heath**
- **Flaky sea salt (optional), for topping**

1. Preheat the oven to 375°F (or 350°F on the convection setting). Line a cookie sheet with parchment paper.
2. In a stand mixer fitted with the paddle, blend together the brown sugar, granulated sugar, and butter until light and creamy, about 3 minutes.
3. Meanwhile, in a separate bowl, stir together the cake flour, baking soda, fine salt, and cinnamon. Set aside.
4. Add the dry pudding mix, egg, and vanilla to the butter/sugar mixture and beat until combined. Scrape down the sides of the bowl to ensure everything is incorporated evenly and blend again on high for another 3 minutes.
5. On low speed, gradually beat the flour mixture into the butter mixture until everything is incorporated. Scrape down the sides of the bowl to make sure it is evenly incorporated.
6. On low speed (or by hand with a wooden spoon), mix in all the chocolate chips, the coconut flakes, potato chips, and toffee bits until just combined. Do not overmix.
7. Using a cookie scoop or a spoon, drop 2-tablespoon balls of dough onto the lined cookie sheet, spacing at least 1 inch apart in case they spread slightly. You want the dough to be in a fairly round, high mound before baking to ensure it gets a nice chewy consistency after baking. If you'd like an extra salty finish, sprinkle a few flakes of sea salt on top of each ball of dough. Transfer to the oven.
8. Bake for 10 minutes. Then, with oven mitts on, carefully rap/bang the pan on the counter to release the air and to assist with spreading slightly. Rotate the pan front to back, return to the oven, and bake for 2 to 3 minutes, until the edges are golden but the cookies are still a bit gooey and soft in the center.
9. Let them cool slightly on the pan before serving. They can be enjoyed warm or cold, they will be soft and chewy regardless!

STORAGE: **Store in an airtight container or tin or wrapped in parchment paper and then aluminum foil at room temperature for up to 5 days. Cookie dough balls can be stored in a ziplock bag in the freezer for up to 6 months. Thaw slightly at room temperature for 30 minutes before baking.**

SCONE QUEEN TIP

For the chocolate chips, you can just use one single type of chocolate chip instead of the three different types called for. Or split the amounts between only two types of chips!

one toff cookies

When my best friend Chris's favorite cookies were no longer being sold at his local general store he of course turned to his "Fairy Baking Mother"—moi! The prerequisite was they had to be thick and chunky with big chunks of white and dark chocolate, and toffee bits. Chris not only approved of the cookies, but said they were better than the original . . . so, mission accomplished! Now what to name them? I called upon my social media followers to help me come up with the name, and the perfect name was born. The One Toff Cookie is dedicated to all the strong, powerful, and passionate women who work behind the scenes at The Hungry Gnome. I wouldn't be where I am today without them!

MAKES 12 GIANT 4-INCH COOKIES

8 tablespoons (4 ounces/1 stick) cold unsalted butter, cut into cubes

¼ cup vegetable shortening, such as Crisco

1 cup packed dark brown sugar

½ cup granulated sugar

2 teaspoons pure vanilla extract

2 large eggs, at room temperature

2¾ cups all-purpose flour

½ teaspoon baking powder

¾ teaspoon fine table salt

⅓ cup Homemade Toffee Chunks (recipe follows) or store-bought (see Tip)

½ cup milk chocolate chips

½ cup dark chocolate chunks or Ghirardelli bittersweet discs

½ cup white chocolate chunks (if you can't find chunks, chop your own)

1. In a stand mixer fitted with the paddle, beat together the butter, shortening, brown sugar, and granulated sugar until light and creamy, 3 to 5 minutes.
2. Add the vanilla and then the eggs and beat until just combined.
3. In a separate bowl, stir together the flour, baking powder, and salt.
4. On low speed, gradually beat the flour mixture into the butter/sugar mixture until everything is incorporated. Scrape down the sides of the bowl and mix again to make sure it is evenly incorporated. Do not overmix.
5. On low speed (or by hand with a wooden spoon), mix in the toffee chunks, milk chocolate chips, and dark and white chocolate chunks.
6. Place a long sheet of plastic wrap on the counter, scoop the dough into the plastic wrap and using floured hands form the dough into a log shape about 9 inches long and 2½ inches in diameter and roll it tightly in the plastic wrap. Gently place the log on a pan or plate and place in the fridge to chill for at least 3 hours or overnight (overnight preferred as it helps the texture).
7. When ready to bake, preheat the oven to 375°F (or 350°F on the convection setting). Line two cookie sheets with parchment paper.
8. Using a sharp knife cut the logs crosswise into rounds 1½ inches thick and place them about 2 inches apart on the lined cookie sheets. Transfer to the oven.
9. Bake for 11 to 13 minutes, until golden brown on the edges but still soft in the center.
10. Let the cookies cool on the pans for about 10 minutes and then enjoy!

STORAGE: **Store in an airtight container or tin or wrapped in parchment paper and then aluminum foil at room temperature for up to 5 days. Cookie dough balls can be stored in a ziplock bag in the freezer for up to 6 months. Thaw slightly at room temperature for 30 minutes before baking.**

HOMEMADE TOFFEE CHUNKS

MAKES 1⅓ CUPS

8 tablespoons (4 ounces/1 stick) unsalted butter

½ cup sugar

¼ teaspoon fine table salt

1. Line a sheet pan or 9 × 13-inch baking pan with parchment paper and have nearby.
2. In a small heavy-bottom saucepan, combine the butter, sugar, salt, and 2 tablespoons water. Set over medium heat and cook, stirring occasionally, until the mixture is a deep caramel color and a candy thermometer reads 300°F, which is the "hard ball/crack stage."
3. Immediately pour onto the lined pan. Let cool at room temperature and then refrigerate until set, about 30 minutes.
4. Carefully place the chilled toffee on a cutting board and chop it into ½-inch chunks using a sharp chef's knife. Store airtight in the refrigerator or freezer. Or store them in a sealed container in a dry place.

SCONE QUEEN TIP

You can use store-bought toffee bits, however they tend to be much smaller, so the toffee will be a little less apparent but still delicious. Making it homemade makes for beautiful chewy and crunchy caramel pools within the cookie.

chocolate baklava

My husband, Dan, and I went to Greece for our honeymoon in June 2019. We had a truly euphoric ten days in Mykonos, Santorini, and Athens, full of sunshine, souvlaki sandwiches, spectacular views, and phyllo dough. In Athens especially, there were bakeries everywhere with gorgeous trays of baklava and traditional Greek pastries in the windows. Of course, I insisted on trying every single one to find the best baklava in Greece. We finally found a restaurant that solely served lavish desserts called Nancy's Sweet Home, which had chocolate baklava on the menu. Being the chocoholic that I am, I knew I *had* to try it, and it was nothing short of incredible. Since I can't easily hop over to Athens, I decided to re-create it at home. With crisp layers of paper-thin phyllo dough, rich melty chocolate, buttery walnuts and pistachios, and sweet, sticky vanilla bean–infused honey syrup poured all over the top, it is an addicting contrast in textures and one of the most craveable recipes in this book.

MAKES ABOUT 30 PIECES, DEPENDING ON HOW BIG YOU CUT THEM

BAKLAVA

- 20 tablespoons (10 ounces/ 2½ sticks) salted butter (no butter substitutes), melted, plus more softened for the baking pan
- ½ pound (about 2 cups) walnuts, finely chopped (pulsed in a food processor is best)
- ½ pound (about 1 cup) lightly salted roasted pistachios, finely chopped (pulsed in a food processor is best)
- 1 (12-ounce) package mini semisweet chocolate chips
- ¾ cup sugar
- 1½ teaspoons ground cinnamon
- 1 (16-ounce) package frozen phyllo dough, thawed

SYRUP

- ¾ cup freshly squeezed orange juice
- ½ cup sugar
- ½ cup honey
- 1½ teaspoons vanilla bean paste or ½ vanilla bean, split lengthwise (2 teaspoons pure vanilla extract OK, but bean or paste is preferred)
- ⅛ teaspoon fine table salt

1. Make the baklava: Preheat the oven to 375°F (or 350°F on the convection setting). Butter a 15 × 10 × 1-inch baking pan (like a jelly-roll pan).
2. In a bowl, combine the walnuts, pistachios, chocolate chips, sugar, and cinnamon.
3. Remove the phyllo dough from the package, unroll it and instantly cover it with a damp, clean kitchen towel to avoid it drying out and becoming brittle.
4. Layer 8 sheets of phyllo dough (one at a time) in the pan, brushing each with some melted butter before adding the next sheet.
5. Sprinkle 1¾ cups of the chocolate/nut mixture over the top layer of phyllo in the pan.
6. Add 4 more sheets of phyllo dough (one at a time), brushing each with butter before adding the next. Top with 1¾ cups more of the nut mixture.
7. Layer and brush 4 more sheets of dough with butter and top with the remaining nut mixture. Top with the last 4 sheets of dough, brushing each sheet with butter. Drizzle any remaining butter over the top.
8. Using a sharp knife, cut the baklava into about 2-inch diamonds. Transfer to the oven.
9. Bake for 40 to 45 minutes, until golden brown.
10. Meanwhile, make the syrup: In a saucepan, combine the orange juice, sugar, honey, and ½ cup water. Add the vanilla bean paste (if using a vanilla bean, scrape the seeds into the pan). Bring to a boil over medium heat, stirring occasionally. Reduce the heat and simmer, uncovered, for about 20 minutes.
11. As soon as the baklava comes out of the oven, pour the syrup over the hot baklava. Cool completely in the pan on a wire rack before you enjoy.

STORAGE: **To store, just leave it at room temperature lightly covered with paper towels and/or aluminum foil. Do not cover with plastic wrap or put it in a plastic container or it may get soggy.**

vegan cookie butter chip cookies

If you are a frequent flyer, you probably know those crisp, spiced cookies in the red packaging that they often give you on board. Whether you're hungry or not, you'll find yourself munching on them because they are just too delicious to resist. When I discovered that my favorite travel snack came in a creamy, spreadable form, I wanted to put it on everything, or just lick it from a spoon like a dog licks peanut butter. My sister Julia, who, like me, is a big "cookie butter" fan, also happens to be dairy-free, so when I realized that Biscoff spread was vegan, my wheels started turning. Like most Americans, I love a classic peanut butter cookie, with its buttery, crumbly texture—so I wondered what would happen if I made a similar recipe but subbed cookie butter for peanut butter and replaced the egg with my go-to substitute of flaxmeal and water. Would it be my next best cookie? Yes, it was! I was hesitant to put the word "vegan" in the name of this recipe because I don't want to deter people from making it. I will go on the record saying that this may be one of my favorite recipes in the whole book, and it just happens to be vegan friendly. The flavor is buttery and sweet and the texture is melt-in-your-mouth. You will never miss the dairy, I promise!

MAKES 8 TO 12 COOKIES

2 tablespoons flaxseed meal

6 tablespoons vegan butter or margarine, preferably Earth Balance

⅓ cup granulated sugar

¼ cup packed dark brown sugar

1 teaspoon pure vanilla extract

½ cup creamy Biscoff spread (or your favorite Speculoos or cookie butter spread)

1 cup cake flour (not self-rising)

½ teaspoon baking soda

¼ teaspoon fine table salt

⅛ teaspoon ground cinnamon

1 cup dairy-free chocolate chunks, such as Enjoy Life

STORAGE: **Store in an airtight container or tin or wrapped in parchment paper and then aluminum foil at room temperature for up to 5 days. Cookie dough balls can be stored in a ziplock bag in the freezer for up to 6 months. Thaw slightly at room temperature for 30 minutes before baking.**

1 Preheat the oven to 375°F (or 350°F on the convection setting). Line a cookie sheet with parchment paper.

2 In a small bowl, stir together the flaxseed meal and 2 tablespoons water and let it sit for 10 minutes to thicken. Set the flax egg aside.

3 In a stand mixer fitted with the paddle, blend together the vegan butter, granulated sugar, and brown sugar until light and creamy, 3 to 5 minutes.

4 Add the vanilla and flax egg and beat until combined. Scrape down the sides of the bowl to ensure everything is incorporated evenly. Add the Biscoff spread and blend again on high for another 2 to 3 minutes.

5 In a separate bowl, stir together the cake flour, baking soda, salt, and cinnamon.

6 On low speed, gradually add the flour mixture to the butter mixture until everything is incorporated. Scrape down the sides of the bowl to mix all the batter.

7 Add the chocolate chunks and mix until just combined. Do not overmix.

8 Using a cookie scoop or a spoon, roll a 2-tablespoon chunk of dough in your hands to smooth it into a round ball. Place on the lined cookie sheet, leaving at least 2 inches space in between to give them room to spread.

9 Bake for 8 minutes. Then, with oven mitts on, carefully rap/bang the pan on the oven rack to release any air and to promote spreading. Rotate the pan front to back, then bake the cookies for 4 to 6 minutes, until the tops have crackled and the bottoms are golden brown but they are still chewy in the center.

10 Let them cool slightly on the pan before serving. They can be eaten warm or at room temperature!

strawberries & cream cookies

My Soft & Chewy Chocolate Chip Cookies (page 64) were such a big hit that I decided to create more variations of the cookie utilizing that magical pudding powder. I incorporated freeze-dried strawberries in both powder and sliced form to get maximum strawberry flavor, without negatively affecting the texture from too much moisture. I use white chocolate chunks because they get super melty and the flavor doesn't compete too much with the fresh, tangy flavor of the berries. These are my brother-in-law Mel's favorite; in fact, his exact words were "That is the best cookie I have ever had."

MAKES ABOUT 12 COOKIES

- **½ cup packed dark brown sugar**
- **2 tablespoons granulated sugar**
- **8 tablespoons (4 ounces/1 stick) unsalted butter, at room temperature**
- **⅓ cup dry vanilla instant pudding mix (I prefer Jell-O)**
- **3½ tablespoons freeze-dried strawberry powder (see Tip)**
- **1 large egg**
- **1 teaspoon pure vanilla extract**
- **1¼ cups cake flour (not self-rising)**
- **½ teaspoon fine table salt**
- **½ teaspoon baking soda**
- **¾ cup white chocolate chunks (or chop up a white chocolate baking bar) or white chocolate chips**
- **⅓ cup freeze-dried strawberry slices, roughly chopped (I use Trader Joe's)**

SCONE QUEEN TIP

You can buy freeze-dried powder online or you can buy freeze-dried strawberry pieces and grind them up in a food processor.

1. Preheat the oven to 375°F (or 350°F on the convection setting). Line a cookie sheet with parchment paper.
2. In a stand mixer fitted with the paddle, blend together the brown sugar, granulated sugar, and butter until light and creamy, 3 to 5 minutes.
3. Add the dry pudding mix, freeze-dried strawberry powder, egg, and vanilla and beat until combined. Scrape down the sides of the bowl to ensure everything is incorporated evenly and blend again on high for another 2 to 3 minutes.
4. In a separate bowl, stir together the cake flour, salt, and baking soda.
5. On low speed, gradually beat the flour mixture into the butter mixture until everything is incorporated. Scrape down the sides of the bowl to make sure it is evenly mixed.
6. Using a rubber spatula, mix in the white chocolate chunks and roughly chopped freeze-dried strawberry pieces. Mix until just combined. Do not overmix.
7. Using a cookie scoop or a spoon, drop about 2-tablespoon balls of dough onto the lined cookie sheet, leaving at least 1 inch between them in case they spread slightly. You want the dough to be in a fairly round, high mound before baking to ensure it gets a nice chewy consistency after baking. Transfer to the oven.
8. Bake for 8 to 9 minutes, until the edges are golden brown but the cookies are still a bit gooey and soft.
9. Let them cool slightly on the pan before serving. They can be enjoyed warm or cold—they will be soft and chewy regardless.

STORAGE: **Store in an airtight container or tin or wrapped in parchment paper and then aluminum foil at room temperature for up to 5 days.**

chocolate molasses cookies

I can still see it clearly. The long red box filled with the soft, chewy chocolate cookies stacked perfectly and all wrapped in clear cellophane that once opened cannot be resealed (which makes it okay to eat the whole box, right?). I'm talking about Archway cookies in the '90s and early 2000s. A staple in the New York tristate-area grocery stores along with its counterpart, the iced oatmeal cookie (yum). When they were no longer readily available in my local grocery stores, I decided to give them a go myself. Although these are a bit smaller than the Archway cookie, they have the same pleasant chew and rich cocoa flavor. I elevate this boxed classic by adding molasses and espresso powder to really amplify the chocolate flavor and balance out the sweetness.

MAKES 16 COOKIES

2 cups all-purpose flour

¾ teaspoon fine table salt

½ cup dark Dutch-process cocoa powder, preferably Hershey's Special Dark, sifted to remove lumps

1½ teaspoons baking soda

8 tablespoons (4 ounces/1 stick) unsalted butter, at room temperature

4 tablespoons vegetable shortening, such as Crisco

1 cup granulated sugar

½ cup packed dark brown sugar

⅓ cup molasses (I like Grandma's)

2½ teaspoons pure vanilla extract

1 teaspoon instant espresso powder

1 large egg, at room temperature

1. Position the middle and top racks and preheat the oven to 350°F (or 325°F on the convection setting). Line two baking sheets with parchment paper.
2. In a bowl, sift together the flour, salt, cocoa powder, and baking soda to ensure there are no lumps. Set aside.
3. In a stand mixer fitted with the paddle, beat the butter, shortening, ½ cup of the granulated sugar, the brown sugar, and molasses until light and creamy, about 3 minutes.
4. Add the vanilla, espresso powder, and egg and beat until combined.
5. On low speed, add the flour mixture to the butter mixture and mix until just combined. Do not overmix. Scrape down the sides of the bowl with a rubber spatula.
6. Spread the remaining ½ cup of granulated sugar in a shallow bowl. Using a spoon or cookie scoop, scoop into 2½-tablespoon mounds of dough and roll between your hands to create smooth balls. Roll the dough balls in the granulated sugar and then place the cookies on the lined cookie sheets spaced about 3 inches apart.
7. Bake for 8 to 10 minutes, until they have puffed up slightly and have begun to crack on the top, rotating the pans front to back and switching racks halfway through. Do not overbake as they will lose their pleasant chew. As soon as you remove them from the oven, rap/bang the pan on the counter three or four times to help the cookies to spread a bit more and to get deeper cracks.
8. Let the cookies cool on the pans for 10 to 15 minutes and then enjoy!

STORAGE: **Store in an airtight container or tin or wrapped in parchment paper and then aluminum foil at room temperature for up to 5 days. Cookie dough balls (without the sugar coating) can be stored in a ziplock bag in the freezer for up to 6 months. Thaw slightly at room temperature for 45 minutes before rolling in the granulated sugar and then baking.**

double-chocolate espresso nut cookies

Every family seems to have their own cookie repertoire, and this here recipe is at the *top* of our list. It is the most requested cookie during the holidays, and really for any occasion. These cookies are a chocoholic's dream. They have the richest chocolate flavor in part due to the addition of espresso powder, which just makes that chocolate really shine. They are fudgy on the inside but have a wonderful, buttery crunch from the walnuts and pecans. To balance out the sweetness and give them a real pop, I top them with flaky sea salt. Just a warning: Try not to eat these at bedtime unless you want to be partying all night, because these puppies give you quite the boost of energy!

MAKES 12 LARGE COOKIES

2 ounces unsweetened baking chocolate

6 ounces semisweet chocolate

6 tablespoons (3 ounces) unsalted butter

¼ cup all-purpose flour, sifted

¼ teaspoon baking powder

½ teaspoon fine table salt

2 large eggs

¾ cup sugar

2 teaspoons instant espresso powder (not coffee grounds)

2½ teaspoons pure vanilla extract

1 cup semisweet chocolate chips

1 cup walnut pieces

1 cup pecan pieces, lightly toasted

Flaky sea salt, for sprinkling

1. Position the middle and top racks and preheat the oven to 375°F (or 350°F on the convection setting). Line two cookie sheets with parchment paper.
2. In a saucepan, bring a couple of inches of water to a simmer. Put the unsweetened chocolate, semisweet chocolate, and butter in a large heatproof bowl. Set the bowl on top of the saucepan so it is sitting just above the hot water but not touching the water. Cook, stirring occasionally, over low heat until the mixture is melted and smooth, about 5 minutes. Remove the bowl from the heat and set it aside to cool.
3. In another bowl, stir together the flour, baking powder, and fine salt.
4. In a stand mixer fitted with the paddle, beat the eggs, sugar, instant espresso powder, and vanilla on medium-high speed for 2 minutes.
5. Slowly beat in the chocolate/butter mixture. The chocolate may still be warm, so be sure to slowly pour it into the mixer while on medium-low speed to prevent the eggs from cooking.
6. Add the flour mixture and beat until just combined, scraping down the sides in between mixing.
7. With a rubber spatula, fold in the chocolate chips, walnuts, and pecans.
8. Scoop about ⅓ cup of dough for each cookie and place the balls on the lined pans, spacing them about 1½ inches apart to ensure they don't spread into one another in the oven. Sprinkle a touch of flaky sea salt on the top of each cookie. Transfer to the oven.
9. Bake for 9 to 11 minutes, until the tops appear to be dry and shiny on the outside but the centers are still fudgy on the inside.
10. Transfer to a wire rack to cool.

STORAGE: **Store in an airtight container or tin or wrapped in parchment paper and then aluminum foil at room temperature for up to 5 days. Once baked, these cookies can be frozen wrapped in parchment and then plastic wrap in ziplock bags for up to 3 months. Thaw at room temperature on wire racks and enjoy.**

mom's toffee almond brittle

It's not Christmas without Mom's brittle, period. The crunchy, buttery texture is totally addictive and the flavor is the perfect blend of sweet, salty, and nutty. I love that this recipe comes together in minutes and the purchase of a simple candy thermometer ensures it comes out perfect every time. The only issue you'll have is that you didn't make enough. We've been guilty of eating it all before Christmas and then my mom has to make more on Christmas Eve. Although it never lasts long in our house, it does have a great shelf life, which makes this a fun treat to put in jars or tins and give away as gifts or party favors.

MAKES 12 TO 15 SERVINGS

1 cup almonds, toasted and chopped

8 ounces (2 sticks) salted butter

1 cup sugar

1 tablespoon light corn syrup

¾ cup semisweet chocolate chips or chopped chocolate

Flaky sea salt (optional)

1. Line a 9 × 13-inch pan with foil or parchment so it extends slightly over the sides of the pan. If using foil, spray it lightly with cooking spray.
2. Sprinkle half of the chopped almonds on the bottom of the pan.
3. In a heavy-bottom medium saucepan, melt the butter over low heat. Stir in the sugar, corn syrup, and 3 tablespoons water. Cook over medium heat, stirring occasionally until boiling.
4. Clip on a candy thermometer and cook over medium heat stirring frequently until the temperature reaches 290°F. This may take 10 to 15 minutes.
5. Quickly pour the mixture into the prepared pan. Spread it out evenly with an offset spatula if need be.
6. Let it stand for 2 to 3 minutes. When the surface is beginning to firm up, sprinkle the semisweet chocolate chips over the top. Wait about 2 minutes. Once the chocolate is melted, use an offset spatula to spread it out evenly over the toffee. Sprinkle the remaining chopped almonds evenly over the top of the chocolate and press lightly with your hands so they adhere. If you like salty/sweet feel free to add a light sprinkling of flaky sea salt over the top as well.
7. Refrigerate for at least 1 hour or until firm.
8. Lift the candy out of the pan and break into pieces.

STORAGE: **Store in an airtight container in the fridge.**

chocolate-dipped butter cookies

This melt-in-your-mouth shortbread-like cookie requires few ingredients and is super simple to make. It has minimal steps and is super hard to mess up, which make it a great starter recipe for new or unconfident bakers. In fact, this was one of the first family recipes I executed on my own as a young child prepping for the Christmas holiday. This dough is super customizable and can be rolled into all sorts of shapes. It can be dipped in chocolate (or not), pressed into a thumbprint and filled with jam, or even made into small sandwich cookies and filled with a ganache or hazelnut spread. The world is your oyster . . . I mean cookie.

MAKES 24 COOKIES

8 ounces (2 sticks) unsalted butter, at room temperature

½ teaspoon fine table salt

½ cup powdered sugar, sifted

1 teaspoon pure vanilla extract

2 cups all-purpose flour

10 ounces semisweet chocolate chips

1 tablespoon vegetable shortening, such as Crisco

Chopped toasted walnuts, for garnish (see Tip)

1 Preheat the oven to 375°F (or 350°F on the convection setting). Line up to three cookie sheets with parchment paper.

2 In a stand mixer fitted with the paddle, beat together the softened butter, salt, and powdered sugar until smooth. Add the vanilla and mix until combined. Slowly add the flour and just mix until the dough comes together and is fairly smooth. Don't overmix.

3 Using your hands, take 1-tablespoon balls of dough and roll them into log shapes about ¾ inch thick and 2 to 2½ inches long. If you'd prefer, you can also make them into round shapes by rolling the dough into balls and then flattening them with your hands. You can even twist the log shapes into an S shape for Santa Claus! The world is your oyster, have fun making shapes!

4 Set the cookies on the lined cookie sheet about 1 inch apart. Transfer to the oven.

5 Bake for 8 to 9 minutes, until the edges and bottoms are golden. The cookie tops will still be fairly pale in color, you don't want to overbake.

6 Cool the cookies completely on wire racks before decorating.

7 Meanwhile, in a microwave-safe bowl, combine the chocolate chips and shortening. Microwave for 1 minute, stir and then microwave again for 20 to 30 seconds, until the chocolate is fully melted and shiny.

8 Dip one end of the cooled cookie logs into the chocolate and then dip in the toasted walnuts. Place the dipped cookies on the prepared sheet pans and refrigerate them for about 15 minutes to set. Once the chocolate is set you are ready to enjoy!

STORAGE: **Store in an airtight container or tin or wrapped in parchment paper and then aluminum foil at room temperature for up to 10 days. These cookies can be wrapped in parchment then plastic wrap in the freezer for up to 6 months. Thaw slightly at room temperature for 30 minutes before baking. Although you can freeze these with the chocolate on them, the chocolate can sometimes become discolored, so I suggest dipping them later.**

SCONE QUEEN TIP

You can dip the cookies in the chocolate any way you like! And use whatever garnishes you like: any kind of chopped nuts, sprinkles, etc.

grandma's gingerbread cookies

Typically, when you hear "gingerbread," you think of Christmas, or at least the winter season, but to Grandma Rosemarie, any holiday warranted these crisp and spicy biscuits. We had bunnies at Easter and turkeys at Thanksgiving, and of course Santas, snowflakes, and gingerbread men at Christmas. One of my most magical childhood memories was decorating Grandma's lavish gingerbread houses in the days leading up to Christmas. Adorned with intricate molding made of royal icing, colorful stained-glass windows made of melted Life Savers candy, and hand-painted shutters and doors, these houses were nothing short of a work of edible art. My grandpa was an architect, so the structure of the house was always sound thanks to his handmade templates, so much so that we would need a hammer to knock it down. Grandma would spend countless hours putting together the basic foundation of the house and then the kids would decorate it with festive colored candies and icicles made of icing. Get creative with this recipe and let your imagination run wild!

MAKES AT LEAST 48 COOKIES, DEPENDING ON THE SIZE OF THE COOKIE CUTTERS

20 tablespoons (10 ounces / 2½ sticks) unsalted butter, at room temperature

1 cup granulated sugar

¼ cup packed dark brown sugar

4 cups all-purpose flour, sifted

1¼ teaspoons fine table salt

4 teaspoons ground cinnamon

1½ teaspoons ground cloves

1 teaspoon ground ginger

1 teaspoon ground nutmeg

2 teaspoons pure vanilla extract

1 teaspoon pure orange extract

2 large eggs, at room temperature

Royal Icing (optional; recipe follows)

Optional decoration: food coloring; sanding sugar, sprinkles, nonpareils

---

STORAGE: Store airtight at room temperature in a cool, dry place for up to 6 weeks or in the freezer for several months (thaw at room temperature on wire racks).

1. In a stand mixer fitted with the paddle, beat together the butter, granulated sugar, and brown sugar until light and creamy, 3 to 5 minutes.
2. Meanwhile, in a separate bowl, whisk together the flour, salt, cinnamon, cloves, ginger, and nutmeg. Set aside.
3. Add the vanilla and orange extracts to the butter/sugar mixture and beat until combined. Add the eggs one at a time, beating to just combine after each addition.
4. On low speed, gradually beat the flour mixture into the butter mixture until everything is incorporated. Scrape down the sides of the bowl and mix again to make sure it is evenly incorporated. Do not overmix!
5. Divide the dough in 2 equal portions and flatten into discs. Wrap the discs in plastic wrap or parchment and refrigerate the dough for at least 1 hour or until it is cold to the touch. Chilling the dough will make it easier to roll out and will also develop the flavor further.
6. When ready to bake, preheat the oven to 375°F (or 350°F on the convection setting). Line up to three cookie sheets with parchment paper.
7. Remove one disc of dough at a time from the fridge. Generously flour a work surface and a rolling pin. Roll the dough until it is about ¼ inch thick. Cut the dough into your desired shapes and carefully place them on the lined cookie sheets about 1 inch apart. The cookies will not spread much but they will need room to brown evenly. Transfer to the oven.
8. Bake for 10 to 12 minutes depending on the size, until golden brown on the bottoms.
9. Enjoy them plain or let them cool completely and decorate them with icing.
10. To decorate, use a piping bag with a small round tip or simply dip the tops of the cookies in the icing and allow the excess to run off. You can also drizzle them or use a spoon or offset spatula to spread some on! While the icing is still wet, feel free to add any candies or sprinkles.

ROYAL ICING

MAKES 3 CUPS

4 cups powdered sugar, sifted

3 tablespoons meringue powder

Pinch of fine table salt

½ teaspoon pure vanilla extract

Food coloring (optional)

In a stand mixer fitted with the whisk, beat together the powdered sugar, meringue powder, salt, and vanilla. Add a few drops of water at a time until you get the desired consistency. You want it fairly opaque so the icing doesn't run off the edge of the cookie. You can also portion the icing into different bowls and dye each one your desired color.

anisette toast

These classic Italian cookies have a subtly crunchy exterior and a slightly chewy center. They are mildly sweet and have the distinct flavor of anise, which to me is quintessential Sicilian. I will be honest in saying this licorice-like flavor is one you love or you hate, but dunked in a strong cup of Italian coffee, they are hard to resist. This recipe was a year-round go-to for my Grandma Rosemarie since they keep well for many days in a tin, and they can be enjoyed for breakfast or dessert.

MAKES 16 COOKIES

Cooking spray

4 large eggs

1½ cups sugar

1½ teaspoons pure anise extract

1 teaspoon baking powder

1 teaspoon fine table salt

2 cups all-purpose flour

¼ cup vegetable oil

1. Preheat the oven to 375°F (or 350°F on the convection setting). Coat a 9 × 13-inch baking pan with cooking spray.
2. In a stand mixer fitted with the paddle, beat the eggs and sugar thoroughly until light and fluffy, about 5 minutes. Add the anise extract, baking powder, and salt and mix until combined.
3. On low speed, gradually add the flour and mix until combined. Add the vegetable oil and beat until just combined.
4. Spread the batter evenly into the pan and transfer to the oven.
5. Bake for about 25 minutes, or until golden and set. Remove from the oven but leave the oven on and increase the oven temperature to 425°F (or 400°F on the convection setting).
6. Right when it comes out of the oven use a sharp knife to slice the "cake" down the center lengthwise, then make 7 evenly spaced cuts crosswise to make 16 rectangular "biscotti."
7. Carefully remove the cookies from the tray with a spatula and place them on their side on an ungreased cookie sheet. Return them to the oven.
8. Bake for 10 to 15 minutes, until golden brown.
9. Let the cookies cool on a wire rack and then enjoy!

STORAGE: **Store in an airtight container or tin or wrapped in parchment paper and then aluminum foil at room temperature for up to 7 days. These can also be stored in parchment paper then plastic wrap or a sealed container in the freezer for 3 to 4 months. Thaw at room temperature on wire racks.**

chocolate-dipped pistachio cherry biscotti

Let me tell you something about Italians: Honey, we love to dunk. I can still hear the sound of my grandpa's mouth, slurping up the soggy baked goods he submerged into his light and sweet coffee. These biscotti are the perfect texture, shape, and flavor for dunking in coffee, tea, milk, and hot cocoa, just to name a few. They are crunchy, but not so hard you'll break your teeth, and the flavor is rich and nutty. The slight chew and tang of the cherries complements the fruity notes of the dark chocolate, and combined with the green pistachios, they also give the biscotti a beautiful appearance. Bag them up during the holidays and give them away as gifts, or put them in a sealed tin and keep them for a couple of weeks! Breakfast, snack, dessert . . . or all three! Delish!

MAKES 24 COOKIES

DOUGH

- 1½ cups lightly salted roasted pistachios
- 3 cups all-purpose flour
- ⅔ cup dark Dutch-process cocoa powder, preferably Hershey's Special Dark, sifted to remove lumps
- 1 teaspoon baking powder
- 1 teaspoon baking soda
- ½ teaspoon fine table salt
- ⅛ teaspoon ground cinnamon
- 8 ounces (2 sticks) unsalted butter, at room temperature
- 1½ cups granulated sugar
- ½ cup packed dark brown sugar
- 2 teaspoons pure vanilla extract
- ¼ teaspoon pure almond extract
- 3 large eggs
- 2 teaspoons instant espresso powder
- ¾ cup dried cherries

CHOCOLATE DIP

- 1 cup bittersweet sweet chocolate chips, preferably Ghirardelli, or semisweet chocolate chips
- 1 teaspoon vegetable shortening, such as Crisco

Finely chopped roasted pistachios (optional), for sprinkling

1. Preheat the oven to 375°F (or 350°F on the convection setting). Line a sheet pan with parchment paper.
2. Make the dough: In a food processor, grind ½ cup of the pistachios until very fine. Lightly chop the remaining pistachios and set aside.
3. In a bowl, whisk together the ground pistachios with the flour, cocoa powder, baking powder, baking soda, salt, and cinnamon. Set aside.
4. In a stand mixer fitted with the paddle, beat the butter, granulated sugar, brown sugar, vanilla, and almond extract until light and fluffy, about 5 minutes.
5. Add the eggs one at a time, beating to just combine after each addition. Beat in the espresso powder.
6. On low speed, add the flour mixture to the butter/sugar mixture and mix until just combined. Add the cherries and the lightly chopped pistachios. Do not overmix.
7. Divide the dough into 2 equal portions and form each into a log 14 inches long and 2½ inches wide. Place the logs on the lined pan at least 3 inches apart.
8. Bake for 35 minutes. Remove from the oven but leave the oven on.
9. Let the logs cool for 15 minutes, then use a serrated knife to slice the logs crosswise into biscotti ½ inch thick. Arrange the biscotti on the lined sheet pans and bake another 15 minutes. Let cool completely on wire racks.
10. Meanwhile, make the chocolate dip: In a microwave-safe bowl, combine the bittersweet chocolate and shortening and microwave for about 1 minute until smooth.
11. Dip half of each biscotti in the melted chocolate and return them to the lined pans to set. You can also add a sprinkle of chopped pistachios on the chocolate before it sets. If you want less chocolate on the biscotti, instead of dipping, you can drizzle them with the chocolate using a piping bag or a spoon.

STORAGE: **Store airtight at room temperature in a cool, dry place for up to 2 weeks or in the freezer for several months (thaw at room temperature on wire racks).**

jumbo chocolate crinkle cookies

Crinkle cookies are an American staple during the holidays, but these are so good you'll be making them year-round. The texture and flavor of these cookies are that of a fudgy, rich brownie, but the powdered sugar exterior coats your lips and tongue in the most pleasant, playful manner. There's just something about that cornstarchy sugar that makes a baked good that much more addictive, am I right? Try to think about powdered donuts, Mexican wedding cookies, and funnel cake without smiling and salivating, so don't skimp on the powdered sugar when you roll the dough balls!

MAKES 12 LARGE COOKIES

- 8 tablespoons (4 ounces/1 stick) cold unsalted butter, cut into small cubes
- ¼ cup vegetable shortening, such as Crisco
- 1 cup packed dark brown sugar
- ½ cup granulated sugar
- 2 teaspoons pure vanilla extract
- 1 teaspoon instant espresso powder
- 2 large eggs
- 2 cups cake flour (not self-rising)
- ¾ cup dark Dutch-process cocoa powder, preferably Hershey's Special Dark, sifted to remove lumps
- ½ teaspoon baking powder
- ¾ teaspoon fine table salt
- 1 cup semisweet chocolate chips
- 1 cup bittersweet chocolate chips

FOR ROLLING

- About ⅓ cup granulated sugar
- About 1 cup powdered sugar

1. In a stand mixer fitted with the paddle, beat together the butter, shortening, brown sugar, and granulated sugar until light and creamy, about 3 minutes.
2. Add the vanilla and espresso powder and beat until just combined. Add the eggs one at a time, beating to just combine after each addition.
3. In a separate bowl, sift together the cake flour, cocoa powder, baking powder, and salt.
4. On low speed, gradually beat the flour mixture into the butter/sugar mixture until just combined. Scrape down the sides of the bowl to make sure it is evenly incorporated.
5. On low speed (or by hand with a wooden spoon), mix in the semisweet and bittersweet chocolate chips.
6. Using a 3-ounce cookie scoop or ⅓-cup measuring cup, scoop the dough and then use your hands to roll each scoop into a smooth ball.
7. Roll the dough balls in the granulated sugar and then in the powdered sugar and place them on two parchment-lined baking sheets and refrigerate for at least 1 hour or overnight.
8. When ready to bake, preheat the oven to 375°F (or 350°F on the convection setting).
9. After the dough chills, roll each dough ball in the powdered sugar again to really coat the outside. This ensures you get that snowy, crackle finish.
10. Place the dough balls on the lined baking sheets at least 2 inches apart. Transfer to the oven.
11. Bake for about 15 minutes, or until they have cracked on the top but are still fudgy in the center.
12. Let them cool on wire racks for 5 to 10 minutes before enjoying!

STORAGE: **Store in an airtight container or tin or wrapped in parchment paper and then aluminum foil at room temperature for up to 3 days. Cookie dough balls (without the powdered sugar coating) can be stored in a ziplock bag in the freezer for up to 6 months. Thaw slightly at room temperature for 45 minutes before rolling in the powdered sugar and then baking.**

pignoli cookies

Pignoli, or pine nut, cookies are a classic cookie that most Italian families have in their repertoire; however, Grandma Rosemarie's is by far my favorite one. These pignolis have a distinct, chewy center from the almond paste and egg white, but also the perfect sugary, crisp outside. They are very easy and quick to make and are the perfect finish to an Italian Sunday supper or a wonderful addition to your holiday cookie tin.

MAKES 12 COOKIES

8 ounces almond paste

2 large egg whites

1 teaspoon pure vanilla extract

½ cup powdered sugar

½ cup granulated sugar

¼ cup all-purpose flour

⅛ teaspoon fine table salt

About 4 ounces pine nuts, for rolling/topping

1. Preheat the oven to 350°F (or 325°F on the convection setting). Line a cookie sheet with parchment paper.
2. Break up the almond paste into the bowl of a stand mixer fitted with the paddle. Add the egg whites and beat until smooth and combined. Add the vanilla and mix until combined.
3. In a separate bowl, whisk together the powdered sugar, granulated sugar, flour, and salt.
4. On low speed, gradually add the flour mixture to the almond paste mixture until everything is combined and the dough comes together.
5. Using a 1-tablespoon cookie scoop, portion out 12 equal cookie dough balls.
6. Roll the cookie dough balls in the pine nuts making sure they are fully coated. The stickiness of the dough should help the pine nuts adhere to the dough.
7. Place the dough balls on the lined cookie sheet at least 2 inches apart. Transfer to the oven.
8. Bake for 22 to 25 minutes, until the cookies spread and the pine nuts are lightly toasted (don't overbake).
9. Let cool on wire racks, then enjoy!

STORAGE: **Store in an airtight container or tin or wrapped in parchment paper and then aluminum foil at room temperature for up to 3 days. Cookie dough balls (without the pine nuts coating) can be stored in a ziplock bag in the freezer for up to 6 months. Thaw slightly at room temperature for 45 minutes before rolling in the pine nuts and then baking.**

maple pecan sandwich cookies

Every October my friends and I do what we call a Girls & Ghouls Movie Night. We watch all of our favorite Halloween movies, like *Hocus Pocus* and *The Witches,* and eat lots of cheesy, carby, delicious foods. One year, I wanted to create a fun and festive cookie that my crew would enjoy. I love the flavors of molasses and warm spices together; it feels so comforting and of course perfect for fall. These cookies are soft and chewy and the filling is the perfect creamy, salty contrast.

MAKES 14 SANDWICH COOKIES

COOKIES

2 cups plus 2 tablespoons all-purpose flour

1½ teaspoons baking soda

2 teaspoons ground ginger

1¼ teaspoons ground cinnamon

¼ teaspoon ground cloves

¼ teaspoon ground nutmeg

½ teaspoon fine table salt

12 tablespoons (6 ounces / 1½ sticks) unsalted butter, at room temperature

½ cup packed dark brown sugar

¼ cup granulated sugar, plus more for rolling

¼ cup robust molasses (*not* blackstrap), preferably Grandma's

2 teaspoons pure vanilla extract

1 large egg, at room temperature

1. Make the cookies: In a bowl, stir together the flour, baking soda, ginger, cinnamon, cloves, nutmeg, and salt until combined. Set aside.
2. In a stand mixer fitted with the paddle, beat together the butter, brown sugar, granulated sugar, molasses, and vanilla until creamy. Add the egg and beat just until fully combined.
3. On low speed, gradually add the flour mixture to the butter/sugar mixture and just beat until combined. Scrape down the sides as needed. Cover the dough and refrigerate for 1 hour. (If you chill it longer be sure to let it sit at room temp for about 45 minutes before you bake the cookies or they will not spread enough.)
4. When ready to bake, preheat the oven to 375°F (or 350°F on the convection setting). Line two baking sheets with parchment paper.
5. Remove the dough from the fridge and scoop 1½ tablespoons of dough and roll into balls. Roll the balls of dough into granulated sugar until fully coated.
6. Arrange the balls of dough on the lined baking sheets about 3 inches apart. Transfer to the oven.
7. Bake for 7 to 9 minutes, until the edges appear set. Remove the baking sheets from the oven and rap/bang them on the counter two or three times. This will release some air and help them to get the beautiful crackled finish. If the cookies didn't spread enough, right when they come out of the oven you can take the flat bottom of a glass, bowl, or sheet pan and press it down gently on top of the cookies to flatten them slightly.
8. Let the cookies cool completely on wire racks before filling (see Tip).

MAPLE PECAN CREME FILLING

6 ounces cream cheese (I prefer Philadelphia), at room temperature

8 tablespoons (4 ounces/1 stick) unsalted butter

½ teaspoon fine table salt

¾ teaspoon vanilla bean paste or 1 teaspoon pure vanilla extract

3 tablespoons pure maple syrup

2½ cups powdered sugar

½ cup chopped toasted pecans, plus more for the cookies

Dash of ground cinnamon

Milk or cream (optional)

9 Meanwhile, make the maple pecan creme filling: In a stand mixer fitted with the whisk (or in a bowl using a hand mixer), beat together the cream cheese, butter, salt, vanilla, and maple syrup. Beat on medium-high speed until creamy and fully combined.

10 On low speed, gradually add the powdered sugar until fully combined and no lumps. Beat in the pecans and cinnamon. You want the cream to be nice and thick, but if it seems to be way too stiff add a tablespoon or so of milk or cream to thin it out.

11 Spread or pipe filling on the bottoms of half of the cookies and then top with remaining cookies. If desired, roll the sides of the cookies in the crushed pecans.

STORAGE: **Store in an airtight container or tin or wrapped in parchment paper and then aluminum foil for up to 2 days at room temperature (in a cool place) or 3 days in the fridge.**

SCONE QUEEN TIP

If you'd prefer, skip the filling and just serve as single cookies.

the dans' cookies

They say opposites attract, and, for my husband and me, that theory has proven to be pretty true. He's a quiet redhead who loves history and backpacking in the mountains. I'm a loud Italian who falls asleep at the word "Gettysburg" and is happiest in the Hamptons. Despite our differences, we are aligned by our values, love of Will Ferrell movies, passion for travel, and obsession with chocolate and peanut butter. We enjoy nurturing our summer vegetable garden, find comfort in eating a warm cookie on the couch after a stressful day, and of course we have our shared names . . . Danielle and Daniel. Ever since we started dating in college, our friends began to refer to us as The Dans, so this cookie is an ode to my husband and a celebration of our relationship. This thick, chewy, yet pleasantly dense cookie has all of Dan's favorite flavors and textures, including rich, creamy chocolate; nutty peanut butter chips; and crunchy, salty pretzels. These cookies are strategically made super thick and large to give them the perfect texture and a real WOW presentation.

MAKES 8 GIANT (4-INCH) COOKIES

- 8 tablespoons (4 ounces/1 stick) cold unsalted butter, cut into small cubes
- ¼ cup vegetable shortening, such as Crisco
- 1 cup packed dark brown sugar
- ½ cup granulated sugar
- 2 teaspoons pure vanilla extract
- 2 tablespoons creamy peanut butter (I prefer Skippy; do not use natural)
- 2 large eggs
- 2¾ cups all-purpose flour
- ½ teaspoon baking powder
- ¾ teaspoon fine table salt
- ⅛ teaspoon ground cinnamon
- ¾ cup semisweet chocolate chips
- ¾ cup peanut butter chips
- ¾ cup roughly chopped hard pretzels, such as Snyder's Olde Tyme or sourdough

1. In a stand mixer fitted with the paddle, beat together the butter, shortening, brown sugar, and granulated sugar until light and creamy, about 3 minutes.
2. Add the vanilla and peanut butter and beat until just combined. Add the eggs one at a time, beating to just combine after each addition.
3. In a separate bowl, stir together the flour, baking powder, salt, and cinnamon.
4. On low speed, gradually beat the flour mixture into the butter/sugar mixture, scraping down the sides of the bowl to make sure all ingredients are evenly incorporated.
5. On low speed (or by hand with a wooden spoon), stir in the chocolate chips, peanut butter chips, and pretzels until just combined. Do not overmix.
6. Place a long sheet of plastic wrap on the counter, scoop the dough into the plastic wrap, and use floured hands to form the dough into a log shape about 12 inches long and 3 inches in diameter. Roll it tightly in the plastic wrap. Gently place the log on a pan or plate and refrigerate for at least 2 hours or overnight.
7. When ready to bake, preheat the oven to 375°F (or 350°F on the convection setting). Line two cookie sheets with parchment paper.
8. Using a sharp knife, cut the log into 8 rounds about 1½ inches thick and place them on the lined cookie sheets about 2½ inches apart. Transfer to the oven.
9. Bake for 11 to 13 minutes, until golden brown on the edges but still soft in the center.
10. Let the cookies cool on the pans.

STORAGE: **Store in an airtight container or tin or wrapped in parchment paper and then aluminum foil at room temperature for up to 5 days.**

gnommies (m&m oatmeal chip) cookies

I think most millennials like myself have memories of M&M cookies, whether they were large sugar cookies encrusted with the colorful candies from a local bakery or even Starbucks, or those Rainbow Deluxe cookies by Keebler that I could eat a whole sleeve of if given a glass of milk. When the time came to grow The Hungry Gnome menu from just scones to muffins, loaves, and cookies, too, I knew I needed to create a playful, candy-coated cookie that would be a magnet for the kiddies and also so nostalgic for adults that they too could not resist.

MAKES 12 GIANT (4-INCH) COOKIES

8 tablespoons (4 ounces/1 stick) cold unsalted butter, cut into small cubes

¼ cup vegetable shortening, such as Crisco

1 cup packed dark brown sugar

¼ cup granulated sugar

2 teaspoons pure vanilla extract

2 large eggs, at room temperature

2¾ cups all-purpose flour

½ teaspoon baking powder

¾ teaspoon fine table salt

½ teaspoon ground cinnamon

½ cup semisweet chocolate chips

1 cup mini M&M's

½ cup rolled oats

1. In a stand mixer fitted with the paddle, beat together the butter, shortening, brown sugar, and granulated sugar until light and creamy, about 3 minutes.
2. Add the vanilla and beat until combined. Add the eggs one at a time, beating to just combine after each addition.
3. In a separate bowl, stir together the flour, baking powder, salt, and cinnamon.
4. On low speed, gradually add the flour mixture to the butter/sugar mixture until just combined. Scrape down the sides of the bowl to make sure it is evenly incorporated.
5. On low speed (or by hand with a wooden spoon), stir in the chocolate chips, ¾ cup of the mini M&M's, and the oats until just combined. Do not overmix.
6. Using a 4-ounce cookie scoop or a ½-cup measure, scoop the dough into balls (or high mounds). Place the balls on a parchment-lined cookie sheet and refrigerate the dough for at least 2 hours or overnight to help develop the flavors further.
7. When ready to bake, preheat the oven to 375°F (or 350°F on the convection setting). Line two cookie sheets with parchment paper.
8. Press or roll the tops of each cookie dough ball into the remaining ¼ cup of mini M&M's and place on the lined cookie sheets 3 inches apart. Transfer to the oven.
9. Bake for 12 to 15 minutes, until golden brown on the edges but still soft in the center.
10. Let the cookies cool on the pans for about 10 minutes, then enjoy!

STORAGE: **Store in an airtight container or tin or wrapped in parchment paper and then aluminum foil at room temperature for up to 5 days. Cookie dough balls (without the M&M's) can be stored in a ziplock bag in the freezer for up to 4 months. Thaw slightly at room temperature for 30 minutes before baking.**

CHAPTER 4

BROWNIES & BARS

UNBOXED BROWNIES . . . 122

CONDENSED MILK BROWNIES . . . 125

GALACTIC BROWNIES . . . 126

BISCOFF APPLE CHEESECAKE BARS . . . 129

BREAKFAST BARS . . . 130

LEMON ICEBOX BARS . . . 133

MUDDY BUDDY BARS . . . 134

S'MORES BLONDIES . . . 137

unboxed brownies

Growing up I hosted a lot of sleepover parties with friends, and no sleepover at the Marullo household was ever complete without some chewy, decadent boxed brownies and some cold rigatoni alla vodka out of the fridge at 2 a.m. (but that's another story). When testing brownie recipes I just kept saying, "I'd still rather have the boxed brownies"—until these. I wanted these classic brownies to have shiny tops, fudgy centers, super-chewy edges, and uber-rich chocolatey flavor. The blend of melted chocolate and dark cocoa powder gives them the right amount of chocolate flavor without resulting in a cakey texture, which sometimes a batter made with all cocoa powder can have. The molasses in the dark brown sugar and the cornstarch also play a crucial role here, as they help us achieve the chewy edge rather than a brittle, dry edge. The process of microwaving the ingredients and whisking until we get a glossy, sticky sugar and butter mixture is what gives these the shiny tops, so be sure to follow closely.

MAKES 9 TO 12 BROWNIES

10 tablespoons (5 ounces) unsalted butter, plus softened butter for the baking pan

¾ cup packed dark brown sugar

½ cup granulated sugar

½ cup bittersweet chocolate chips, preferably Ghirardelli

2 teaspoons pure vanilla extract

2 large eggs, at room temperature

⅓ cup all-purpose flour

¾ cup dark Dutch-process cocoa powder, preferably Hershey's Special Dark, sifted to remove lumps

2 teaspoons cornstarch

½ teaspoon fine table salt

¾ cup semisweet chocolate chips

1. Preheat the oven to 350°F (or 325°F on the convection setting). Grease an 8 × 8-inch metal pan with the softened butter and line the pan with parchment paper, then butter the top of the paper slightly.
2. In a microwave-safe bowl, combine the butter, brown sugar, and granulated sugar and microwave in 30-second increments, whisking after each until the mixture is melted and slightly glossy and grainy, about 1 minute total. Add the bittersweet chocolate chips and microwave again for 30 seconds. Whisk again to see if the chocolate is melted. If it isn't, microwave in 10-second increments until it is.
3. Whisk in the vanilla and eggs, making sure you are quick so the eggs do not scramble.
4. In a separate bowl, whisk together the flour, cocoa powder, cornstarch, and salt until blended.
5. Pour the flour mixture into the butter/chocolate mixture and whisk until just combined. Fold in the semisweet chocolate chips and then spread the batter into the prepared pan. Be sure to spread it out evenly, the batter is very thick and will need your assistance to get it into an even layer.
6. Bake for 22 to 25 minutes, until the edges are set and when you stick a table knife in the center of the brownies a bit of batter still sticks to the knife. You don't want to overbake brownies in order to get that fudgy chew we all look for.
7. Allow them to cool slightly in the pan before cutting (if you can wait that long).

STORAGE: **Store in an airtight container or tin or wrapped in parchment paper and then plastic wrap at room temperature for up to 7 days.**

150

condensed milk brownies

Condensed milk on its own is just a delight and, in my opinion, totally underutilized in the US. When I was dreaming up fudgy brownie recipes, a can of the sticky stuff caught my eye while perusing my pantry. Could it add the right amount of sweetness while simultaneously adding a chewy yet dense quality to the brownies? Yes—but no. It resulted in a brownie with a slightly cakey exterior and a fudgy core. These aren't cloyingly sweet and the chocolate flavor is beautifully enhanced by the subtle caramel and nutty notes of the milk. They're perfect on their own, but I can't help but think they would be the perfect base to a warm brownie sundae with vanilla ice cream, chocolate sauce, and, hey, maybe a drizzle of condensed milk!

MAKES 12 BROWNIES

Cooking spray

1¾ cups semisweet chocolate chips

8 tablespoons (4 ounces/1 stick) unsalted butter

¼ cup virgin coconut oil

1 (14-ounce) can sweetened condensed milk

2 large eggs

2 teaspoons pure vanilla extract

⅔ cup all-purpose flour

1 tablespoon cornstarch

½ cup dark Dutch-process cocoa powder, preferably Hershey's Special Dark, sifted to remove lumps

¾ teaspoon fine table salt

⅛ teaspoon baking soda

1. Preheat the oven to 375°F (or 350°F on the convection setting). Coat an 8 × 8-inch metal pan with cooking spray, then line the pan with parchment paper and spray lightly again on top.
2. In a large microwave-safe bowl (preferably glass), combine 1 cup of the chocolate chips, the butter, and coconut oil. Microwave for 1 minute and stir. Then microwave in 30-second increments, stirring after each, until the mixture is melted.
3. Whisk in the condensed milk by hand until combined. Then whisk in the eggs and vanilla until incorporated.
4. In a separate bowl, stir together the flour, cornstarch, cocoa powder, salt, and baking soda.
5. Stir the flour mixture into the butter mixture by hand until just combined and there are no more flour streaks. Fold in the remaining ¾ cup of chocolate chips. Spread the batter into the prepared pan.
6. Bake for 25 to 30 minutes, just until a tester inserted in the center comes out mostly clean. It's okay to have some wet crumbs come off on the knife or toothpick, but not fully raw batter.
7. Cut into 12 pieces and enjoy them warm or at room temperature!

STORAGE: **Store in an airtight container or tin or wrapped in parchment paper and then plastic wrap at room temperature for up to 5 days.**

galactic brownies

A take on the classic '90s packaged treat, these brownies have the nostalgic fudgy chew but a more elevated, rich flavor. As impressive as they look, they're easy to throw together and are always the first to go at a party. Adults and kids alike will enjoy these addictive and playful sweets!

MAKES 16 BROWNIES

BROWNIE BASE

- **Cooking spray**
- **10 tablespoons (5 ounces) unsalted butter**
- **1 cup granulated sugar**
- **⅓ cup packed dark brown sugar**
- **¾ cup dark Dutch-process cocoa powder, preferably Hershey's Special Dark, sifted to remove lumps**
- **¾ teaspoon pure vanilla extract**
- **2 large eggs**
- **1 large egg yolk**
- **1 tablespoon light corn syrup**
- **⅔ cup all-purpose flour**
- **1 tablespoon cornstarch**
- **½ teaspoon fine table salt**

TOPPING

- **1½ cups semisweet chocolate chips**
- **½ cup heavy cream**
- **¼ cup rainbow-colored candy-coated chocolate chips, mini M&M's, or even sprinkles!**

1. Make the brownie base: Preheat the oven to 375°F (or 350°F on the convection setting). Line an 8 × 8-inch metal baking pan with parchment paper and coat it with cooking spray.
2. In a large microwave-safe bowl, microwave the butter for 60 to 90 seconds to melt. Stir in the granulated sugar, brown sugar, and cocoa powder with a wooden spoon.
3. Add the vanilla, whole eggs, egg yolk, and corn syrup and stir until combined.
4. Add the flour, cornstarch, and salt and stir just until it comes together. The batter will be thick! Spread the batter into the lined pan and transfer to the oven.
5. Bake for about 20 minutes, or until just set. You will see that the edges begin to appear dryer and crack ever so slightly.
6. Let the brownies cool in the pan completely.
7. Meanwhile, make the topping: Place the semisweet chocolate chips in a heatproof bowl. Pour the heavy cream into a small microwave-safe bowl or measuring cup and microwave on high for 1 minute.
8. Pour the hot cream over the chocolate chips and let it stand for 2 to 3 minutes, until the chips melt. Stir together until the ganache is smooth.
9. Pour the ganache over the cooled brownies and spread it out evenly. Sprinkle the top with rainbow chips. Refrigerate for 1 to 2 hours to set the chocolate.
10. Remove the brownies from the fridge and cut into 16 squares.

STORAGE: **Store in an airtight container or tin or wrapped in parchment paper and then plastic wrap for up to 5 days at room temperature, or in the fridge if you prefer a more dense, fudgy texture.**

biscoff apple cheesecake bars

From the moment I tried my first Biscoff cookie on an airplane flight I knew I was in love. Simple yet so dynamic, crisp yet buttery, with a comforting warmth of spices—man, that's good. Its similarities to a graham cracker made these cookies the perfect candidate for a cheesecake crust, and the addition of the apples . . . well, that happened during a workday snack break. This is the perfect dessert for the holidays or just in the fall when you have an abundance of apples. Cut them into small squares for the perfect shareable party treat!

MAKES 9 LARGE SQUARES OR 12 TO 15 SMALL BARS

CRUST

1 cup Biscoff cookie crumbs (finely crushed)

¼ cup packed dark brown sugar

4 tablespoons (2 ounces) unsalted butter, melted

Cooking spray

CHEESECAKE FILLING

12 ounces cream cheese (I prefer Philadelphia), at room temperature

¾ cup granulated sugar

1 teaspoon pure vanilla extract

1 large egg, at room temperature

1 large egg yolk, at room temperature

¼ cup Biscoff smooth cookie butter spread (can also use Speculoos spread)

APPLE LAYER

1½ cups diced peeled Honeycrisp apples (about 2 medium apples)

¼ teaspoon ground cinnamon

1 tablespoon granulated sugar

STREUSEL TOPPING

¼ cup packed dark brown sugar

½ cup all-purpose flour

½ cup rolled oats

Pinch of fine table salt

4 tablespoons (2 ounces) unsalted butter, melted

Garnish: ¼ cup Biscoff smooth cookie butter spread (can also use Speculoos brand), melted

1. Preheat the oven to 375°F (or 350°F on the convection setting).
2. Make the crust: In a medium bowl, whisk together the cookie crumbs and brown sugar. Add the melted butter and stir until moistened and combined.
3. Coat an 8 × 8-inch square pan lightly with cooking spray and then line it with parchment paper, leaving 1 inch overhang on all sides. Press the crust mixture into the bottom of the pan in one even layer. Transfer to the oven.
4. Bake for 10 minutes just to set it slightly. Remove and cool completely. Leave the oven on, but reduce the temperature to 350°F (or 325°F on the convection setting).
5. Meanwhile, make the cheesecake filling: In a stand mixer fitted with the paddle, beat together the cream cheese, granulated sugar, and vanilla until light and fluffy and there are no harsh granules of sugar.
6. Beat in the whole egg, egg yolk, and Biscoff spread until just combined. Pour the filling over the cooled crust and spread it out evenly. Set aside.
7. Prepare the apple layer: In a bowl, toss together the apple chunks, cinnamon, and granulated sugar. Sprinkle the apple mixture evenly over the cheesecake layer.
8. Make the streusel topping: In a small bowl, stir together the brown sugar, flour, oats, and salt. Add the melted butter and toss everything together with a fork to create crumbs. Sprinkle the crumbs over the top of the apple layer evenly. Transfer to the oven.
9. Bake for 35 to 40 minutes, until just set. You want the center to be slightly jiggly but not completely loose. Let it cool completely and then refrigerate for at least 2 hours.
10. Use the parchment paper edges to carefully lift the cheesecake out of the pan and cut into squares or any size bars you would like.
11. Use a spoon or a piping bag with a small round tip to drizzle the melted Biscoff spread over the top. Let set in the fridge for at least 15 minutes and then enjoy!

STORAGE: **Store in the fridge in an airtight container or wrapped in parchment paper and then plastic wrap at room temperature for up to 5 days. You can also freeze the bars for up to 3 months.**

breakfast bars

It's no secret that gluten-free and dairy-free baking are not my preferred styles of baking, so when I bake such a recipe, I make sure it is so tasty you don't miss the butter and flour. These soft baked oatmeal bars are packed with nutrients, so they are the perfect grab-and-go breakfast, preworkout snack, or lunch box treat! And hey, it doesn't hurt that they taste like a delicious oatmeal cookie! This recipe was inspired by something I enjoyed on my honeymoon in Santorini, Greece. Each morning the hotel would place an overflowing basket of baked goods on our breakfast table and their soft and chewy oat bars were surprisingly one of my most memorable bites of the trip. Have a busy week ahead? Make a batch (or two), cut them into bars, and you have a nutritious and stress-free breakfast on the go! Feel free to customize with different kinds of nuts, seeds, and spices!

MAKES 9 TO 12 BARS

Cooking spray

3 tablespoons ground flaxseeds

¼ cup coconut sugar

⅓ cup pure maple syrup

¼ cup virgin coconut oil, melted

1 teaspoon pure vanilla extract

½ teaspoon ground cinnamon

½ teaspoon fine table salt

½ teaspoon baking powder

1 cup rolled oats

1 cup blanched almond flour

½ cup chopped walnuts

¼ cup sunflower seeds

3 tablespoons pumpkin seeds

½ cup dried cranberries or dried cherries

¼ cup mini chocolate chips or cacao nibs (optional)

1. Preheat the oven to 350°F (or 325°F on the convection setting). Coat an 8 × 8-inch square baking pan with cooking spray and line it with parchment paper leaving a 1-inch overhang all around.
2. In a large bowl, mix together the flaxseeds and 2 tablespoons water until combined. Stir in the coconut sugar, maple syrup, coconut oil, and vanilla until blended. Whisk in the cinnamon, salt, and baking powder.
3. Stir in the oats, almond flour, walnuts, sunflower seeds, pumpkin seeds, cranberries, and chocolate chips (if using) until moistened and combined.
4. Scrape the batter into the prepared pan and spread evenly. Transfer to the oven.
5. Bake for 20 to 25 minutes, until golden brown and the top appears dryer and set.
6. Let cool completely in the pan and then refrigerate for at least 1 to 2 hours to make them easier to cut.
7. Carefully lift the bars out of the pan and place them on a cutting board. Cut into squares or bars and enjoy!

STORAGE: **Store airtight at room temperature (or in the fridge if you prefer cold) for 7 to 10 days. You can also freeze them tightly wrapped in parchment paper and plastic wrap for 2 to 3 months.**

lemon icebox bars

These are super lemony and bright with the perfect creamy custard on the top and a buttery crunchy crust on the bottom. The best part is this custard doesn't involve the tempering of any eggs, which can be a daunting task even for the most advanced bakers. These bars come together in a flash, which is why they have become summertime staple in my house, when you just can't bear to stand in front of the oven all day.

MAKES 9 TO 12 BARS

Cooking spray

CRUST

1 cup plus 3 tablespoons graham cracker crumbs (I like Honey Maid)

⅓ cup granulated sugar

¼ teaspoon ground cinnamon

Pinch of fine table salt

6 tablespoons (3 ounces) unsalted butter, melted

FILLING

3 large egg yolks

2 teaspoons finely grated lemon zest

1 (14-ounce) can sweetened condensed milk

⅔ cup freshly squeezed lemon juice

⅛ teaspoon fine table salt

½ teaspoon pure vanilla extract

WHIPPED CREAM

2 cups cold heavy cream

⅓ cup powdered sugar

1 teaspoon pure vanilla extract

Garnish: Grated lemon zest

1. Preheat the oven to 375°F (or 350°F on the convection setting). Coat an 8 × 8-inch baking pan with cooking spray and line it with parchment paper leaving 1 inch of overhang on all sides.
2. Make the crust: In a bowl, combine the cookie crumbs, granulated sugar, cinnamon, salt, and melted butter and just stir until it resembles wet sand. Pour the crust mixture into the prepared pan and use your hands to pat down the crust into an even layer. You can also use a flat-bottom measuring cup to flatten the crumbs.
3. Bake the crust for 9 to 10 minutes, until it's golden brown and set. Remove from the oven to cool completely. Leave the oven on, but reduce the temperature to 350°F (or 325°F on the convection setting).
4. Make the filling: In a stand mixer fitted with the whisk, beat the egg yolks and lemon zest until pale yellow in color and slightly fluffy, 4 to 5 minutes.
5. Whisk in the condensed milk, lemon juice, salt, and vanilla until smooth and combined.
6. Pour the filling into the pan over the crust and use an offset spatula to spread it out evenly. Return the pan to the oven.
7. Bake for 10 to 15 minutes, until set. The center should be just slightly jiggly but not too loose.
8. Let it cool on a wire rack and then refrigerate for at least 1 hour.
9. Meanwhile, make the whipped cream: In a stand mixer fitted with the whisk, beat together the heavy cream, powdered sugar, and vanilla until stiff peaks form.
10. Once chilled, carefully lift the lemon custard–topped crust out of the pan using the parchment paper edges, place it on a cutting board, and use a sharp knife to cut into bars.
11. To serve, top the bars with a dollop of whipped cream and a bit of lemon zest.

STORAGE: **Store in the fridge in an airtight container or wrapped in parchment paper and then plastic wrap for up to 3 days.**

muddy buddy bars

WE ARE . . . PENN STATE! As a Penn State University alum, I have a duty to yell that. They call Penn State football the greatest Show in football and that is partly because of our impressive tailgating setups. It was at my first college tailgate that I was introduced to Muddy Buddies, also known as Puppy Chow. Puppy Chow is Rice Chex cereal that has been coated with a creamy mixture of chocolate and peanut butter that is then tossed with copious amounts of powdered sugar. The texture and flavor is nothing short of addictive and I can honestly say it's in my Top 10 favorite foods of all time. In a group setting, the bowls of Muddy Buddies can get messy and unsanitary—since dozens of hands are entering the bowl—so I decided to create a sliceable, bar version that still tastes just as heavenly.

MAKES 12 BARS

10 ounces mini marshmallows

4 tablespoons (2 ounces) salted butter

½ cup creamy peanut butter (Skippy is my favorite)

5½ cups Rice Chex cereal

1 cup semisweet chocolate chips

¼ cup heavy cream

About ¼ cup powdered sugar, for dusting

1. Line an 8 × 8-inch baking pan with parchment paper leaving 1 inch overhang on all sides.
2. In a small saucepan, combine the marshmallows, butter, and peanut butter and melt over low heat until smooth, about 5 minutes.
3. Using a silicone spatula, fold in the Rice Chex cereal.
4. Press the mixture into the parchment-lined pan. Set aside.
5. Place the chocolate chips in a heatproof bowl. In a microwave-safe bowl or measuring cup, microwave the heavy cream for 30 to 45 seconds, until hot. Pour the heavy cream over the chocolate chips and let sit for 2 to 3 minutes, then whisk the ganache until smooth.
6. Pour the ganache over the top of the Chex mixture in the pan and spread it out evenly with an offset spatula.
7. Place the pan in the fridge for 20 to 30 minutes, until the chocolate is set but not super hard.
8. Carefully lift the parchment paper to release the bars from the pan. Heavily dust the top with the powdered sugar and then cut into 12 bars (though you can cut them into whatever size bars you'd like).

STORAGE: **Store in an airtight container at room temperature for up to 1 week.**

SCONE QUEEN TIP

Cut each marshmallow into 4 to 6 pieces. Use clean kitchen scissors or a knife sprayed with cooking spray to cut them more easily.

s'mores blondies

My husband's family has a cabin in a beautiful secluded area called Ricketts Glen State Park in Pennsylvania. We try to make a trip to the cabin a few times a year to disconnect from our busy, sometimes stressful lives back in New York. One of my favorite things to do there is to raid the cabinets and bake something using whatever ingredients I can find. I must say, some pretty delicious desserts have been created over the years, but sadly, since they are so impromptu, I will never be able to re-create most of them. One October we went down to the cabin with some friends, and in the evening, while playing our favorite board games, I had a craving for a little something sweet . . . as per usual. Some of the group wanted traditional s'mores and some wanted cookies, so I decided to create the perfect happy medium: S'Mores Blondies. I used all the ingredients you'd find in a s'more including the extra-large marshmallows. The "marshies" seemed too large to be baked into a cookie bar, so I decided to cut them up, and to my surprise, the sticky centers of the marshmallows actually melted and caramelized in the oven. They turned toffee-like in consistency and flavor, which was WOWEE delicious. I also didn't have brown sugar on hand, which I would typically put in a blondie, so I used regular granulated sugar and pure maple syrup, which resulted in the perfect chewy texture. Our friends loved these so much that, unusually for this chatty and opinionated group, we were all at a loss for words the second they touched our mouths.

MAKES 16 THIN BLONDIES OR 12 THICK BLONDIES

Cooking spray, for the pan

8 ounces (2 sticks) unsalted butter, at room temperature

1½ cups sugar

¼ cup pure maple syrup

2 large eggs, at room temperature

1 teaspoon pure vanilla extract

1½ cups all-purpose flour

1½ cups coarsely crushed graham cracker crumbs (I prefer Nabisco)

¼ teaspoon baking powder

¾ teaspoon fine table salt

½ teaspoon ground cinnamon

1½ cups semisweet, bittersweet, or milk chocolate chunks (or a mixture)

1¼ cups standard-size marshmallow pieces (see Tip)

1. Preheat the oven to 375°F (or 350°F on the convection setting). Line a 9 × 13-inch baking pan or glass baking dish with parchment paper, leaving 1 inch of overhang on the two long sides. Grease the paper with cooking spray. (For thicker blondies, use an 8 × 8-inch pan.)
2. In a stand mixer fitted with the paddle, beat the butter, sugar, and maple syrup until light and fluffy, about 4 minutes.
3. Add the eggs one at a time, beating to just combine after each addition. Beat in the vanilla.
4. In a separate bowl, stir together the flour, graham cracker crumbs. baking powder, salt, and cinnamon.
5. On low speed, slowly add the flour/graham mixture to the butter/sugar mixture just until fully incorporated. Using a rubber spatula, stir in the chocolate chunks and marshmallow pieces.
6. Spread the batter evenly in the prepared pan and transfer to the oven.
7. Bake for 30 to 40 minutes, until it is golden brown and set. (Add 10 to 15 minutes to the bake time if using the smaller pan.) The center may be slightly gooey due to the marshmallows.
8. Let the blondies cool slightly in the pan before cutting into bars or squares. You can enjoy these hot, however I find that they are even better at room temperature.

STORAGE: **Store in an airtight container or tin or wrapped in parchment paper and then plastic wrap at room temperature for up to 5 days.**

CHAPTER 5

ROLLS & BREADS

CHOCOLATE DATE CINNAMON BUNS WITH TAHINI FROSTING . . . 140
ITALIAN RAINBOW BUNS . . . 143
BACI BUNS . . . 148
POPPYSEED DANISH BUNS . . . 151
PB&J CINNAMON BUNS WITH FLUFF FROSTING . . . 155
Homemade Marshmallow Fluff . . . 157
COCO LOCO BABKA . . . 158
CHOCOLATE CHUNK BRIOCHE WITH PEARL SUGAR . . . 162
RAISIN TEA BISCUITS . . . 166
EASY CHOCOLATE PEAR STRUDEL . . . 168
MOM'S SNOW DAY BREAD . . . 170
HOT CROSS BUNS . . . 172
FRENCH TOAST MONKEY BREAD . . . 174
CINNAMON & SUGAR MALL PRETZELS . . . 179
CINNAMON RAISIN LOAF WITH CINNAMON SUGAR CRUST . . . 182
IRISH SODA BREAD . . . 184
ITALIAN EASTER BREADS . . . 186
CINNAMON SUGAR POPOVERS WITH MAPLE PECAN BUTTER . . . 189

chocolate date cinnamon buns with tahini frosting

About ten years ago I started the tradition of making homemade cinnamon buns for my family on Christmas morning (as if I don't have enough to worry about that day, LOL!). Even though it does take a little time, I find making this dough therapeutic to work with; it's so soft, so pillowy, and the rolling and cutting of the rolls—don't even get me started! Cancel my therapy appointment . . . pure bliss! I started with a traditional cinnamon bun but then began to get creative with the flavors when I did a pop-up event in Brooklyn with my friend Edy Massih, a Lebanese chef. He introduced me to great products like date molasses and some of the best tahini and halva candy I had ever tasted. This was one of those recipes that took me one try: It just felt like magic. The plush interior; the rich, slightly bitter flavor of the dark cocoa and date molasses combined; the nutty, velvety tahini mixed with tangy cream cheese in the frosting—this is 100 percent shopping mall cinnamon bun nostalgia but 100 percent elevated. See why people line up for these . . .

MAKES 9 BUNS

DOUGH

1 cup whole milk

8 tablespoons (4 ounces/1 stick) unsalted butter

⅓ cup granulated sugar

1 (7g) envelope active dry yeast (2¼ teaspoons)

2 large eggs

1 large egg yolk

1 teaspoon pure vanilla extract

2 teaspoons fine table salt

4 to 4¼ cups all-purpose flour, plus more for dusting

FILLING

4 tablespoons (2 ounces/ ½ stick) unsalted butter, at room temperature

1 cup packed dark brown sugar

½ cup date molasses

½ teaspoon pure vanilla extract

⅓ cup tahini

2 tablespoons dark Dutch-process cocoa powder, preferably Hershey's Special Dark, sifted to remove lumps

1 tablespoon ground cinnamon

2 tablespoons white sesame seeds

½ teaspoon fine table salt

1 Make the dough: In a small saucepan, bring the milk to a boil. The moment it reaches a boil, remove from the heat. (This process is called scalding, and it ensures the milk doesn't affect the yeast's ability to rise. Don't skip it!)

2 Pour the hot milk into the bowl of a stand mixer and add the butter. Stir, allowing the butter to melt completely. Then stir in the sugar. Wait until the mixture is just warmer than room temperature, then stir in the yeast. Allow the yeast to sit for 10 to 20 minutes to activate and get bubbly and frothy. (If the yeast does not bubble up after 30 minutes, start again with fresh ingredients, as the yeast may be dead.)

3 Attach the dough hook to the mixer and turn the mixer to low. Add the whole eggs, egg yolk, vanilla, salt, and 4 cups flour. Beat the dough until it pulls away from the sides. Run the mixer for about 10 minutes to allow the dough to stretch and develop the gluten. If the dough seems too sticky after the first 2 to 3 minutes, add an additional ¼ cup flour. After mixing for 10 minutes, turn the mixer off. Move the dough to a separate bowl, cover with plastic, and allow the dough to rise until doubled in size, about 1½ hours in a warm kitchen.

4 Make the filling: In a stand mixer fitted with the paddle, beat together the butter, brown sugar, date molasses, and vanilla until smooth and creamy. Add the tahini and beat until smooth.

5 Add the cocoa powder, cinnamon, white sesame seeds, and salt. Beat until blended together.

6 Once the dough has risen, dump it onto a lightly floured surface. Press it flat with your hands and fold into thirds. Press flat again, turn, and fold into thirds again. Roll the dough out into a 16 × 20-inch rectangle.

♥ *recipe continues on page 142*

TAHINI FROSTING

4 ounces cream cheese (I prefer Philadelphia), at room temperature

4 tablespoons (2 ounces/ ½ stick) unsalted butter, at room temperature

¼ cup tahini

2 cups powdered sugar

2 teaspoons pure vanilla extract

Milk, if needed

TOPPING (OPTIONAL)

Pistachio halva, broken into pieces

Black sesame seeds

7 Use a large offset spatula to spread the filling over the dough in a thin layer. Leave 1 inch of dough bare on one of the long edges of the rectangle. Starting with the filling-covered long edge of the dough, roll the dough tightly toward the uncovered edge to form a tight log.

8 Line a 9 × 13-inch glass baking dish with parchment paper.

9 Cut the log crosswise into 12 equal rolls. Tuck the loose end of each roll underneath the roll to secure it so it doesn't unravel in the oven and place the rolls in the baking dish. Cover the dish with plastic wrap and a kitchen towel and let rise for about 45 minutes, or until puffed up slightly.

10 Preheat the oven to 350°F (or 325°F on the convection setting).

11 Bake for 20 to 25 minutes, until the edges are just slightly golden and the centers of the rolls puff up.

12 Meanwhile, make the tahini frosting: In a stand mixer fitted with the paddle, beat together the cream cheese, butter, and tahini until smooth and creamy. Sift in the powdered sugar, add the vanilla, and beat until smooth and creamy. If it is too thick to spread, add a splash or two of milk.

13 The moment the rolls come out of the oven, gently spread half of the frosting over the tops and allow it the melt and seep into the cracks and layers. Wait 5 to 10 minutes and add more frosting if desired. Sprinkle with halva and black sesame seeds and serve warm or at room temp.

STORAGE: **Store airtight in the refrigerator for up to 3 days. To reheat, microwave on a plate for about 30 seconds or until warm and softened.**

italian rainbow buns

These are the baked good mash-up you didn't know you needed. They have all the flavors of the Italian American staple, the rainbow cookie, but in a soft, pillowy bun. This is one of the more laborious recipes in this book, but the buns are certainly worth it! The almond-infused dough is dyed the three signature colors of pink, green, and yellow, and once rolled it's filled with apricot jam and a sweet almond frangipane filling similar to that of an almond croissant. When they come out of the oven, they are topped with a rich chocolate glaze that settles in the cracks and has a gorgeous, glossy sheen. Although my favorite way to enjoy a bun is to unravel it slowly, pulling away pieces, and eat it bit by bit, for this one I recommend you first cut it in half to reveal the "rainbow" within.

MAKES 8 JUMBO OR 10 LARGE BUNS

DOUGH

1 cup whole milk

8 tablespoons (4 ounces/1 stick) unsalted butter

⅓ cup granulated sugar

1 (7g) envelope active dry yeast (2¼ teaspoons)

2 large eggs

1 large egg yolk

½ teaspoon pure vanilla extract

1½ teaspoons pure almond extract

2 teaspoons fine table salt

4 to 4¼ cups all-purpose flour, plus more for dusting

Food coloring: red (or pink), yellow, and green

1 Make the dough: In a small saucepan, bring the milk to a boil. The moment it reaches a boil, remove from the heat. (This process is called scalding, and it ensures the milk doesn't affect the yeast's ability to rise. Don't skip it!)

2 Pour the hot milk into the bowl of a stand mixer and add the butter. Stir, allowing the butter to melt completely. Then stir in the sugar. Wait until the mixture is just warmer than room temperature, then stir in the yeast. Allow the yeast to sit for 10 to 20 minutes to activate and get bubbly and frothy. (If the yeast does not bubble up after 30 minutes, start again with fresh ingredients, as the yeast may be dead.)

3 Attach the dough hook to the mixer and turn the mixer to low. Add the whole eggs, egg yolk, vanilla, almond extract, salt, and 4 cups flour. Beat the dough until it pulls away from the sides. Run the mixer for about 10 minutes to allow the dough to stretch and develop the gluten. If the dough seems too sticky after the first 2 to 3 minutes add an additional ¼ cup flour.

4 Divide the dough into 3 equal portions the best you can and place in separate bowls. (Weigh it if you have a kitchen scale.) Add a few drops of red (or pink) dye to one bowl of dough, yellow to another, and green to the last. Using a stand mixer fitted with the dough hook (or by hand with disposable gloves), knead the food coloring into the dough balls leaving you with one pink ball, one pale yellow, and one green. Cover the top of the bowls with plastic and allow the dough to rise until doubled in size, about 1½ hours in a warm kitchen.

♥ *recipe continues*

ALMOND FRANGIPANE FILLING

9 tablespoons (4½ ounces) unsalted butter, at room temperature

¾ cup granulated sugar

¼ teaspoon fine table salt

½ teaspoon pure vanilla extract

2 teaspoons pure almond extract

2 large eggs

1½ cups blanched almond flour

4½ tablespoons all-purpose flour

APRICOT GLAZE

¾ cup apricot preserves (see Tip)

CHOCOLATE GLAZE

2 tablespoons dark Dutch-process cocoa powder, preferably Hershey's Special Dark, sifted to remove lumps

½ cup powdered sugar

2 tablespoons heavy cream

Pinch of fine table salt

SCONE QUEEN TIP

If the preserves are thick and not pourable, melt it in the microwave for 20 to 30 seconds to thin it out. You could also use raspberry preserves instead.

5 Make the almond frangipane filling: In a stand mixer fitted with the paddle, beat together the butter, granulated sugar, salt, vanilla, and almond extract until smooth and creamy, about 2 minutes.

6 Add the eggs, almond flour, and all-purpose flour and beat until just combined. Set aside while you roll out the risen doughs.

7 Once the doughs have risen, dump them onto a lightly floured surface. Place the doughs side by side in this order: green, yellow, pink. Pat and pull the dough into rough rectangles that overlap one another by a half inch. Roll the dough out into a 16 × 20-inch rectangle.

8 With the green side (short side) of the dough rectangle facing you, use a large offset spatula to spread the almond frangipane filling over the dough in a thin layer. Next, pour or spread the melted apricot preserves all over the almond layer. Leave 1 inch of dough bare at the pink end of the rectangle. Starting with the green end of the dough, roll the dough tightly toward the pink end to form a tight log.

9 Carefully place the log on a plate and place in the freezer for 15 minutes to make it easier to cut.

10 Line a 9 × 13-inch glass baking dish with parchment paper.

11 Cut the log crosswise into 9 equal rolls. Tuck the loose end of each roll underneath the roll to secure it so it doesn't unravel in the oven and place the rolls in the baking dish with only 1 inch between them. Cover the dish with plastic wrap or a kitchen towel and let them proof again for 45 minutes, until they puff up slightly.

12 Preheat the oven to 375°F (or 350°F on the convection setting).

13 Bake for 22 to 25 minutes, until the edges are just slightly golden and the centers of the rolls puff up. If you have a thermometer, the centers should read at least 195°F to ensure doneness.

14 Meanwhile, make the chocolate glaze: In a bowl, whisk together the cocoa powder, powdered sugar, heavy cream, and salt until smooth.

15 The moment the rolls come out of the oven, gently spread half of the glaze over the tops and allow it to melt and seep into the cracks and layers. Wait about 10 minutes and add the remaining glaze. Serve warm or at room temperature.

STORAGE: **Store airtight in the refrigerator for up to 3 days. To reheat, microwave on a plate for about 30 seconds, or until warm and softened.**

baci buns

January 6 is the Epiphany, a Christian holiday that commemorates the three kings' visit to baby Jesus. In Italy, the Epiphany is synonymous with a "Santa-like" character called La Befana, aka the Christmas Witch. The story goes that on the night of the Epiphany, La Befana would travel to the children and give the good ones treats like candy, fruits, nuts, etc. in their stockings or shoes, and coal to the naughty ones. After learning about La Befana in middle school Italian class, my older sister Christiana and I decided to start this tradition in our home for our much younger little sister, Julia. We would stuff her shoes with whole nuts, fruits like pomegranates, and of course Italian candies like Perugina Baci! The word *baci* in Italian means "kisses," and these classic Italian confections truly are the much tastier version of the chocolate kisses we know in the states. They are truffle-like chocolates that have a creamy yet crunchy hazelnut center and a rich dark chocolate coating. These Baci Buns are my interpretation: soft, tender buns have a crunchy chocolate hazelnut filling and a super-creamy, luscious frosting that has the perfect amount of hazelnut flavor from the Frangelico liqueur.

MAKES 9 BUNS

BUN DOUGH

- **1 cup whole milk**
- **8 tablespoons (4 ounces/1 stick) unsalted butter, cut into 1-inch chunks**
- **⅓ cup granulated sugar**
- **1 (7g) envelope active dry yeast (2¼ teaspoons)**
- **2 large eggs**
- **1 large egg yolk**
- **4 to 4¼ cups all-purpose flour, plus more for dusting**
- **2 teaspoons fine table salt**
- **1 teaspoon pure vanilla extract**

FILLING

- **½ cup semisweet chocolate chips (mini chips also do well here)**
- **½ cup chopped roasted unsalted hazelnuts (ideally skinless)**
- **½ cup Nutella spread**
- **4 tablespoons (2 ounces/ ½ stick) unsalted butter**
- **1 tablespoon dark Dutch-process cocoa powder, preferably Hershey's Special Dark, sifted to remove the lumps**

1. Make the bun dough: In a small saucepan, bring the milk to a boil. The moment it reaches a boil, remove from the heat. (This process is called scalding, and it ensures the milk doesn't affect the yeast's ability to rise. Don't skip it!)
2. Pour the hot milk into the bowl of a stand mixer and add the butter. Stir, allowing the butter to melt completely. Then stir in the sugar. Wait until the mixture is just warmer than room temperature, then stir in the yeast. Allow the yeast to sit for 10 to 20 minutes to activate and get bubbly and frothy. (If the yeast does not bubble up after 30 minutes, start again with fresh ingredients, as the yeast may be dead.)
3. Attach the dough hook to the mixer and turn the mixer to low. Add the whole eggs, egg yolk, 4 cups flour, the salt, and vanilla. Beat the dough until it pulls away from the sides. Run the mixer for about 10 minutes to allow the dough to stretch and develop the gluten. Stop the mixer every minute or two and scrape down the sides of the bowl with a rubber spatula. If the dough seems too sticky after the first 2 to 3 minutes, add an additional ¼ cup flour. After mixing for 10 minutes, turn the mixer off. Cover the top of the bowl with plastic wrap and allow the dough to rise until doubled in size, about 1½ hours in a warm kitchen.
4. Once the dough has risen, make the filling: Place the chocolate chips in a heatproof bowl and make a double boiler by setting it over a pan of simmering water (do not let it touch the bottom) over medium heat until the chocolate is melted.
5. In a stand mixer fitted with the paddle, stir together the melted chocolate, hazelnuts, Nutella, butter, cocoa powder, brown sugar, vanilla, and salt until combined. It will look like a thick paste.
6. Once the dough has risen, dump it onto a very lightly floured surface. Press it flat with your hands and fold into thirds. Press flat again, turn, and fold into thirds again. Roll the dough out into a 16 × 20-inch rectangle.

recipe continues on page 150

½ cup packed dark brown sugar

½ teaspoon pure vanilla extract

⅛ teaspoon fine table salt

TOPPING

4 tablespoons (2 ounces/ ½ stick) unsalted butter, at room temperature

3 ounces cream cheese (I prefer Philadelphia), at room temperature

⅛ teaspoon fine table salt

1 tablespoon dark Dutch-process cocoa powder, preferably Hershey's Special Dark, sifted to remove lumps

½ teaspoon pure vanilla extract

1½ cups powdered sugar

1½ tablespoons Frangelico liqueur

Chopped roasted hazelnuts (salted or unsalted), for sprinkling

7 Use a large offset spatula to spread the filling over the dough in a thin layer. (The paste is very thick, so don't stress if it feels difficult to spread cleanly and appears a bit patchy.) Leave 1 inch of dough bare on one of the long edges of the rectangle. Starting with the filling-covered long edge of the dough, roll the dough tightly toward the uncovered edge to form a tight log.

8 Line a 9 × 13-inch glass baking dish with parchment paper.

9 Cut the log crosswise into 9 equal rolls. Tuck the loose end of each roll underneath the roll to secure it so it doesn't unravel in the oven and place it in the baking dish. Cover the dish with plastic wrap and a kitchen towel and let rise again for about 45 minutes, or until puffed up slightly.

10 Preheat the oven to 375°F (or 350°F on the convection setting).

11 Bake for 20 to 25 minutes, until the edges are just slightly golden and the centers of the rolls puff up.

12 Meanwhile, make the topping: In a stand mixer fitted with the paddle (or in a bowl using a hand mixer), beat together the butter, cream cheese, salt, cocoa powder, vanilla, and powdered sugar until smooth. Beat in the Frangelico until creamy and spreadable.

13 The moment the rolls come out of the oven, gently spread half of the frosting over the tops and allow it to melt and seep into the cracks and layers. Wait 10 to 15 minutes and add the remaining frosting (or put it in a bowl on the side for dunking). Sprinkle them with chopped hazelnuts and serve them warm or at room temperature.

STORAGE: **Store airtight in the refrigerator for up to 3 days. To reheat, microwave on a plate for about 30 seconds or until warm and softened.**

poppyseed danish buns

One of my fondest memories of my Grandpa Vincent (aka Jim) is our summertime crabbing trips. My cousins, sisters, and I would all pile into Grandpa's car at the crack of dawn and head out to the docks with a trunk full of rusty old nets and plastic grocery bags full of raw chicken legs (the best bait). On our way to the beach we would stop at a bakery for sustenance . . . the only kind of food Grandpa ever wanted: sweets. He would get a couple of turnovers and the other kids would grab sprinkle cookies as big as their faces. Me on the other hand, I'd get a Danish filled with a mildly sweet poppyseed filling, coated with a simple, sticky glaze. These poppyseed Danish buns have that wonderful crunchy poppyseed filling I remember but with an even more pleasant dough texture as they are in the style of a plush cinnamon bun. The hint of citrus balances out the subtle earthiness of the seeds, and the mild sweetness makes these the perfect baked good for those who prefer a less sweet offering.

MAKES 12 BUNS

DOUGH

1¼ cups whole milk

8 tablespoons (4 ounces/1 stick) unsalted butter

⅓ cup granulated sugar

1 (7g) envelope active dry yeast (2¼ teaspoons)

2 large eggs

1 large egg yolk

4 to 4¼ cups all-purpose flour, plus more for dusting

2 teaspoons fine table salt

½ teaspoon pure vanilla extract

½ teaspoon finely grated orange zest

FILLING

½ cup poppyseeds

¼ cup hot whole milk (microwave about 30 seconds)

¼ cup granulated sugar

¼ cup packed dark brown sugar

1½ tablespoons unsalted butter, melted

1½ teaspoons freshly squeezed orange juice

1 teaspoon pure vanilla extract

Pinch of fine table salt

1 Make the dough: In a small saucepan, bring the milk to a boil. The moment it reaches a boil, remove from the heat. (This process is called scalding, and it ensures the milk doesn't affect the yeast's ability to rise. Don't skip it!)

2 Pour the hot milk into the bowl of a stand mixer and add the butter. Stir, allowing the butter to melt completely. Then stir in the sugar. Wait until the mixture is just warmer than room temperature, then stir in the yeast. Allow the yeast to sit for 10 to 20 minutes to activate and get bubbly and frothy. (If the yeast does not bubble up after 30 minutes, start again with fresh ingredients, as the yeast may be dead.)

3 Attach the dough hook to the mixer and turn the mixer to low. Add the whole eggs, egg yolk, 4 cups of the flour, the salt, vanilla, and orange zest. Beat the dough until it pulls away from the sides. Run the mixer for about 10 minutes to allow the dough to stretch and develop the gluten. If the dough seems too sticky after the first 2 to 3 minutes add an additional ¼ cup flour. After mixing for 10 minutes, turn the mixer off. Cover the top of the bowl with plastic and allow the dough to rise until doubled in size, about 1½ hours in a warm kitchen.

4 Meanwhile, make the filling: In a bowl, use a wooden spoon or whisk to stir together the poppyseeds, milk, granulated sugar, brown sugar, melted butter, orange juice, vanilla, and salt. Cover with plastic wrap and refrigerate for at least 30 minutes.

5 Dump the dough onto a lightly floured surface. Press it flat with your hands and fold into thirds. Press flat again, turn, and fold into thirds again. Roll the dough out into a 16 × 20-inch rectangle.

♥ *recipe continues*

FROSTING AND GARNISH

- **4 ounces cream cheese (I prefer Philadelphia), at room temperature**
- **1 tablespoon unsalted butter, at room temperature**
- **1 tablespoon freshly squeezed lemon juice**
- **½ teaspoon pure vanilla extract**
- **Pinch of fine table salt**
- **1½ cups sifted powdered sugar**
- **Grated lemon zest, for garnish**

6 Use a large offset spatula to spread the chilled filling over the dough in a thin layer. Leave 1 inch of dough bare on one of the long edges of the rectangle. Starting with the filling-covered long edge of the dough, roll the dough tightly toward the uncovered edge to form a tight log.

7 Line a 9 × 13-inch glass baking dish with parchment paper.

8 Cut the log crosswise into 12 equal rolls. Tuck the loose end of each roll underneath the roll to secure it so it doesn't unravel in the oven and place in the baking dish. Cover the dish with plastic wrap and a kitchen towel and let rise for about 45 minutes, or until they have puffed up slightly.

9 Preheat the oven to 375°F (or 350°F on the convection setting).

10 Bake for 20 to 25 minutes, until the edges are just slightly golden and the centers of the rolls puff up.

11 Meanwhile, make the frosting: In a stand mixer fitted with the paddle (or in a bowl using a hand mixer), beat together the cream cheese, butter, lemon juice, vanilla, salt, and powdered sugar until smooth and creamy.

12 The moment the rolls come out of the oven, gently spread half of the frosting over the tops and allow it to melt and seep into the cracks and layers. Wait 5 to 10 minutes and add more frosting if desired. Sprinkle the top with the lemon zest to garnish.

STORAGE: **Store in the pan wrapped in plastic wrap in the fridge or at room temperature in a cool place for up to 3 days. Reheat by placing a bun on a plate and microwave for 30 seconds or until warmed through.**

pb&j cinnamon buns with fluff frosting (for dan levy)

If you watched *The Big Brunch,* you may remember the moment in the finale when Sohla El-Waylly and Dan Levy had a friendly argument about these very buns, which resulted in Dan's final statement: "This is greatest thing I have ever eaten in *my life*!" These buns are soft and plush and they taste like an elevated peanut butter, jelly, and Marshmallow Fluff sandwich. The base of the frosting is a more traditional cream cheese frosting, but then the marshmallow is folded in at the end, giving it a lighter, airier texture that has all the goo-factor you ever desired. These are a thank-you to Dan, who gave me the opportunity of a lifetime that truly changed me, both personally and professionally. I adore you, "HEARD?!"

MAKES 9 JUMBO BUNS

DOUGH

1 cup whole milk

8 tablespoons (4 ounces/1 stick) unsalted butter

⅓ cup granulated sugar

1 (7g) envelope active dry yeast (2¼ teaspoons)

2 large eggs, at room temperature

1 large egg yolk, at room temperature

4 to 4¼ cups all-purpose flour, plus more for dusting

2 teaspoons fine table salt

1 teaspoon pure vanilla extract

FILLING

½ cup packed dark brown sugar

¾ cup strawberry preserves (I prefer Smucker's)

4 tablespoons (2 ounces/ ½ stick) unsalted butter, at room temperature (not melted)

2 teaspoons cornstarch

½ teaspoon ground cinnamon

1 cup peanut butter chips (I prefer Reese's)

1 Make the dough: In a small saucepan, bring the milk to a boil. The moment it reaches a boil, remove from the heat. (This process is called scalding, and it ensures the milk doesn't affect the yeast's ability to rise. Don't skip it!)

2 Pour the hot milk into the bowl of a stand mixer and add the butter. Stir, allowing the butter to melt completely, then add in the sugar. Wait until the mixture is just warmer than room temperature, then stir in the yeast. Allow the yeast to sit for 10 to 20 minutes to activate and get bubbly and frothy. (If the yeast does not bubble up after 30 minutes, start again with fresh ingredients, as the yeast may be dead.)

3 Attach the dough hook to the mixer and turn the mixer to low. Add the whole eggs, egg yolk, 4 cups of the flour, the salt, and vanilla. Beat the dough until it pulls away from the sides. Run the mixer for about 10 minutes to allow the dough to stretch and develop the gluten. If the dough seems too sticky after the first 2 to 3 minutes, add an additional ¼ cup flour. After mixing for 10 minutes, turn the mixer off. Cover the top of the bowl with plastic wrap or a kitchen towel and allow the dough to rise until doubled in size, about 1½ hours in a warm kitchen.

4 Make the filling: In a stand mixer fitted with the paddle (or in a bowl with a wooden spoon), mix together the brown sugar, strawberry preserves, butter, cornstarch, and cinnamon until smooth.

5 Dump the dough onto a lightly floured surface. Press it flat with your hands and fold into thirds. Press flat again, turn, and fold into thirds again. Roll the dough out into a 16 × 20-inch rectangle.

♥ *recipe continues*

FROSTING

2 ounces cream cheese (I prefer Philadelphia), at room temperature

4 tablespoons (2 ounces/ ½ stick) unsalted butter, at room temperature

1 teaspoon pure vanilla extract

Pinch of fine table salt

1 cup powdered sugar

1 heaping cup Homemade Marshmallow Fluff, store-bought or homemade (recipe follows; see Tip)

GARNISH (OPTIONAL)

Warmed peanut butter

Strawberry jam

Crumbled freeze-dried strawberries and/or chopped roasted peanuts

A dollop of extra Marshmallow Fluff

6 Use a large offset spatula to spread the filling over the dough in a thin layer. Leave 1 inch of dough bare on one of the long edges of the rectangle. Sprinkle the peanut butter chips evenly all over the filling. Starting with the filling-covered long edge of the dough, roll the dough tightly but gently (this filling can get a bit messy, don't fret) toward the uncovered edge to form a tight log. Carefully place the log onto a tray and place it in the freezer for 10 minutes to make it a bit easier to cut.

7 Line a 9 × 13-inch glass baking dish with parchment paper.

8 With a sharp knife, cut the log crosswise into 9 equal rolls. Tuck the loose end of each roll underneath the roll to secure it so it doesn't unravel in the oven and place the rolls in the baking dish. Cover the dish lightly with plastic wrap and a kitchen towel and let the buns proof for about another 45 minutes, or until puffed up slightly.

9 Preheat the oven to 375°F (or 350°F on the convection setting).

10 Bake for 22 to 25 minutes, until the edges are golden and the centers of the rolls start to puff up. (You can also take the internal temperature of the buns, which should be at 195°F when done.)

11 Meanwhile, make the frosting: In a stand mixer fitted with the paddle (or in a bowl using a hand mixer), beat together the cream cheese, butter, vanilla, salt, and powdered sugar until smooth and creamy. Finally, fold in the Marshmallow Fluff until just combined.

12 The moment the rolls come out of the oven, gently spread three-quarters of the frosting over the tops and allow it to melt and seep into the cracks and layers. Wait 5 to 10 minutes and then add more frosting if desired.

13 To garnish (if desired): Top with a drizzle of warmed peanut butter and jam, and a sprinkle of chopped roasted peanuts or crumbled freeze-dried strawberries. For a little extra pizzazz, top each bun with a dollop of extra fluff and toast it using a kitchen torch!

STORAGE: **Store airtight in the refrigerator for up to 3 days. To reheat, microwave on a plate for about 30 seconds, or until warm and softened.**

SCONE QUEEN TIP

Trust me on this, you can use store-bought Marshmallow Fluff here, but I strongly encourage you to make the homemade version as it is fairly easy to execute and the taste and texture are really something special.

HOMEMADE MARSHMALLOW FLUFF

Use to make Fluffernutter sandwiches! Homemade Marshmallow Fluff is a game changer!

MAKES 5 CUPS

4 egg whites

1 cup sugar

½ teaspoon cream of tartar

½ teaspoon pure vanilla extract

⅛ teaspoon coconut extract (optional, but encouraged)

Pinch of fine table salt

1. Pour the egg whites into a heatproof bowl and set the bowl over a pot of simmering water (the water should not be touching the bottom of the bowl). Whisk vigorously and stream the sugar and the cream of tartar into the egg whites. Keep whisking over the double boiler until the egg whites thin out, become whitish in color and there are no more noticeable granules of sugar when you rub some of the mixture between your fingers.

2. Remove from the heat and pour the mixture into the bowl of a stand mixer fitted with the whisk (or into a bowl and using a hand mixer or whisk). Add the vanilla, coconut extract (if using), and salt and whisk on high until stiff peaks form. This will take about 5 minutes.

STORAGE: **Store in a sealed container or bowl in the fridge until you are ready to use it. It will keep for about 7 days in the fridge.**

SCONE QUEEN TIP

Use the Marshmallow Fluff on peanut butter sandwiches, layer it with Nutella in a dish and dip graham crackers in it for a gooey s'mores dip, add it to raspberry jam on a toasted English muffin, or put a big dollop on a mug of hot cocoa (you can even torch it to get the toasted marshmallow effect). You can even use it to make the Snowball Icebox Cake on page 207.

coco loco babka

For about twelve years I lived in Manhattan, and like most young New Yorkers I spent my weekends gallivanting around SoHo and the Lower East Side, shopping, sipping cocktails, and brunching. You already know I love brunch, mostly because it's the meal period that allows me to have a big stack of pancakes and a cheeseburger and fries all at once. When you're brunching in New York, you mustn't forget to always order the pastry and bread basket "for the table," because you never know what buttery gems you might encounter. At a popular downtown brunch brasserie, I discovered a chocolate-, banana-, and coconut-stuffed croissant that was so perfect it lived in my head rent free. Although this establishment still has many desirable desserts, this one has since disappeared, inspiring me to create my own rendition. This sweet, fluffy yet flaky bread has a fudgy filling consisting of rich chocolate, ripe banana, and chewy coconut. This recipe makes two loaves, because if you're going to go through the effort, you might as well make two, plus it'll be one you want to show off to your friends at your next brunch. Just wait for the oohs and aahs as you cut the first slice, revealing that signature marbling within the folds of the dough.

MAKES TWO 9 × 5-INCH LOAVES

DOUGH

⅔ cup warm milk (90° to 100°F)

1 tablespoon active dry yeast

⅓ cup plus 2 teaspoons granulated sugar

3¾ cups all-purpose flour, plus more as needed

1¼ teaspoons fine table salt

2 large eggs

1 large egg yolk

1 teaspoon pure vanilla extract

2 tablespoons honey, preferably clover

2 tablespoons vegetable shortening, such as Crisco

5 tablespoons (2½ ounces) unsalted butter, cut into small cubes, plus more for greasing the pan

1. Make the dough: In a small bowl, combine the milk, yeast, and 2 teaspoons of the granulated sugar. Allow the yeast to sit for 10 to 15 minutes to activate and get bubbly and frothy. (If the yeast does not bubble up after 30 minutes, start again with fresh ingredients, as the yeast may be dead.)
2. In a stand mixer fitted with the dough hook, mix together the flour, remaining ⅓ cup of sugar, and the salt. In a separate bowl, whisk together the whole eggs, egg yolk, milk/yeast mixture, vanilla, and honey until just combined.
3. With the mixer on low speed, add the egg mixture to the flour mixture until the dough comes together in a soft dough mass, about 2 minutes. You may need to stop the mixer and push the flour down the sides of the bowl with a rubber spatula to ensure everything gets incorporated. If the dough seems super sticky and doesn't come away from the sides of the bowl, add a tablespoon more of flour at a time until it pulls away, beating after each addition.
4. With the mixer on medium speed, add the shortening and then the butter, cube by cube until it is all incorporated into the dough. Continue to mix on medium speed for 10 minutes to help the dough become elastic. If the dough is very sticky and stuck to the sides of the bowl, add a tablespoon or two of flour again.
5. Lightly grease a clean bowl with softened butter and place the dough in the center. Cover the bowl lightly with plastic wrap and a kitchen towel and place it in a warm place to rise. (I like to place mine in an oven that is off.) Allow the dough to rise and almost double in size, 1½ to 2 hours. About 1 hour into the dough rising, make the filling.
6. Make the filling: In a bowl, stir together the melted butter, vanilla, powdered sugar, the mashed banana, coconut flakes, cocoa powder, salt, cinnamon, and chocolate chips. Once it is blended and resembles a thick, chunky paste, fold in the ⅔ cup diced banana.

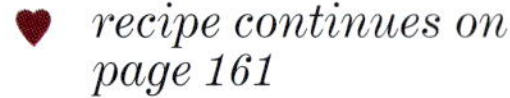
recipe continues on page 161

FILLING

4 tablespoons (2 ounces/ ½ stick) unsalted butter, melted

1 teaspoon pure vanilla extract

½ cup powdered sugar

⅓ cup mashed plus ⅔ cup diced very ripe banana (the riper they are, the sweeter and more pronounced the flavor)

¾ cup sweetened coconut flakes

¼ cup dark Dutch-process cocoa powder, preferably Hershey's Special Dark, sifted to remove lumps

½ teaspoon fine table salt

½ teaspoon ground cinnamon

⅓ cup mini semisweet chocolate chips

ASSEMBLY

Softened butter, for the loaf pans

⅔ cup granulated sugar

⅛ teaspoon vanilla bean paste

2 tablespoons sweetened coconut flakes, for sprinkling

7 To assemble: Butter two 9 × 5-inch loaf pans and line them with parchment paper leaving 2 inches of overhang over the two long sides.

8 Press down the risen dough and do your best to divide it in half. On a lightly floured surface roll one piece into a 9 × 15-inch rectangle. Spread with half the filling and then starting with a long side, roll the dough into a tight coil (like a cinnamon roll). Put it on a tray and place it in the freezer for 10 minutes to make it easier to cut. Repeat this rolling process with the second piece of dough and remaining filling.

9 Once the dough has chilled for 10 minutes, slice one of the dough logs in half lengthwise to expose the filling. Twist the halves together like a 2-plait braid and then coil the braid into one of the pans in an S shape. Repeat this with the second dough log in the second pan. Cover the pans loosely with kitchen towels and allow them to rise in a warm place again for 1 hour to 1 hour 20 minutes, until puffed up. (You can also cover them with plastic wrap and let them rise in the fridge overnight and then bring them back to room temperature for an hour before baking.)

10 Preheat the oven to 375°F (or 350°F on the convection setting).

11 Transfer the babkas in their pans to the oven and bake for 40 to 45 minutes, until a tester goes into the center without any resistance. If they are undercooked you will feel stretchy dough in the center when you use the tester. If you have a thermometer, stick it in the center; if it reads 200°F, it's done.

12 Meanwhile, in a small saucepan, combine the sugar, ⅔ cup water, and vanilla bean paste. Bring to a simmer and cook for about 3 minutes, or until the sugar dissolves.

13 As soon as the babkas come out of the oven, gently remove them from the pans and pour or brush the syrup all over the tops, making sure to use half the syrup for each loaf. Sprinkle the tops with the coconut flakes while they're still sticky.

14 Transfer the babkas to wire racks to cool, then slice and serve.

STORAGE: **Store in an airtight container or wrapped in parchment paper and then aluminum foil at room temperature for up to 2 days. The bread can be frozen wrapped in parchment then plastic wrap for up to 2 months.**

chocolate chunk brioche with pearl sugar

I spent my twenties living in Manhattan, and one of my fondest memories is of the sleepovers I used to have with my sister Christiana at her West Village apartment. Even though we lived in the same city, I lived uptown on West 75th Street and downtown just had a different vibe and almost felt like a little vacation for me. There was nothing like waking up on beautiful, sunny Greenwich Street. We would start the day with a workout, followed by a matcha latte and then a stroll to find the latest and greatest treats. There was a tiny French bakery near her place that had the most incredible pain au chocolat and my favorite, fluffy brioche loaves dotted with rich chocolate callets or pearl sugar. Pearl sugar has a special texture that is delicate yet crunchy, but when baked, the exterior melts slightly, creating mysterious, sweet little pockets throughout the baked good. This recipe isn't difficult, but it results in a super-special, almost "fancy" confection that is a dream on any breakfast or brunch table. Bake the loaves off right before your guests arrive to fill your home with the most intoxicating aroma. Use your hands to tear the warm bread apart to reveal the melty chocolate and pearl sugar, and dare I say slather it with some softened, salty French butter?! Note: This dough needs to rise in the fridge overnight.

MAKES TWO 8-INCH ROUND LOAVES

YEAST MIXTURE

- **⅓ cup warm water (like bathwater, or 105° to 115°F)**
- **2 teaspoons active dry yeast**
- **1 teaspoon granulated sugar**

DOUGH

- **1⅓ cups all-purpose flour, plus more for dusting**
- **2 to 2¼ cups bread flour**
- **3 tablespoons granulated sugar**
- **1¼ teaspoons fine table salt**
- **1 cup whole milk**
- **1 large egg**
- **2 large egg yolks**
- **1 teaspoon pure vanilla extract**
- **6 tablespoons unsalted butter, cut into cubes, at room temperature**
- **1 cup Ghirardelli bittersweet chocolate discs (semisweet works, too)**
- **¼ cup pearl sugar**
- **Egg wash: 1 large egg beaten with 2 teaspoons water**

1. Make the yeast mixture: In a small bowl, combine the warm water, yeast, and granulated sugar. Allow the yeast to sit for 10 to 15 minutes to activate and get bubbly and frothy. (If the yeast doesn't bubble up after 30 minutes, start again with fresh ingredients, as the yeast may be dead.)
2. Make the dough: In a stand mixer fitted with the dough hook, whisk together the all-purpose flour, 2 cups of the bread flour, the granulated sugar, and salt. Stir together until combined.
3. In a small saucepan, bring the milk to a boil. Once it starts to boil, shut it off immediately. (This process is called scalding, and it ensures the milk doesn't affect the yeast's ability to rise. Don't skip it!) Allow the milk to cool slightly to avoid scrambling the eggs in the next step.
4. With the mixer on low speed, add the scalded milk, whole egg, egg yolks, vanilla, and yeast mixture. Mix until the dough starts to come together.
5. With the mixer on medium speed, add the cubed butter a little at a time (about 1 cube every 30 seconds), until the butter is fully incorporated into the dough. Continue to knead the dough on medium speed in the mixer for 10 to 15 minutes, until the dough is smooth and very stretchy. If after 5 minutes the dough appears very wet and is sticking to the sides of the bowl, add ¼ cup more bread flour, but no more than that.
6. Gather the dough together into a smooth ball with your hands and place the dough in a clean bowl and cover it with plastic wrap. Place the bowl in the fridge for at least 12 hours and up to 24 hours (or overnight). The dough will rise slowly in the fridge and the flavor will grow stronger and richer.

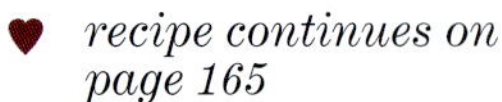
recipe continues on page 165

7 After the dough has spent at least 12 hours in the fridge, transfer the dough ball to a very lightly floured surface. Cut the dough ball in half and lightly flatten each piece with your hands into a disc. Evenly distribute the chocolate chips and pearl sugar over the 2 discs of dough. Fold the edges toward the center and use the heel of your hand to gently knead the chips and sugar into the dough. Gather each piece of dough into a ball using both hands, stretching the dough downward and tucking the seam at the bottom. You want the top to be as smooth as possible.

8 Place the dough balls at least 6 inches apart on a parchment-lined sheet pan. Loosely cover them with kitchen towels and place in a warm place to rise. I like to keep mine in the oven that is off for a nice and cozy place for it to rise. Allow the dough to rise until doubled in size, about 2 hours.

9 Preheat the oven to 350°F (or 325°F on the convection setting). Position the oven rack in the middle but with no rack above it to give the breads room to grow. Brush the tops of the breads with the egg wash.

10 Place the breads in the oven and bake for 20 to 25 minutes, until golden brown and nicely risen.

11 Allow the breads to cool on a wire rack for at least 20 minutes before you eat them.

STORAGE: **Store wrapped in parchment paper and then aluminum foil at room temperature for up to 3 days. I prefer to warm up the bread in the oven for 5 to 7 minutes on 350°F before serving.**

SCONE QUEEN TIP

You can also leave the bread plain with no chips or pearl sugar, or add whatever mix-ins you prefer! I also like to omit the chocolate and make this with just pearl sugar. For a plain pearl sugar brioche, divide 1 cup pearl sugar between the discs of dough and knead them in.

raisin tea biscuits

If you're not familiar with tea biscuits, they live somewhere between a scone and a buttermilk biscuit. For some reason, they are a bit of a Long Island staple, as they are prominently found on the shelves of local bakeries and in plastic clamshell boxes on grocery store shelves. I rarely see them in other states and there are very few recipes on the internet, which brought me to this conclusion: I believe that someone attempted to make an English-style scone and didn't think the people of Long Island would know what a scone was, so they called it a "tea biscuit." I am no food historian but this is my assumption, and I'm stickin' to it! For as long as I could remember, my grandmother and mother would pick up fresh, iced, raisin tea biscuits from the bakery that had been cut in half and filled with a generous amount of softened butter spread. They aren't overly sweet and the texture is moist and soft on the inside and slightly crisp and crumbly on the outside. The raisins plump up slightly in the oven and add the perfect contrasting chew. With a cup of hot coffee or tea, it's a real breakfast treat. Feel free to swap out the raisins for currants, dried cranberries, or even chocolate or cinnamon chips!

MAKES 7 LARGE BISCUITS

DOUGH

- 1 heaping cup raisins
- 1¼ cups bread flour
- 1½ cups all-purpose flour, plus more for dusting
- ⅓ cup granulated sugar
- 1 teaspoon fine table salt
- 3½ teaspoons baking powder
- 10 tablespoons (4 ounces) vegetable shortening, such as Crisco, cut into small pieces
- ¾ cup plus 1 to 2 tablespoons very cold whole buttermilk, plus more for brushing
- 1 large egg
- 1 large egg yolk
- 1 teaspoon pure vanilla extract
- 1½ teaspoons distilled white vinegar

GLAZE

- 1 cup powdered sugar
- Pinch of fine table salt
- ⅛ teaspoon vanilla bean paste or ¼ teaspoon pure vanilla extract

1. Preheat the oven to 425°F (or 400°F on the convection setting).
2. Make the dough: Pour hot, but not boiling, water (at least 150°F) over the raisins and let them soak while you start the dough.
3. In a stand mixer fitted with the dough hook (or in a large bowl with a wooden spoon), combine the bread flour, the all-purpose flour, granulated sugar, salt, and baking powder.
4. With the mixer on low speed, add the shortening and mix until it blends into the flour mixture and resembles fine crumbs, about 2 minutes. Be sure to scrape the sides of the bowl to ensure all the dry mix gets mixed with the shortening.
5. Drain the raisins in a fine-mesh sieve. Add them to the flour mixture and stir just until they are evenly distributed throughout the mix.
6. In a separate bowl or measuring cup, whisk together ¾ cup of the buttermilk, the whole egg, egg yolk, vanilla, and vinegar just until blended. If the dough feels very wet and sticks easily onto your hands, add the remaining ¼ cup of bread flour.
7. On medium-low speed, add the buttermilk mixture to the flour mixture and mix until the dough just comes together, about 2 minutes. If the dough appears to be too dry add another tablespoon or two of buttermilk just to bring it together. You want the dough moist but not so sticky that it comes off on your hands.
8. Dump the dough onto a lightly floured surface and roll it out until it is 1 inch thick. Flour a 3-inch round cutter and cut straight down into the dough, don't wiggle or twist the cutter or else it may not rise evenly. Gather the scraps, reroll, and cut out more biscuits. You should get 7 biscuits. Place the biscuits ½ inch apart on a parchment-lined baking sheet. Lightly brush the tops of the biscuits with buttermilk and transfer to the oven.
9. Bake for 12 minutes. Rotate the pan front to back, reduce the oven temperature to 375°F (or 350°F on the convection setting), and continue to bake for another 8 to 10 minutes, until the edges and bottoms are golden and the centers are baked through.

10 Let the tea biscuits cool for 10 to 15 minutes on the pan while you make the glaze.

11 Make the glaze: In a small bowl, whisk together the powdered sugar and salt. Add a tablespoon of water at a time until you get a paste-like consistency. Add the vanilla bean paste. Add a few drops of water at a time if needed until the glaze becomes a spreadable texture. You still want it fairly opaque so it sets beautifully on top of the biscuits.

12 Take a spoon and spread about 1 tablespoon of the glaze on top of each biscuit. Let the glaze set for 10 to 15 minutes at room temperature (if you can wait!) before serving.

STORAGE: **Store in a sealed container or wrapped in parchment paper and then aluminum foil at room temperature for 3 days. Reheat in the oven at 325°F for a few minutes or even on a plate in the microwave for 15 to 20 seconds.**

SCONE QUEEN TIP

You can serve them as is or cut them horizontally, butter the insides generously with softened, salted butter, and place the tops back on, then enjoy!

easy chocolate pear strudel

One of my favorite flavor combinations is pear and chocolate. My love of this duo started when I was studying abroad as a college student in Florence, Italy. I frequented a local trattoria that had the perfect finale to every perfect meal: an insanely rich poached pear and chocolate ganache cake. Years later, I discovered a bakery in Hoboken, New Jersey, with a pear and chocolate pastry that reunited me with my lost love! Here I've re-created my favorite dessert using store-bought puff pastry to save time, filled with chocolate and a pear compote so delicious that you can put it on top of ice cream, too.

SERVES UP TO 8

PEAR FILLING

4 large ripe pears (see Tip)

2 tablespoons freshly squeezed lemon juice or orange juice

2 tablespoons unsalted butter

⅓ cup packed dark brown sugar

1½ tablespoons cornstarch

1 teaspoon ground cinnamon

½ teaspoon fine table salt

⅛ teaspoon ground nutmeg

1 teaspoon vanilla bean paste or 2 teaspoons pure vanilla extract

ASSEMBLY

Flour, for dusting

1 sheet frozen puff pastry dough, thawed but still cold

4 ounces semisweet or bittersweet chocolate (I use Baker's chocolate bars), chopped up in small chunks, or just use 3 ounces or a heaping ⅓ cup chips (I use Ghirardelli bittersweet chips)

Egg wash: 1 egg beaten with 1 tablespoon milk or water

1 tablespoon raw or turbinado sugar (optional)

1. Make the pear filling: Peel, core, and cut the pears into ½-inch dice, toss them in the lemon juice as you work (so they don't brown).
2. In a nonstick skillet, melt the butter over medium heat. Add the pears and sauté for 5 to 7 minutes, until the pears begin to release their juices and soften but there are still some chunks.
3. In a small bowl, stir together the brown sugar, cornstarch, cinnamon, salt, nutmeg, and vanilla bean paste.
4. Add the sugar mixture to the pears in the pan and cook over medium-low heat for about 3 minutes, or until the mixture thickens.
5. Let the pear mixture cool to room temperature or you can chill it covered in the fridge.
6. Preheat the oven to 425°F (or 400°F on the convection setting).
7. Assemble the strudel: Roll out the puff pastry with a rolling pin on a lightly floured surface to about 12 × 10 inches. With a long side facing you, mark the puff pastry vertically into 3 equal sections. Sprinkle the chocolate in the center section of the dough and then top the chocolate with the pear filling. Fold over the section on the left side and brush the top with a little of the egg wash. Then fold the right section on top, like a letter.
8. Brush the top of the strudel gently with the egg wash and then use a sharp paring knife to make some shallow diagonal slits on the top of the pastry. This will help the pastry cook properly. Sprinkle the top with a little bit of raw sugar (if desired).
9. Bake for 25 to 30 minutes, until golden brown and crispy on the top and bottom.
10. Allow to cool for a few minutes before eating.

STORAGE: **Best eaten same day! If you do have leftovers, store at room temperature in a container that is loosely covered and not airtight, as it will get very soggy.**

SCONE QUEEN TIP

You want the pears to be ripe and sweet but not overly soft and mushy.

mom's snow day bread

When I was a kid growing up on the East Coast, nothing was more thrilling than waking up on a cold winter's morning to look out the window and see a blanket of snow on the ground. We would rush to the television in my parents' bedroom, standing just inches from the screen, hoping, praying, that our school name would appear on the moving banner at the bottom of the newsfeed. Sachem East . . . Sachem North . . . Smithtown . . . YES! Snow day! Although I was fond of school, I loved snow days because it meant I was "stuck," cozy inside with my mom and sisters. One of my fondest cooking traditions was Mom's "Daisy Braid" bread (I have no idea where the name came from), which I renamed "Snow Day Bread," as it was only made on snow days. If the weather forecast called for snow, I remember her checking the pantry to make sure she was prepared with packets of yeast. The four girls would gather together in our pajamas at the kitchen island, kneading and braiding the dough while watching the beautiful snowfall. The second it came out of the oven, we would sit at the table with a whole stick of butter and a jar of honey, slathering each crumb and devouring it all. I hope all of you start this tradition in your homes, and if you're not from a snowy climate, I give you permission to make it during the next rainstorm with a hot cup of cocoa.

MAKES 1 BRAIDED LOAF

3 cups all-purpose flour

1 (7g) envelope active dry yeast (2¼ teaspoons)

¼ cup sugar

¾ teaspoon fine table salt

4 tablespoons (2 ounces / ½ stick) unsalted butter, at room temperature

¾ cup warm water (110° to 115°F)

1 large egg, at room temperature, lightly beaten

Canola or other vegetable oil, for oiling and brushing the top of the loaf

Salted butter and honey, for serving

1 In a stand mixer fitted with the dough hook or paddle, combine 1 cup of the flour, the yeast, sugar, and salt. With the mixer on medium speed, beat in the butter and then the warm water and beat for 2 minutes, or until combined.

2 Add the beaten egg and ½ cup more of flour. Beat at high speed for 1 minute until thick and elastic.

3 With a wooden spoon, gradually stir in just enough of the remaining 1½ cups of flour to make the soft dough leave the sides of bowl. Turn out onto a well-floured board or countertop. Shape the dough into a ball and knead it for 10 minutes or less until the dough is smooth and the bubbles are out.

4 Place the dough in a clean lightly oiled bowl and cover it lightly with plastic wrap and a clean towel. Let it rise until has doubled in size, about 1 hour in a warm kitchen.

5 Punch the dough down and divide into 3 fairly equal pieces. Roll them into logs and then braid them like you would hair. You will be left with roughly an 11-inch-long dough braid.

6 Place the dough braid on a lightly greased cookie sheet. Lightly brush the braid with canola oil and then loosely cover it with plastic wrap. Allow to rise in a warm place again for about 1 hour, until it has puffed up slightly, or in the fridge overnight.

7 When ready to bake, preheat the oven to 400°F (or 375°F on the convection setting).

8 Bake the bread for about 30 minutes, or until golden and cooked through.

9 Let cool just slightly before enjoying with salted butter and a drizzle of honey if you please.

STORAGE: **Store wrapped in parchment paper and then aluminum foil at room temperature for up to 2 days.**

hot cross buns

Lightly spiced, sweet, and eggy bread rolls dotted with candied orange peel and topped with a sweet orange glaze, hot cross buns are a spring and Easter time treat!

MAKES 12 BUNS

DOUGH

- 1 cup whole milk
- 8 tablespoons (4 ounces/1 stick) unsalted butter, plus more for greasing
- ½ cup sugar
- 3½ teaspoons active dry yeast
- 2 large eggs
- 2 large egg yolks
- 2 teaspoons fine table salt
- ½ teaspoon pure vanilla extract
- ½ teaspoon grated orange zest
- ½ teaspoon grated lemon zest
- 1 teaspoon ground cinnamon
- ¼ teaspoon ground nutmeg
- ¼ teaspoon ground cloves
- ¼ teaspoon ground allspice
- 4 to 4¼ cups all-purpose flour, plus more as needed
- ½ cup dried currants
- ¼ cup candied orange peel (see Tip)

TOPPINGS

- 2 tablespoons apricot jam
- 1 tablespoon hot water
- 1 cup powdered sugar
- Pinch of fine table salt
- ⅛ teaspoon vanilla bean paste or ¼ teaspoon vanilla extract
- A few tablespoons orange juice, as needed

1. Make the dough: In a small saucepan, bring the milk to a boil. The moment it reaches a boil, remove from the heat. (This process is called scalding, and it ensures the milk doesn't affect the yeast's ability to rise. Don't skip it!)

2. Pour the hot milk into the bowl of a stand mixer and add the butter. Stir, allowing the butter to melt completely. Then stir in the sugar. Wait until the mixture is just warmer than room temperature, then stir in the yeast. Allow the yeast to sit for 10 to 20 minutes to activate and get bubbly and frothy. (If the yeast does not bubble up after 30 minutes, start again with fresh ingredients, as the yeast may be dead.)

3. Attach the dough hook to the mixer and turn the mixer to low. Add the whole eggs, egg yolks, salt, vanilla, orange zest, lemon zest, cinnamon, nutmeg, cloves, and allspice. Once that is incorporated, beat in 4 cups of the flour, the currants, and candied orange peel and continue to beat the dough until it pulls away from the sides. Run the mixer for about 10 minutes to allow the dough to stretch and develop the gluten. If the dough seems too sticky after the first 2 to 3 minutes add an additional ¼ cup flour. After mixing for 10 minutes, turn the mixer off. Cover the top of the bowl with plastic and allow the dough to rise until doubled in size, about 1½ hours in a warm kitchen.

4. Punch the dough down and dump it out onto a lightly floured surface. Using your hands roll the dough into a log shape that is about 3 inches in diameter and then using a sharp knife, slice the log crosswise into 12 equal pieces. You can also use a kitchen scale to weigh the dough and figure out what each portion should weigh.

5. Grease a 9 × 13-inch glass baking dish with butter. Next, carefully shape each piece of dough into a smooth ball, pinching them on the bottom to seal them. Then arrange them in the baking dish in a 3-by-4 grid. Cover with plastic wrap and a kitchen towel. Allow them to rise again until they are puffy, about 1 hour.

6. Preheat the oven to 375°F (or 350°F on the convection setting).

7. Bake for 20 to 25 minutes, until golden brown. To ensure the buns are properly baked, you can take the internal temperature of one of them. The center of the bun should read 190°F.

8. While the buns are baking, prepare the toppings: In a small bowl, whisk together the apricot jam and hot water and if it is too thick, microwave it for 30 seconds to loosen it.

9 Right when the buns come out of the oven, baste them with the apricot jam mixture and then allow them to cool in the pan.

10 While the buns are cooling, in a small bowl, whisk together the powdered sugar, salt, and vanilla bean paste. Add a tablespoon of orange juice at a time until it is a thick but pipeable texture. Pour the icing into a piping bag or a zip-seal plastic bag and cut a small tip.

11 Pipe the icing in a straight line across the rows of buns, first in one direction and then perpendicular to that, so that the top of each bun ends up with a cross shape. Allow the icing to set for a few minutes before eating.

STORAGE: **Store in the pan wrapped with plastic wrap for up to 3 days. To reheat, I like to put a bun on a plate and microwave for 20 to 30 seconds to maintain its moisture.**

SCONE QUEEN TIP

I use the candied orange peel that comes already cut into small dice, but if you have larger pieces you can chop it up small yourself.

french toast monkey bread

I must confess that, despite my sweet tooth, French toast was never a favorite of mine as a child. Unfortunately, the version I grew up with (sorry, Mom!) was typically a soggy, greasy metallic-tasting piece of white bread, saturated in egg and then slathered in syrup, which made it, well, soggier. It wasn't until I moved to New York City after college that I was introduced to the magic of properly made French toast, which I learned to make while working at the iconic Waldorf Astoria Hotel. I'll never forget Miss Elsie, who soaked hundreds of pieces of uber-thick brioche overnight in a rich custard and then cooked them in the morning in browning butter on a griddle top. This French toast was perfect: custardy, pillowy on the inside, and buttery, yet crisp on the outside.

Since my favorite gathering to host with friends is a carb-heavy brunch, I wanted to create something that would check all the boxes in the flavor and texture departments but would also let me enjoy the company of my friends with a mimosa in hand. Here, soft, cinnamon bun–like dough is rolled into balls, coated in cinnamon sugar, and layered into a Bundt pan. A sinful maple sauce that's poured on top seeps in and creates a magical glaze while it bakes. Flip this over onto a tall cake stand and watch your guests' mouths drop as they see the luscious maple caramel cascade down the sides. The dough can even be prepared the night before and then assembled and baked the morning of your gathering. Let the record reflect that this is one of my favorite recipes in the entire book and is worth every bit of effort.

SERVES 8 TO 12

DOUGH

1 cup whole milk

8 tablespoons (4 ounces/1 stick) unsalted butter

⅓ cup sugar

1 (7g) envelope active dry yeast (2¼ teaspoons)

2 large eggs

1 large egg yolk

4 to 4¼ cups all-purpose flour

2 teaspoons fine table salt

2 teaspoons pure vanilla extract

¼ teaspoon ground nutmeg

Cooking spray

ASSEMBLY

1⅓ cups sugar

⅛ teaspoon ground nutmeg

1 tablespoon ground cinnamon

8 tablespoons (4 ounces/1 stick) unsalted butter, melted

1. Make the dough: In a small saucepan, bring the milk to a boil. The moment it reaches a boil, remove from the heat. (This process is called scalding, and it ensures the milk doesn't affect the yeast's ability to rise. Don't skip it!)
2. Pour the hot milk into the bowl of a stand mixer and add the butter. Stir, allowing the butter to melt completely. Then stir in the sugar. Wait until the mixture is just warmer than room temperature, then stir in the yeast. Allow the yeast to sit for 10 to 20 minutes to activate and get bubbly and frothy. (If the yeast does not bubble up after 30 minutes, start again with fresh ingredients, as the yeast may be dead.)
3. Attach the dough hook to the mixer and turn the mixer to low. Add the whole eggs, egg yolk, 4 cups of the flour, the salt, vanilla, and nutmeg. Beat the dough until it pulls away from the sides. Run the mixer for about 10 minutes to allow the dough to stretch and develop the gluten. If the dough seems too sticky after the first 2 to 3 minutes add an additional ¼ cup flour. After mixing for 10 minutes, turn the mixer off. Cover the top of the bowl with plastic, and allow the dough to rise until doubled in size, about 1½ hours in a warm kitchen. (You can make the dough ahead of time and allow it to proof slowly in the fridge overnight, then take the dough out to sit at room temperature for 2 hours before continuing on to the next step.)
4. Generously grease a 10- to 12-cup Bundt pan with cooking spray.
5. To assemble: In a medium bowl, mix together the sugar, nutmeg, and cinnamon. Place the melted butter in a bowl. Set both aside for coating the dough balls.

recipe continues on page 178

MAPLE CARAMEL SAUCE

12 tablespoons (6 ounces/ 1½ sticks) unsalted butter

¾ cup pure maple syrup

1 teaspoon pure vanilla extract

Pinch of fine table salt

6 Punch the dough down to release the air. Roll the dough out to a rectangle about 12 × 16 inches. With a short side facing you, cut the rectangle lengthwise into 4 equal strips. Make 9 evenly spaced crosswise cuts so you end up with 40 pieces of dough. Take each piece of dough and roll into a ball about 1¼ inches in diameter.

7 Dip each ball, one by one, into the melted butter, letting the excess drip off. Then generously roll in the spice-sugar mixture to coat them heavily. Fill the Bundt pan with the coated dough balls as you go.

8 Cover the pan with a kitchen towel or plastic wrap and allow the shaped monkey bread to rest for 45 minutes. The balls will rise ever so slightly during this time.

9 Preheat the oven to 375°F (or 350°F on the convection setting).

10 Make the maple caramel sauce: Melt the butter in a microwave-safe bowl or large glass measuring cup. Whisk in the maple syrup, vanilla, and salt.

11 Just before you slide the bread into the oven, pour the maple caramel sauce over the top of the entire bread. Place the Bundt pan on a cookie sheet, as some of the maple caramel sauce may drip over the sides of the pan while baking.

12 Bake for about 35 minutes, or until the bread is a bit puffed up and golden brown and the internal temperature reads 195°F.

13 Let cool in the pan for 10 minutes, then carefully flip onto a plate or cake stand. Be sure to get all of the maple caramel sauce poured over the top of the bread. This is best enjoyed by pulling each ball off one by one. Serve warm!

STORAGE: **Store in an airtight container at room temperature for up to 2 days or in the fridge for up to 4 days. To reheat, wrap the monkey bread in parchment paper then aluminum foil and place in a 300°F oven until warm to the touch, or heat individual servings for 20 to 30 seconds in the microwave.**

cinnamon & sugar mall pretzels

Picture this: It's the year 2002 and your mom drops you off at the local shopping mall on a Saturday afternoon with friends. You're doing a few things on this trip, such as trying on the latest trends at Delia's, popping in to Abercrombie to scope out the hot "models" and to catch a whiff of that signature scent, secretly perusing the back area of Spencer's Gifts (IYKYK), and, of course, giving in to the tantalizing aroma of those Auntie Anne's pretzels at the food court. Oh to be twelve again, when your caloric intake didn't quite matter and you could house a buttery cinnamon sugar pretzel and wash it down with a double chocolate chip Frappuccino. This recipe will bring you right back to these memorable Mall Moments, and the dough is so soft and pillowy you'll thoroughly enjoy the assembly. I may not be that twelve-year-old girl anymore, but I did marry a pretzel-obsessed Pennsylvanian, so we have made it our annual Super Bowl Sunday tradition to make these together. You can see from the photos, we have just a little bit of fun making these, and you will, too. Note: This dough needs to rise in the fridge overnight.

MAKES 12 LARGE PRETZELS

DOUGH

2 cups warm water (105° to 110°F)

2 tablespoons granulated sugar

2 (7g) envelopes active dry yeast (4½ teaspoons)

2 tablespoons barley malt syrup

6½ cups bread flour

2 tablespoons fine table salt

10 tablespoons (5 ounces/ 1¼ sticks) cold unsalted butter, cut into small cubes

PRETZEL BOILING LIQUID

½ cup baking soda

⅓ cup packed dark brown sugar

1 (12-ounce) bottle ale

COATING

1 cup granulated sugar

1 tablespoon ground cinnamon

12 tablespoons (6 ounces/ 1½ sticks) unsalted butter, melted

1 Make the dough: In a bowl, whisk together the warm water, sugar, yeast, and barley malt syrup until combined. Allow the yeast to sit for 10 minutes to activate and get bubbly and frothy. (If the yeast does not bubble up after 30 minutes, start again with fresh ingredients, as the yeast may be dead.)

2 In a stand mixer fitted with the dough hook, combine the bread flour and salt. Add the cubes of butter and allow the mixer to run on medium/low speed until the flour resembles coarse sand.

3 Pour the yeast mixture into the mixer and mix on low speed until a shaggy dough ball forms. Increase the mixer to medium speed and allow the dough to knead for 7 to 8 minutes, or until it is smooth and elastic.

4 Cover the bowl with plastic wrap. At this point, you can place it in the fridge to cold-proof overnight, which will result in a more flavorful dough. Or you can make them same day, by letting the dough rise in a warm place until it has doubled in size, about 2 hours. (If you cold-proof the dough in the fridge, take it out of the fridge 1 hour before you want to cook the pretzels to allow the dough to soften slightly.)

5 After the dough has proofed, preheat the oven to 425°F (or 400°F on the convection setting).

6 Set up the pretzel boiling liquid: In a large Dutch oven or pot, combine 8 cups water, the baking soda, brown sugar, and ale. Bring to a boil over medium heat, then reduce to a simmer. While you are waiting for it to boil, roll out the dough.

♥ *recipe continues on page 181*

7 Meanwhile, roll the pretzel dough into a 14 × 12-inch rectangle. With a long side facing you, cut the rectangle into 12 strips about 1 inch wide. Roll each strip into a long rope about ¾ inch thick. When forming the ropes, it is easiest to start from the center and work your way to the ends. Loop the ropes into pretzel shapes by first forming a U-shape with the rope and then crossing the ends over each other in the middle, twisting them slightly before pressing the ends down to secure the shape at the bottom part of the U. (You can also make simple knots, twists, nuggets, or sticks with this dough, just watch the baking time as smaller shapes will bake more rapidly.)

8 Set up the pretzel coating station: On a plate or shallow baking dish, stir together the sugar and cinnamon. Pour the melted butter into a bowl. Set both aside.

9 Spray 2 or 3 baking sheets with cooking spray and set them near the stove. Working in batches of only 2 or 3 pretzels, gently lower them one at a time into the simmering ale mixture. Boil for about 30 seconds, or until they float. Use a slotted spatula or spider strainer to carefully transfer the pretzels to the prepared baking sheets.

10 Bake the pretzels for 5 minutes. Rotate the baking sheets front to back and continue to bake for 5 to 6 minutes, until a deep brown color.

11 Remove the pretzels from the oven and immediately baste them with the melted butter and then dunk them in the cinnamon-sugar mixture to coat completely.

12 Serve them warm!

STORAGE: **These are best eaten immediately, however if there are leftovers, store them airtight at room temperature and then reheat on a sheet pan in the oven for 5 minutes at 350°F.**

SCONE QUEEN TIP

Opt for a more salty/savory pretzel by swapping the cinnamon-sugar coating for a sprinkling of pretzel salt, flaky sea salt, everything bagel seasoning, or even Middle Eastern za'atar! If you opt for a salty pretzel rather than sweet, sprinkle on the pretzel salt, flaky sea salt, everything bagel seasoning, or za'atar as soon as they come out of the boiling beer bath and before going into the oven.

cinnamon raisin loaf with cinnamon sugar crust

In my hometown of Saint James, New York, there once was a bakery café on our main street (Lake Avenue) that had not only the best pancakes but also the best cinnamon raisin bread, period. Sadly, this establishment closed many years ago, but the memories of this soft, flavorful cinnamon-scented bread with the sugary exterior lived rent free in my head for years to come. I'll never forget the bakers pulling the fresh loaves off a wooden shelf behind them, placing them in the slicing machine, and then carefully sliding the loaf into a pink paper bag. I could never wait until we got home to eat it, so I would reach into the bag in the back of my dad's car and take out a fluffy center slice, eating the edges first to ensure I got as much of the crunchy crystallized sugar before it fell to my lap. This is everything that bread was and more. Just wait until you smell it baking . . .

MAKES ONE 9 × 5-INCH LOAF

DOUGH

- ¼ cup warm water (100° to 110°F)
- ⅓ cup plus 1 teaspoon sugar
- 2½ teaspoons active dry yeast
- 8 tablespoons (4 ounces/1 stick) unsalted butter, melted
- 2 tablespoons vegetable oil
- ¾ cup milk, whole or 2%
- 1½ teaspoons fine table salt
- 1 teaspoon pure vanilla extract
- 2 large eggs, at room temperature
- 1¼ cups raisins, regular or golden
- 4 to 4¼ cups all-purpose flour
- Cooking spray

ASSEMBLY

- Flour, for dusting
- Softened butter, for the loaf pan
- 2 tablespoons milk or water
- ¾ cup sugar
- 1½ tablespoons ground cinnamon
- 2 to 3 tablespoons unsalted butter, melted

1 Make the dough: In a stand mixer fitted with the dough hook (you can also do this in a large bowl and knead it by hand!), combine the warm water and 1 teaspoon of the sugar. Pour the yeast on top and mix it into the water. Allow the yeast to sit for 10 to 15 minutes to activate and get bubbly and frothy. (If the yeast does not bubble up after 30 minutes, start again with fresh ingredients, as the yeast may be dead.)

2 Pour in the melted butter, vegetable oil, remaining ⅓ cup of sugar, the milk, salt, vanilla, and eggs. Break up the eggs with a fork and then allow the dough hook to mix it up a bit, about 30 seconds on medium-low speed. Add the raisins.

3 Pour 4 cups of the flour in all at once and run the machine for about 5 minutes on medium speed, until the dough is soft and smooth. If it gets very sticky and is stuck to the hook and bowl sides, add ¼ cup more flour, but no more than that or it will affect the texture. (If you're doing this by hand, once the dough comes together, you'll want to dump it out onto a floured counter and knead it for about 10 minutes, until it's nice and smooth.)

4 Rub a large bowl with oil or spray it with cooking spray and place the dough in the center of the bowl. Cover it with a clean kitchen towel and allow it to rise until doubled in size, about 1½ hours in a warm kitchen.

5 Assemble the loaf: Grease a 9 × 5-inch loaf pan with butter.

6 Punch the dough down and then roll out on a lightly floured surface into a 9 × 13-inch rectangle about ½ inch thick. Moisten the top of the dough rectangle with the milk.

7 In a small bowl, whisk together the sugar and cinnamon. Sprinkle ½ cup of the mixture evenly on top of the moistened dough. (Reserve the remaining mixture.)

8 With a long side facing you, roll the dough into a log. Tuck the ends under and place it in the buttered loaf pan. Brush the top lightly with some of the melted butter (reserve the rest). Place in a warm spot to rise again for 1 hour.

9 Preheat the oven to 350°F (or 325°F on the convection setting). Place the loaf pan on top of a baking sheet to catch any sugar that may fall while it bakes. Transfer to the oven.

10 Bake for 30 minutes. Remove from the oven and brush the top again with the reserved melted butter and sprinkle the reserved cinnamon sugar mixture evenly over the top.

11 Return to the oven and bake 10 to 15 minutes, until golden brown. When you tap the top it should sound a bit hollow.

12 Let cool for 10 minutes in the pan and then release gently from the pan, slice, and enjoy it warm!

STORAGE: **Store wrapped in parchment paper and then aluminum foil at room temperature for up to 3 days.**

SCONE QUEEN TIP

Toast a slice and spread some cream cheese or salted butter on top—hello, heaven! My husband likes his with peanut butter . . . also heaven! It makes great French toast, too!

irish soda bread

Just like most Americans, this Italian girl becomes Irish once a year on Saint Patrick's Day. For as long as I can remember, I have been asking my Italian grandmother to make me corned beef and cabbage for my birthday dinner, since it is just before Saint Paddy's. She seeks out a specific brand of corned beef, always adding half of the seasoning it comes with because it's "too salty" (funny because nothing is ever salty enough for her) and pounds and pounds of peeled red potatoes. She would serve me up a few slices of the tender beef in a soupy, steaming bowl of the cabbage and potatoes, topping each piece of potato with a pat of butter. Meat and potatoes . . . the epitome of comfort, especially when it's served with a hunk of bread. Irish soda bread and scones are actually very similar in ingredients and process, so one day I had an aha! moment and realized if I swapped out the heavy cream for the more acidic alternative of buttermilk and added some baking soda, we might get the tender and spongy yet crisp texture and tangy flavor that makes the perfect loaf of soda bread. I add currants to mine because my family prefers a small bite of raisin, but you can customize this recipe by adding larger raisins, some caraway seeds, or even a small amount of chopped fresh rosemary. As the Irish say, Sláinte!

MAKES 1 ROUND LOAF

- 2 cups all-purpose flour, plus more for dusting
- ⅓ cup sugar
- ¾ teaspoon baking soda
- ¾ teaspoon baking powder
- ¾ teaspoon fine table salt
- 6 tablespoons (3 ounces) very cold unsalted butter, cut into small cubes
- ¾ cup dried Zante currants
- ¾ cup buttermilk, reduced-fat or whole
- 2 large egg yolks
- ¼ teaspoon pure vanilla extract
- Butter, for the sheet pan

CRUST

- 2 tablespoons buttermilk
- 2 to 3 tablespoons sugar

1. Preheat the oven to 425°F (or 400°F on the convection setting).
2. In a large bowl, whisk together the flour, sugar, baking soda, baking powder, and salt.
3. Using a pastry cutter, cut the cold cubes of butter into the flour mixture until it resembles coarse meal and the butter is a little smaller than a pea size. Stir in the currants.
4. In a measuring cup or bowl, beat together the buttermilk, egg yolks, and vanilla.
5. Make a well in the center of the flour mixture, add the buttermilk mixture, and use a fork to incorporate until it forms a shaggy dough ball. You don't want to overmix, you just want it to all come together.
6. Use floured hands to gather the dough into a ball (it should be a bit sticky). Transfer the dough to a lightly floured surface and shape it into a round loaf about 2 inches thick.
7. Lightly grease a sheet pan or 8-inch cast-iron skillet with butter.
8. Transfer the dough to the pan or skillet. Using a sharp or serrated knife, score the top of the dough about 1 inch deep in an "X" shape. This helps the center cook properly.
9. For the crust: Brush the top with the buttermilk and generously sprinkle with the sugar (you want a nice crust). Transfer to the oven.
10. Bake for 15 minutes. Then, while keeping the oven closed, reduce the oven temperature to 350°F (or 325°F on the convection setting), and continue to bake for another 10 to 12 minutes, until golden brown and a skewer inserted in the center comes out clean. If it starts to get too dark for your liking, cover the top loosely with aluminum foil.
11. Transfer the bread to a wire rack and let the bread cool for 15 to 20 minutes before eating.

STORAGE: **Store wrapped in parchment paper and then aluminum foil at room temperature for up to 2 days. Leftovers are best enjoyed slightly toasted with butter.**

italian easter breads

One of my all-time favorite family traditions is making this Easter bread on Good Friday. This recipe is over one hundred years old (probably even two hundred years old!) and is very traditional of Sicilian culture, although it has many variations! It is a slightly sweet and eggy bread that has a texture that is both crisp yet chewy. My mom and I make the dough a few hours before the family arrives and then we all gather around the kitchen island and make the dough into Easter basket shapes, baking a dyed Easter egg right into the center of dough baskets. This recipe has come a long way, partly because when I first read this recipe in my grandmother's cookbook it made absolutely no sense! My great-grandma had scratched some notes on a piece of loose-leaf paper that resembled a recipe, but it had virtually no measurements. After years of trial and error—and a culinary degree—I think I mastered it. It does take practice, as you need to understand the feel of the dough, but I always tell people to not get stressed about it because as long as you've got yeast, flour, and egg, it will become some sort of bread . . . so let's give it a whirl!

MAKES 6 TO 8 BREADS

½ cup lukewarm water

1½ packets (10½ grams) active dry yeast

1½ cups plus 1½ teaspoons sugar

9 to 10 cups all-purpose flour, plus more as needed

1½ teaspoons fine table salt

½ cup lukewarm milk

6 large eggs, at room temperature

8 ounces (2 sticks) unsalted butter, at room temperature

Canola or vegetable oil, for greasing the bowl

6 to 8 Easter eggs (hard-boiled and dyed; see Tip)

Egg wash: 1 egg beaten with 1 tablespoon milk or cream

Nonpareils (optional), for decorating

Softened salted butter and honey, for serving

1. Pour the warm water into a measuring cup. Sprinkle in the yeast and 1½ teaspoons of the sugar and stir together. Allow the yeast to sit for 10 minutes to activate and get bubbly and frothy. (If the yeast does not bubble up, start again with fresh ingredients, as the yeast may be dead.)
2. In a stand mixer fitted with the dough hook (or by hand in a large bowl with a wooden spoon), stir together 6 cups of the flour, the remaining 1½ cups of sugar, and the salt.
3. In a separate bowl, combine the warm milk and eggs. Beat them together with a whisk until just combined.
4. With the mixer on low speed, add the yeast/water mixture and mix until just combined, about 1 minute.
5. On low speed, gradually add the egg/milk mixture until the dough ball starts to form. At first the dough will be very sticky, so add another 1 cup flour slowly with the mixer still running. Using floured hands or a rubber spatula, pull the dough from the sides of the bowl, and if it is still too sticky, add another 1 cup flour and mix until incorporated. You want the dough to be coming away from the sides of the bowl and forming a nice ball, so if still too sticky add another 1 cup flour. I generally end up using 9 cups of flour.
6. Once the ball of dough is formed, with the mixer on medium-low speed, add the butter 2 tablespoons at a time, allowing it to mostly incorporate after each addition. After all the butter is added, the dough should be nice and smooth and not so sticky that it comes off onto your hands when you touch it. If it is too sticky still add another 1+ cups flour slowly until it is just right.

♥ *recipe continues on page 188*

7 Lightly grease a large bowl with canola oil. Remove the ball of dough from the bowl and place it on a clean surface dusted with flour. Knead the dough by hand for a few minutes until it gets nice and smooth and then place in the greased bowl. Cover the bowl loosely with plastic wrap and let it rise in a warm place until almost doubled in size, about 3 hours in a warm kitchen. I cover my dough with towels or blankets to help keep it warm.

8 Punch down the dough, place on a floured surface, and knead a few times just to release any air. Now it's time to make your desired shapes! Here are some choices:

FOR A TRADITIONAL SHAPE

9 Cut the dough into 6 equal portions. Cut each portion in half for a total of 12. Roll each out to a log about 9 inches long.

10 Pinch one end together. Now twist the two ropes together. Pinch the other end together.

11 Next, join the ends to each other to form a ring, twisting the ends under so they don't unravel. Place a colored egg into the center of the ring. Place on a parchment-lined sheet pan.

FOR BASKET SHAPES

12 Take a baseball-size ball of dough and lightly flatten it with your hand. Place an Easter egg right in the center and press down gently. Next, make a smaller twist or braid (but with only 2 strands of dough not 3) and place the twist across the top of the egg in the center like a basket handle.

13 After the breads are shaped, place them on parchment paper–lined sheet pans. Be sure not to crowd the pans, the breads will grow quite a bit when they bake. Cover them again with plastic wrap and set them aside for 30 minutes to proof or rise again slightly.

14 Meanwhile, preheat the oven to 375°F (or 350°F on the convection setting).

15 Using a pastry brush, lightly brush the tops of the breads with the egg wash, trying to avoid the dyed eggs. You can also sprinkle on some nonpareils at this stage if you'd like. Transfer to the oven.

16 Bake for 35 to 40 minutes for the smaller wreath shapes and up to 50 to 55 minutes for the larger ones. You may have to adjust the bake time based on the shape and size.

17 Let cool for 5 to 10 minutes before enjoying with some salted butter and even a drizzle of honey if you'd like!

STORAGE: **Allow the breads to cool on wire racks and then tightly wrap them in aluminum foil. Keep them on the counter at room temperature. Warm them in the oven before enjoying if you prefer, they will keep about 3 days.**

SCONE QUEEN TIPS

- Make sure you make the Easter eggs a day ahead so they're dry.
- Remember that the eggs will be cooked twice in this recipe, so if you want to end up with hard-boiled eggs that are fully cooked but not dry and gray, try this technique: Put 6 to 8 eggs in a medium saucepan and cover the eggs with room temperature water. Cover the pot and bring the water to a boil. Once the water is boiling, shut off the heat and let the eggs sit in the pot for 10 minutes. Drain and place the eggs in an ice water bath to cool.
- Use only food dye to dye the eggs. Don't use any glitter or any nonedible decorations because you'll be baking them into the bread.

cinnamon sugar popovers with maple pecan butter

Popovers are a light "roll" made from an egg batter that puffs up in the oven to create a crunchy exterior and an airy, almost hollow center. This classic puff can be made savory with flavorings like cheese and herbs, or left plain and eaten with jam or butter. My version features a crunchy cinnamon sugar infusion and the rich creaminess of maple pecan butter. This recipe was inspired by my late grandfather Vincent, a retired New York City Fire Department captain who would rave about the popovers baked by the firehouse cooks. He first introduced me to popovers when I was a child. In the final months of his life, I developed this recipe and got to watch him enjoy it. When I bake them now, I can still imagine him saying his signature phrase: "VERRRYYY GOOD!"

MAKES 12 POPOVERS

BATTER

3 cups milk, 1%, 2%, or whole

3 cups all-purpose flour

1 tablespoon fine table salt

⅓ cup plus 2 tablespoons granulated sugar

1¼ teaspoons ground cinnamon

6 large eggs

Cooking spray

Powdered sugar (optional), for dusting

MAPLE PECAN BUTTER

5 tablespoons (2½ ounces) unsalted butter, at room temperature

2 tablespoons finely chopped pecans

4 teaspoons pure maple syrup

¼ teaspoon fine table salt

STORAGE: Wrap in aluminum foil and store at room temperature. Reheat in a 350°F oven on a sheet pan for 5 to 7 minutes, or until warm to the touch.

1 Place a 6-cup popover pan in the bottom third of the oven (note that this will be baked in two batches, for a total of 12 popovers). Put a baking sheet on the rack underneath in case anything drips. Preheat the oven to 425°F (or 400°F on the convection setting) with the popover pan inside.

2 Make the batter: In a small saucepan, warm the milk over medium-high heat until small bubbles form around the edges. Set aside.

3 Sift the flour into a bowl. Stir in the salt, 2 tablespoons of the granulated sugar, and 1 teaspoon of the cinnamon.

4 In a separate bowl, stir together the remaining ⅓ cup of granulated sugar and remaining ¼ teaspoon of cinnamon. Set the bowl of cinnamon sugar near the stove, at the ready.

5 In a large bowl, whisk the eggs until frothy, about 2 minutes. Slowly whisk in the hot milk, whisking constantly so the eggs don't cook, then gradually whisk in the flour mixture until almost smooth. Pour the batter into a liquid measuring cup or small pitcher with a spout to make it easier to pour into the pan.

6 Remove the popover pan from the oven and spray the cups with cooking spray. Quickly fill the prepared cups about three-quarters full with batter and spoon 1 teaspoon of the cinnamon-sugar right on top in the center of the batter of each popover cup.

7 Return the pan to the oven and bake for 15 minutes. Rotate the pan front to back, reduce the oven temperature to 375°F (or 350°F on the convection setting), and bake for 20 to 25 minutes more, until the popovers are browned and puffed. Do not open the oven after rotating the pan.

8 Meanwhile, make the maple-pecan butter: In a small bowl, stir together the butter, pecans, maple syrup, and salt. Super simple!

9 Remove the popovers from the oven, dust with a little powdered sugar (if desired). To eat, just break open with your hands and lather on some of the maple-pecan butter. Remember, popovers are like snowflakes—they don't last very long and each one looks different!

10 Using a paper towel, wipe out the excess fat from the popover cups. Heat the pan in the oven for 5 to 10 minutes. Repeat the filling and baking process with the remaining batter and remaining cinnamon sugar to make the second batch of popovers. (You will have cinnamon sugar left over.)

CHAPTER 6

QUICK BREADS & SNACKING CAKES

NUTELLA POUND CAKE 194
CLASSIC TOP-HEAVY DELI CRUMB CAKE 197
PISTACHIO CHOCOLATE CHIP CRUMB CAKE 198
COOKIES & CREAM CRUMB CAKE 200
BANANA CHIP CRUMB CAKE 202
BANANA CREAM ICEBOX CAKE 204
SNOWBALL ICEBOX CAKE 207
CANNOLI ICEBOX CAKE 208
PEACH ALMOND UPSIDE-DOWN CAKE 211
COCONUT CRUNCH BUNDT CAKE 212
DOUBLE-CHOCOLATE SHEET CAKE 215

BANANA NUTELLA SNACKING CAKE 218
CRAIG'S CAKE (CHOCOLATE SNACKING CAKE WITH PEANUT BUTTER GANACHE) 220
FUDGE ICED GOLDEN CAKE 223
GREAT-GRANDMA LENA'S APPLESAUCE CAKE 224
COOKIE BUTTER SWIRLED PUMPKIN BREAD 227
DAD'S DATE NUT BREAD 228
ZUCCHINI BREAD 230
CHOCOLATE CHIP CRUMB LOAF 232
MADELEINE LOAF 235
SPUMONI LOAF 236
PUMPKIN YOGURT LOAF 239
MATCHA ALMOND LOAF 240

nutella pound cake

Every year my best friends Jon and Chris host a holiday brunch in their New York City apartment. Everyone brings a signature dish, and we all crowd around, elbow to elbow, while listening to Mariah Carey and Celine Dion . . . it's kinda perfect. Although this crowd isn't keen on carbs 364 days a year, on this day all the carbs are welcome, guilt-free . . . okay, there is definitely some guilt, but they give in, because who could resist French toast, fresh-baked cookies, biscuits, and Nutella-swirled pound cake?! Ever since I introduced them to this pound cake, it has been requested year after year. Just make sure you have aluminum foil around, because guests will be asking to wrap slices to take home for their morning breakfast.

MAKES ONE 9 × 5-INCH LOAF

Softened butter and flour, for the pan

8 ounces (2 sticks) unsalted butter, at room temperature

1¼ cups sugar

2½ teaspoons pure vanilla extract

4 large eggs, at room temperature

1½ cups all-purpose flour

¾ teaspoon baking powder

½ teaspoon fine table salt

1 (13-ounce) jar Nutella

1 Preheat the oven to 350°F (or 325°F on the convection setting). Butter and lightly flour a 9 × 5-inch loaf pan, tapping out any excess flour.

2 In a stand mixer fitted with the paddle (or in a bowl using a hand mixer), beat the butter, sugar, and vanilla at medium speed until light and fluffy, about 4 minutes.

3 Gradually beat in the eggs one at a time until fully incorporated.

4 In a medium bowl, whisk the together the flour, baking powder, and salt.

5 On low speed, add the flour mixture to the butter/sugar mixture in three additions, beating after each addition until just incorporated. Be sure to scrape down the sides of the bowl after each addition to ensure everything gets mixed properly. Do not overmix.

6 Spread one-third of the batter in the prepared pan. Spread half of the Nutella on top. Use a wooden skewer or knife to gently swirl the Nutella into the batter slightly. Repeat with another one-third of the batter and the remaining Nutella. Top with the remaining batter. Transfer to the oven.

7 Bake for about 1 hour 15 minutes, or until a toothpick inserted in the center comes out clean.

8 Let the cake cool in the pan for 15 minutes and then carefully invert the cake onto a wire rack to further cool. I prefer this cake served at room temp rather than warm. Cut the cake into slices and serve.

STORAGE: **Store in an airtight container or wrapped in parchment paper and then aluminum foil at room temperature for up to 5 days.**

classic top-heavy deli crumb cake

I dedicate these crumb cake recipes to the people of Long Island, where crumb cake is a staple treat you find on nearly every bakery, deli, and bagel shop shelf. When I was growing up, you couldn't go to a friend's house and not find a box of the stuff sitting in the back corner of their kitchen counter. I use the word "cake" loosely, because the typical variation has 80 percent crumb and 20 percent cake—and that's just the way we like it. My version consists of a satisfyingly dense, moist cake topped with tender yet slightly crunchy crumbs. The only thing you have to worry about with this cake is the constant sneaking and picking off of the buttery crumbs bit by bit while you're not looking. Whether you want to go classic cinnamon crumb cake with a yellow cake base or you opt for one of my other fun flavors, they are all crowd-pleasers and the first thing to go at a party.

SERVES 8 TO 12

CAKE

- Cooking spray
- 12 tablespoons (6 ounces/1½ sticks) unsalted butter, at room temperature
- ½ cup packed dark brown sugar
- ½ cup granulated sugar
- 2 teaspoons pure vanilla extract
- 3 large eggs
- 1¼ cups all-purpose flour
- ½ teaspoon fine table salt
- ½ teaspoon baking powder
- ½ cup sour cream

CRUMB TOPPING

- 3½ cups cake flour (not self-rising)
- ⅔ cup packed dark brown sugar
- ⅔ cup granulated sugar
- 1½ teaspoons ground cinnamon
- ½ teaspoon fine table salt
- 8 ounces (2 sticks) unsalted butter, melted
- Powdered sugar, for dusting

1. Preheat the oven to 375°F (or 350°F on the convection setting). Grease an 8 × 8-inch pan with cooking spray.
2. Make the cake: In a stand mixer fitted with the paddle (or in a bowl using a hand mixer), beat together the butter, brown sugar, and granulated sugar on medium speed until creamy and fluffy, 3 to 4 minutes.
3. Beat in the vanilla. Add the eggs one at a time and beat well after each addition.
4. In a medium bowl, stir together the all-purpose flour, salt, and baking powder. Add the flour mixture to the butter/sugar mixture in three additions, alternating with the sour cream, beginning and ending with the flour. Beat on low speed until each addition is just combined.
5. Pour the batter into the prepared pan and smooth the top with an offset spatula.
6. Make the crumb topping: In a medium bowl, combine the cake flour, brown sugar, granulated sugar, cinnamon, and salt. Pour in the melted butter and use a fork to toss it all together until it creates large crumbs. (Do not overmix or whisk rapidly as it will become a paste rather than thick crumbs. You want a gentle tossing motion.)
7. Sprinkle the crumbs over the top of the batter starting at the perimeter and then moving to the center. Transfer to the oven.
8. Bake for 30 to 35 minutes, until a cake tester inserted in the center comes out clean.
9. Let cool in the pan on a wire rack. Dust heavily with powdered sugar, cut into squares, and serve!

STORAGE: **Store airtight at room temperature for up to 5 days.**

pistachio chocolate chip crumb cake

As a chef, I am often asked to name my favorite restaurant, and I consistently turn to my hometown hot spot, Maureen's Kitchen. Maureen's is a diner-style eatery serving up massive portions of classic American breakfast and lunch dishes. An Arnold Palmer, Moe's Famous Homemade Baked Oatmeal, crispy Corned Beef Hash, Cranberry Chicken Salad, and creamy Potato Salad will without a doubt be on my table, and upon departure, I can never resist a "3 Lb" slab of their crumb cake. My pistachio crumb cake is inspired by Maureen's and is so addictive you won't be able to stop eating it. The cake is subtly nutty, and the dark chocolate crumbs are tender and buttery and have the perfect bitterness from the cocoa, which offsets the sweetness.

SERVES 9 TO 12

CAKE

Cooking spray

2 cups all-purpose flour

1 teaspoon baking soda

1 teaspoon baking powder

1 teaspoon fine table salt

8 tablespoons (4 ounces/1 stick) unsalted butter, melted

6 tablespoons vegetable or canola oil

1 cup granulated sugar

1 teaspoon pure vanilla extract

1½ teaspoons pure almond extract

1 (3.4-ounce) box pistachio instant pudding mix (I like Jell-O)

3 large eggs, at room temperature

1 cup sour cream

5 to 7 drops green food coloring (optional)

1 cup mini semisweet chocolate chips

1 Preheat the oven to 375°F (or 350°F on the convection setting). Coat a 9 × 9-inch baking pan with cooking spray and line it with parchment paper and allow a slight overhang.

2 Make the cake: In a medium bowl, stir together the all-purpose flour, baking soda, baking powder, and salt. Set aside.

3 In a stand mixer fitted with the paddle (or in a bowl using a hand mixer), beat together the melted butter, vegetable oil, granulated sugar, vanilla, and almond extract on medium speed until creamy and fluffy, about 3 minutes.

4 Add the pistachio pudding mix and beat just until incorporated, about 2 minutes. Add the eggs one at a time, beating to just combine after each addition.

5 Add the sour cream in two additions, alternating with the flour mixture, mixing on low speed until just combined. If desired, add some green food coloring to enhance the pistachio green color. By hand, fold in the mini chocolate chips.

6 Scoop the batter into the prepared pan and smooth the top with an offset spatula.

7 Make the chocolate crumb topping: In a medium bowl (you can use the same one that held the flour mixture!), combine the cake flour, brown sugar, granulated sugar, cocoa powder, cinnamon, and salt. In a small bowl, stir the vanilla into the melted butter and then slowly pour the butter into the dry mix and use a fork to toss it all together until large crumbs form.

8 Sprinkle the crumbs over the top of the batter starting at the perimeter and then moving to the center. Transfer to the oven.

9 Bake for 55 minutes to 1 hour 5 minutes, until a table knife inserted into the center comes out clean.

10 Let cool in the pan on a wire rack.

CHOCOLATE CRUMB TOPPING

3 cups cake flour (not self-rising)

⅔ cup packed dark brown sugar

⅔ cup granulated sugar

⅓ cup dark Dutch-process cocoa powder, preferably Hershey's Special Dark, sifted to remove lumps

½ teaspoon ground cinnamon

½ teaspoon fine table salt

2 teaspoons pure vanilla extract

8 ounces (2 sticks) unsalted butter, melted

GARNISH

½ cup semisweet chocolate chips

1 teaspoon vegetable shortening

Powdered sugar, for dusting

2 tablespoons finely ground salted roasted pistachios (optional)

11 To garnish: Melt the semisweet chocolate chips with the shortening in the microwave for about 1 minute, or until smooth. Dust the top of the cake lightly with powdered sugar and then use a spoon or pastry bag to drizzle the top with the melted chocolate. For an extra nutty crunch, you can sprinkle the melted chocolate with the finely chopped pistachios (if desired). Let the chocolate set and then cut into squares and serve!

STORAGE: **Store airtight at room temperature for up to 5 days.**

cookies & cream crumb cake

One of my favorite candy bars growing up were Hershey's Cookies 'n' Cream chocolate bars. I love the crispy crunch of the slightly bitter chocolate cookies combined with the super sweet and creamy white chocolate. This crumb cake incorporates these cherished flavors and textures but in thick slices of tender, New York–style crumb cake.

MAKES ONE 9-INCH SQUARE CAKE THAT SERVES 9 TO 12

CAKE

Cooking spray

1¼ cups all-purpose flour

½ teaspoon fine table salt

½ teaspoon baking powder

12 tablespoons (6 ounces/ 1½ sticks) unsalted butter, at room temperature

½ cup packed dark brown sugar

½ cup granulated sugar

2 teaspoons pure vanilla extract

2 large eggs, at room temperature

½ cup sour cream

⅓ cup white chocolate chips or chunks

10 double-stuffed sandwich cookies, chopped into small pieces and divided equally into 2 bowls

CRUMB TOPPING

3 cups cake flour (not self-rising)

½ cup dark Dutch-process cocoa powder, preferably Hershey's Special Dark, sifted to remove lumps

⅔ cup packed dark brown sugar

⅔ cup granulated sugar

¼ teaspoon ground cinnamon

½ teaspoon fine table salt

1. Preheat the oven to 375°F (or 350°F on the convection setting). Grease a 9 × 9-inch pan with cooking spray and line with parchment paper, allowing a 1-inch overhang for easy releasing later on.
2. Make the cake: In a medium bowl, stir together the all-purpose flour, salt, and baking powder. Set aside.
3. In a stand mixer fitted with the paddle (or in a bowl using a hand mixer), beat together the butter, brown sugar, granulated sugar, and vanilla on medium speed until creamy and fluffy.
4. Add the eggs one at a time, beating to just combine after each addition.
5. Add the flour mixture in two additions, alternating with the sour cream, mixing on low speed until just combined. By hand, fold in the white chocolate chips and half of the chopped sandwich cookies.
6. Pour the batter into the prepared pan and smooth the top with an offset spatula. Sprinkle the top with the remaining cookie pieces.
7. Make the crumb topping: In a medium bowl, combine the cake flour, cocoa powder, brown sugar, granulated sugar, cinnamon, and salt. In a separate bowl, mix together the vanilla and melted butter. Pour the butter mixture over the dry mix and use a fork to toss it all together until it creates large crumbs. (Do not overmix or whisk rapidly as it will become a paste rather than thick crumbs. You want a gentle tossing motion.) You will end up with some large and some small crumbs.
8. Sprinkle the crumbs over the top of the batter starting at the perimeter and then moving to the center to ensure proper weight distribution.
9. Bake for 45 to 55 minutes, until a cake tester inserted into the center comes out clean.

2 teaspoons pure vanilla extract

8 ounces (2 sticks) unsalted butter, melted

GARNISH

Powdered sugar, for dusting

½ cup white chocolate chips or chunks

1 teaspoon vegetable shortening or canola oil

3 to 4 sandwich cookies, crushed into small pieces

10 Let the cake fully cool in the pan on a wire rack.

11 To garnish: Lightly dust the top with powdered sugar. In a small microwave-safe bowl, melt the white chocolate chips and vegetable shortening for about 1 minute. Using a spoon or a piping bag with a small round tip, drizzle the top of the cake with the white chocolate and then sprinkle with the chopped sandwich cookies.

12 Allow the white chocolate drizzle to set and then cut the cake into squares and serve!

STORAGE: **Keep the cake in the pan and cover it with aluminum foil or keep it in a sealed container at room temperature for up to about 5 days.**

banana chip crumb cake

Here's another cake that is inspired by a grocery store boxed cake classic—but with no offensive artificial banana flavorings and a much more substantial crumb topping (the best part always). My dad says the tender, spongy banana cake brings him right back to his elementary school cafeteria days in the best way possible. If you are someone who really wants to double down on the banana flavor, feel free to swap out the vanilla pudding mix for banana pudding mix! For best results, be sure to use very ripe bananas that are soft and have a peel that is speckled or beginning to brown.

MAKES ONE 9-INCH SQUARE CAKE

Cooking spray

2 cups all-purpose flour

1 teaspoon baking soda

1 teaspoon baking powder

½ teaspoon fine table salt

¼ teaspoon ground cinnamon

8 tablespoons (4 ounces/1 stick) unsalted butter, at room temperature

6 tablespoons vegetable oil or canola oil

½ cup packed dark brown sugar

½ cup granulated sugar

1 (3.4-ounce) box vanilla or banana instant pudding mix (I prefer Jell-O)

2 teaspoons pure vanilla extract

2 large eggs, at room temperature

1 cup mashed very ripe banana (about 2 large bananas)

¾ cup sour cream

1 cup mini semisweet chocolate chips

1. Preheat the oven to 375°F (or 350°F on the convection setting). Grease a 9 × 9-inch pan with cooking spray.
2. In a medium bowl, stir together the all-purpose flour, baking soda, baking powder, salt, and cinnamon. Set aside.
3. In a stand mixer fitted with the paddle (or in a bowl using a hand mixer), beat together the butter, vegetable oil, brown sugar, and granulated sugar on medium speed until creamy and fluffy, 3 to 4 minutes.
4. Add the vanilla pudding mix and beat for about 3 minutes, until creamy.
5. Beat in the vanilla. Add the eggs one at a time, beating to just combine after each addition. Beat in the mashed banana until just combined.
6. Add the flour mixture in three additions, alternating with the sour cream, mixing on low speed until just combined. By hand, fold in the mini chocolate chips.
7. Pour the batter into the prepared pan and smooth the top with an offset spatula.

CINNAMON CRUMB TOPPING

3 cups cake flour (not self-rising)

⅔ cup packed dark brown sugar

⅔ cup granulated sugar

2 teaspoons ground cinnamon

½ teaspoon fine table salt

2 teaspoons pure vanilla extract

8 ounces (2 sticks) unsalted butter, melted

GARNISH

¼ cup mini semisweet chocolate chips

Powdered sugar, for dusting

8 Make the cinnamon crumb topping: In a medium bowl, combine the cake flour, brown sugar, granulated sugar, cinnamon, and salt. In a separate bowl, mix together the vanilla and melted butter. Pour the butter mixture into the dry mix and use a fork to toss it all together until it creates large crumbs. (Do not overmix or whisk rapidly as it will become a paste rather than thick crumbs. You want a gentle tossing motion.)

9 Sprinkle the crumbs over the top of the batter starting at the perimeter and then moving to the center.

10 Bake for 1 hour to 1 hour 5 minutes, until a cake tester inserted into the center comes out clean.

11 To garnish: When you remove the cake from the oven, sprinkle the mini chocolate chips evenly over the top and then let the cake cool in the pan on top of a wire rack.

12 Lightly dust the top with powdered sugar, cut the cake into squares, and serve.

STORAGE: **Store airtight at room temperature for up to 5 days.**

banana cream icebox cake

Banana cream pie was a Grandma Rosemarie staple. It was one of the most requested desserts at any family gathering, and I remember her being embarrassed when people asked for the recipe, since it was barely homemade. I have inherited the recipe and a similar sentiment, as it could be taken as an insult to my culinary degree and baking abilities, but what's good is good! This is a layered, icebox version of Grandma's easy banana cream pie, and it's great for beginners and for those who want minimal effort but maximum accolades!

SERVES 9 TO 12

BANANA PUDDING

2 (3.4-ounce) boxes instant vanilla pudding mix (I prefer Jell-O)

3 cups milk, 2% or whole

½ cup heavy cream

½ teaspoon vanilla bean paste, ½ vanilla bean, or 1 teaspoon pure vanilla extract

2 cups ¼-inch slices banana (4 to 5 medium bananas)

WHIPPED CREAM TOPPING

1½ cups heavy cream

⅓ cup powdered sugar

½ teaspoon vanilla bean paste, ½ vanilla bean, or 1 teaspoon pure vanilla extract

ASSEMBLY

2 sleeves original graham crackers (about 15 sheets, unbroken)

1. Make the banana pudding: In a stand mixer fitted with the paddle (or in a bowl using a hand mixer), combine the pudding mixes, milk, heavy cream, and vanilla bean paste (if using a vanilla bean, split it lengthwise and scrape in the vanilla seeds). Beat on medium-low speed until the mixture thickens slightly and can coat the back of a spoon, 5 to 7 minutes.
2. Using a rubber spatula, fold in the sliced bananas. Set the pudding aside.
3. Make the whipped cream topping: In a bowl, with an electric mixer, combine the heavy cream, powdered sugar, and vanilla bean paste (if using a vanilla bean, split it lengthwise and scrape in the vanilla seeds). Beat until stiff peaks form.
4. To assemble: In an 8 × 8- or 9 × 9-inch square baking pan, place a single layer of graham crackers. It should be 4½ to 5 sheets of graham crackers to cover the bottom of the pan. (It's okay if there are little spaces between the crackers, this is not a fussy dessert.)
5. Next layer half of the banana pudding (about 3 cups) on top of the graham crackers and use an offset spatula to spread it out evenly. Top with another layer of the graham crackers (another 4½ to 5 sheets). Top the crackers with the remaining banana pudding and spread evenly. Top with the remaining graham crackers (4½ to 5 sheets) to cover the pudding.
6. Using a spoon and an offset spatula or a piping bag with your favorite tip, cover the top graham cracker layer completely with the whipped cream topping.
7. Refrigerate the icebox cake for at least 6 hours or overnight to set. You want the moisture of the pudding to soften the graham crackers to create a cake-like consistency.
8. Serve by scooping with a big spoon or spatula.

STORAGE: **Wrap the pan with plastic wrap and store in the fridge for up to 3 days.**

snowball icebox cake

Although we lived in the charming town of Huntington, Long Island, my mom, who was a teacher, drove us an hour each way to her school in Port Jefferson. To make the long commute more enjoyable, we often stopped at local bakeries or delis for breakfast. I still dream about the buttered kaiser rolls from the dingy deli across the street or the warm chocolate croissants and muffins from Strawberry Fields in Stony Brook. My favorite indulgence, though, was always the pink, squishy, coconut-covered Hostess Snoballs by the deli register. This no-bake cake channels all the nostalgic flavors of my guilty pleasure snack but in a celebratory dessert that's easy to prep ahead—and perfect for getting kids involved.

MAKES ONE 9-INCH ROUND CAKE

"CAKE"

- **2½ cups heavy cream**
- **4 ounces mascarpone cheese**
- **½ cup sugar**
- **½ teaspoon pure vanilla extract**
- **¼ teaspoon coconut extract**
- **Pinch of fine table salt**
- **75 to 80 Oreo Thins (you can also use regular Oreos, but you will need to separate them or they will be too thick)**

COCONUT TOPPING

- **10 ounces Homemade Marshmallow Fluff, store-bought or homemade (page 157)**
- **¼ teaspoon coconut extract**
- **About 2 drops pink or red food coloring**
- **1½ cups sweetened coconut flakes**

STORAGE: Store in an airtight cake container or wrap with plastic wrap and store in the fridge for up to 3 days.

1. Make the "cake": In a stand mixer fitted with the whisk (or in a bowl using a hand mixer), beat together the heavy cream, mascarpone, sugar, vanilla, coconut extract, and salt until stiff peaks form.
2. Carefully pull 10 Oreo thins in half and line the bottom of a 9-inch springform pan with the cookies in a single flat layer. For the sides that have the cream on them, place in the pan cream-side up. If some of the cookies break, don't fret, this cake is very forgiving. You want to make sure the cookies are close together and there is little to no space between them.
3. Spread one-quarter of the whipped cream carefully and evenly over the first cookie layer. Top the cream layer with another layer of the Oreo thins, but this time keep them whole. You will need 20 cookies to cover the layer of cream.
4. Layer another one-quarter of the cream over the cookies, followed by the next quarter of cookies, the final quarter of cream, then the final layer of cookies.
5. For the top layer, pull the cookies apart again and layer the top of the cake with the cookies, cookie side facing up. Set the cake aside.
6. Make the coconut topping: In a stand mixer fitted with the whisk (or in a bowl using a hand mixer), beat together the Marshmallow Fluff, coconut extract, and 1 drop of pink or red food coloring. Blend just until smooth and combined, about 30 seconds. Adjust the color to your liking.
7. Carefully pour the marshmallow mixture over the top of the top cookie layer of the cake. Use an offset spatula to spread it out evenly over the top.
8. In a small bowl, add 1 drop of the pink or red food coloring into the shredded coconut and use your hands to rub/mix the food coloring into the coconut to dye it pink. I like to use food-safe disposable gloves here to avoid dying my hands.
9. Sprinkle the pink coconut all over the top of the cake and then loosely cover the top with plastic wrap and refrigerate overnight. The cookies need time to soften from the moisture of the cream and ultimately give you a cake-like consistency.
10. Once the cake has chilled overnight and you are ready to serve, carefully remove the sides of the springform pan, slice, and serve!

cannoli icebox cake

As a 50-percent Sicilian and 100-percent New Yorker, I know a good cannoli. But like most, I don't have the desire to go through the laborious and fragile task of making homemade cannoli shells. Thus, the Cannoli Icebox Cake! Icebox cake is great for entertaining, because you have to make it in advance in order to get the proper texture. This version has all the flavors of a perfect cannoli without the fuss and the presentation is rustic but elegant when served in perfectly scooped squares so you can see the distinct layers.

MAKES ONE 8-INCH SQUARE CAKE

CANNOLI CREAM

8 ounces mascarpone cheese, at room temperature

2 cups whole-milk ricotta cheese, preferably Galbani (see Tip)

1¼ cups powdered sugar

½ teaspoon ground cinnamon

1 tablespoon pure vanilla extract

¼ teaspoon fine table salt

¾ cup mini semisweet chocolate chips

ASSEMBLY

20 to 25 graham crackers (whole sheets, not broken in half)

1½ cups semisweet chocolate chips

1 cup heavy cream

2 tablespoons light corn syrup

1 teaspoon pure vanilla extract

¼ cup chopped lightly salted roasted pistachios (optional)

1. Make the cannoli cream: In a stand mixer fitted with the whisk, beat together the mascarpone, ricotta, powdered sugar, cinnamon, vanilla, and salt until smooth and creamy, about 2 minutes. By hand, fold the mini chocolate chips in with a rubber spatula.
2. To assemble: Line an 8 × 8-inch square pan with a layer of graham crackers (about 5½ crackers). Evenly spread one-third of the cannoli cream over the top of the crackers.
3. Top the cream with another layer of the graham crackers (about 5½ crackers). Evenly spread another third of the cream over the top of the crackers and then another layer of graham crackers (about 5½ crackers). Add the remaining cream and spread evenly over the crackers. Add one final layer of graham crackers on top (about 5½ crackers). Set aside while you make the ganache.
4. Place the chocolate chips in a heatproof bowl. In a microwave-safe bowl, microwave the heavy cream in 30-second increments until piping hot (1 to 1½ minutes). Pour the hot cream over the chocolate chips and let sit for 3 to 4 minutes until melted, then whisk until smooth. Whisk in the corn syrup and vanilla.
5. Pour the ganache over the top of the icebox cake and spread evenly. Immediately sprinkle the ganache layer with the chopped pistachios, if desired.
6. Cover with plastic wrap (being sure to not let the plastic touch the ganache layer) and refrigerate for at least 6 hours or overnight. The graham crackers need time to soften.
7. Cut into squares and serve with a cake spatula or scoop with a large serving spoon and enjoy!

STORAGE: **Wrap the pan with plastic wrap and store in the fridge for up to 4 days.**

SCONE QUEEN TIP

If you use a different brand of ricotta, line a sieve with cheesecloth, spoon in the ricotta, and let it drain for at least 1 hour or overnight in the refrigerator to remove the excess liquid.

peach almond upside-down cake

Summer baking can be less than ideal, as the scorching temperatures don't exactly make standing in front of a hot oven or stove very enjoyable. With warmer weather also comes an abundance of invites to parties and gatherings. As someone who was taught to never show up empty-handed, this has become one of my go-to summer recipes. It isn't very difficult or time-consuming to make and the peaches and almond flour result in a light texture and beautiful flavor. You can swap the peaches for other stone fruits, such as plums or apricots or both—or even the retro classic, sliced pineapple and cherries. I love to use a blend of white and yellow peaches for a sweet yet floral flavor profile.

MAKES ONE 8-INCH ROUND CAKE

Softened butter, for the pan

2 to 3 peaches, cut into ½-inch-thick slices (enough to cover the bottom of the cake pan)

½ cup sugar

BATTER

8 tablespoons (4 ounces/1 stick) unsalted butter, plus more for greasing

¾ cup sugar

1 teaspoon vanilla bean paste or pure vanilla extract

3 large eggs, at room temperature

½ cup blanched almond flour

½ cup all-purpose flour

¾ teaspoon baking powder

¼ teaspoon fine table salt

¼ teaspoon ground cinnamon

Pinch of ground nutmeg

SERVING OPTIONS

Whipped cream or crème fraîche, sweetened with powdered sugar

Ice cream (I suggest vanilla, raspberry, green tea, or butter pecan!)

1. Preheat the oven to 375°F (or 350°F on the convection setting). Heavily grease an 8-inch springform pan with butter, line the bottom with a round of parchment paper, and then grease the paper with butter again. (Note: You can also bake this in an 8-inch cake pan without removable sides, just heavily butter the pan and line the bottom with parchment paper.)
2. Arrange the peach slices close together in one layer all over the bottom of the pan.
3. In a small saucepan, combine the sugar and ¼ cup water and stir over medium heat until the sugar dissolves and the mixture turns an amber color. Immediately pour the caramel all over the peaches in the pan using up all of it. Set the pan aside while you make the cake batter.
4. Make the batter: In a stand mixer fitted with the paddle (or in a bowl using a hand mixer), beat together the butter, sugar, and vanilla bean paste until light and fluffy, about 5 minutes.
5. Add the eggs one at a time, beating to just combine after each addition.
6. In a separate bowl, whisk together the almond flour, all-purpose flour, baking powder, salt, cinnamon, and nutmeg.
7. On low speed, add the flour mixture to the butter/sugar mixture and blend until just combined. Do not overmix.
8. Spread the batter evenly over the peaches and caramel in the pan and then transfer to the oven.
9. Bake for 30 to 35 minutes, until the cake is set and a toothpick just comes out clean.
10. Let the cake cool slightly in the pan for 10 minutes and then place a plate or cake stand on top of the cake and flip it upside down. Remove the sides of the springform pan and then carefully remove the bottom piece and parchment paper, revealing the peach layer, which will now become the top.
11. Serve warm or room temperature with or without fresh whipped cream or your favorite ice cream!

STORAGE: **Store leftovers in an airtight container or wrap the cake with plastic wrap and store in the fridge for up to 3 days.**

coconut crunch bundt cake

A take on a classic store-bought Louisiana Crunch Cake, this pound cake–style Bundt has the subtle essence of coconut and is the perfect afternoon snack with a warm cup of tea. Make this cake your own by swapping out the extracts or by adding toasted nuts to the glaze (see Tips for suggestions).

SERVES 12 TO 14

Softened butter and flour, for the Bundt pan

12 ounces (3 sticks) unsalted butter, at room temperature

2 cups granulated sugar

2 teaspoons pure vanilla extract

½ teaspoon coconut extract

4 large eggs, at room temperature

3 cups cake flour (not self-rising)

1 teaspoon fine table salt

2 teaspoons baking powder

1 cup buttermilk

COCONUT CRUNCH GLAZE

1½ cups powdered sugar

⅓ cup unsweetened large coconut flakes, lightly toasted (see Tips)

⅓ cup sweetened shredded coconut

1½ tablespoons unsalted butter, melted

¼ teaspoon pure vanilla extract

Pinch of fine table salt

About 2 tablespoons milk (just enough to thin out the glaze)

1. Preheat the oven to 350°F (or 325°F on the convection setting). Generously grease and lightly flour a 15-cup Bundt pan and set aside.
2. In a stand mixer fitted with the paddle (or in a bowl using a hand mixer), beat together the butter and granulated sugar until light and fluffy, about 5 minutes.
3. Add the vanilla and coconut extract and beat until combined. Add the eggs one at a time, beating to just combine after each addition, scraping the sides of the bowl each time.
4. In a separate bowl, stir together the cake flour, salt, and baking powder.
5. Add the flour mixture to the butter/sugar mixture in three additions, alternating with the buttermilk. Do not overmix, just blend until there are no more flour streaks. Let the batter sit at room temperature for 20 to 30 minutes to allow the ingredients to really meld together.
6. Spread the batter evenly in the prepared Bundt pan and transfer to the oven.
7. Bake for 50 to 60 minutes, until a toothpick inserted in the center comes out clean.
8. Meanwhile, make the coconut crunch glaze: In a bowl, whisk together the powdered sugar, toasted coconut flakes, sweetened shredded coconut, melted butter, vanilla, and salt. Add the milk 1 tablespoon at a time until it is a thick but pourable texture.
9. When the cake is done, let it cool in the pan for 10 to 15 minutes, then carefully flip it out onto a wire rack. Pour the glaze on top of the cake when it is still slightly warm but not piping hot. Use a spoon or offset spatula to spread it evenly all over the cake.
10. Allow the glaze to set for about 45 minutes and then slice and enjoy!

STORAGE: **Store in an airtight cake container or wrapped in parchment paper and then aluminum foil at room temperature for up to 3 days.**

SCONE QUEEN TIPS

- Toast the coconut in a skillet over medium heat, tossing constantly.
- Try almond extract in the cake with an orange glaze and sliced almonds, or vanilla bean paste and a pecan crunch glaze.

double-chocolate sheet cake

Most of the memories I have of public school lunch are pretty negative. The only things I could muster up the courage to eat were the soggy, salty French fries, the underbaked cookies, and the chocolate sheet cake with sprinkles. I remember being in second grade, digging through my backpack for change so I could buy a hunk of the moist chocolate cake that had been wrapped so tightly in plastic wrap you had to lick off the frosting. There's just something so comforting, reliable, and straightforward about a one-layer sheet cake format. This cake is good enough to use for a celebration, but it's also one of those cakes you want to eat on a weeknight, cuddled up on the couch with just a fork eating your way from the center outward. (I know, what kind of crazy person starts in the center . . . cough . . . me!) My mother calls this cake "the best chocolate cake" she's ever had!

MAKES ONE 8-INCH SQUARE CAKE

Softened butter and flour, for the pan

1 cup all-purpose flour

1 cup granulated sugar

⅓ cup dark Dutch-process cocoa powder, preferably Hershey's Special Dark, sifted to remove lumps

½ teaspoon baking powder

½ teaspoon baking soda

¾ teaspoon fine table salt

¾ teaspoon instant espresso powder

1 large egg, at room temperature

2 teaspoons pure vanilla extract

¼ cup buttermilk

¼ cup vegetable or canola oil

½ cup boiling hot water

½ cup sour cream

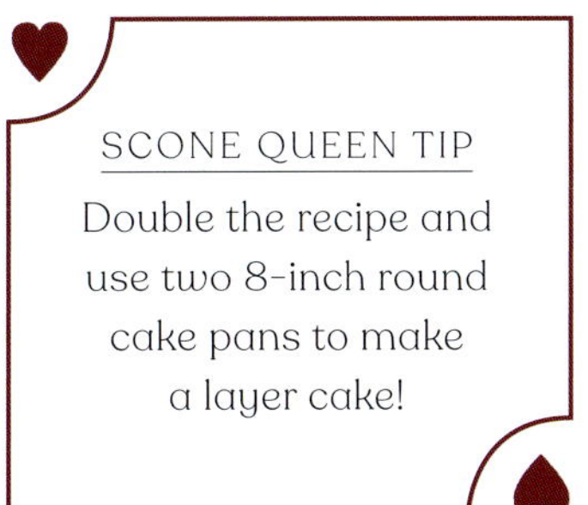

1 Preheat the oven to 375°F (or 350°F on the convection setting). Grease and lightly flour an 8 × 8-inch pan and set aside.

2 In a stand mixer fitted with the whisk (or in a large bowl by hand with a whisk), whisk together the flour, granulated sugar, cocoa powder, baking powder, baking soda, salt, and espresso powder.

3 In a separate bowl, whisk together the egg, vanilla, buttermilk, and vegetable oil. Whisk the wet ingredients into the flour mixture until combined.

4 Whisk in the hot water until blended. Finally, whisk in the sour cream until incorporated. Do not overmix. Pour the batter into the prepared pan.

5 Bake for 25 to 30 minutes, until a toothpick inserted in the center comes out clean.

6 Let the cake cool completely in the pan on a wire rack before frosting.

♥ *recipe continues*

CHOCOLATE FROSTING

8 ounces bittersweet chocolate chips (I prefer Ghirardelli)

1 cup heavy cream

4 tablespoons (2 ounces/ ½ stick) unsalted butter, cut in ½-inch cubes, at room temperature

2 cups powdered sugar

¼ cup dark Dutch-process cocoa powder, preferably Hershey's Special Dark, sifted to remove lumps

⅛ teaspoon fine table salt

1½ teaspoons pure vanilla extract

Garnish: Sprinkles (optional)

7 Make the chocolate frosting: Place the chocolate chips in the bowl of a stand mixer (or other heatproof bowl). In a small saucepan, heat the heavy cream until it comes to a simmer. Pour the hot cream over the chocolate chips and let it sit for 2 to 3 minutes, until they melt.

8 In a stand mixer fitted with the whisk (or in a bowl using a hand mixer), beat the chocolate on low speed until it is smooth and combined with the heavy cream. On medium speed, gradually beat in the cubes of butter, piece by piece until it's all blended in.

9 On low speed, add the powdered sugar, cocoa powder, salt, and vanilla and blend until smooth. The frosting should be a fudgy and spreadable texture. If it appears to be too loose, let it sit for 30 to 40 minutes to thicken.

10 Once the cake is fully cooled, spread the frosting evenly on top of the cake and top with sprinkles (if desired).

STORAGE: **Store in an airtight cake container at room temperature for up to 3 days; or if you prefer a more firm ganache frosting, refrigerate before serving up to 5 days.**

banana nutella snacking cake

One of my recurring late-night cravings is sheet cake of any kind, topped with creamy chocolate frosting and classic nonpareil sprinkles. One summer evening my anxiety was high and so were the cravings, so I willingly surrendered. Neglected, brown, speckled bananas typically decorate my countertop, so in an effort to reduce waste I decided on a moist, fluffy banana rendition. One of the greatest flavor combos of all time is chocolate hazelnut spread and banana in any form, so I turned to the six-pound tub of Nutella I store proudly in the cupboard and got baking. This cake is the texture of your dreams, so fluffy and moist it probably couldn't hold up as a layer cake, but it doesn't matter in this case. The fuss-free style of a single-layer snacking cake makes this the ultimate stress-free dessert that hits every single time.

MAKES ONE 8-INCH SQUARE CAKE

Cooking spray

4 tablespoons (2 ounces/ ½ stick) unsalted butter, at room temperature

2 tablespoons canola oil or vegetable oil

½ cup granulated sugar

¼ cup packed dark brown sugar

1 teaspoon pure vanilla extract

1 large egg, at room temperature

¾ cup very ripe mashed bananas (about 2 medium bananas)

1 cup cake flour (not self-rising)

½ teaspoon baking soda

½ teaspoon baking powder

¼ teaspoon fine table salt

¼ teaspoon ground cinnamon

½ cup sour cream

1. Preheat the oven to 350°F (or 325°F on the convection setting). Spray an 8 × 8-inch square baking pan with cooking spray.
2. In a stand mixer fitted with the paddle, beat the butter, canola oil, granulated sugar, brown sugar, and vanilla until light and fluffy, about 5 minutes.
3. Add the egg and then the mashed banana and beat until incorporated.
4. In a separate bowl, stir together the cake flour, baking soda, baking powder, salt, and cinnamon.
5. Add the flour mixture to the butter/sugar mixture in two additions, alternating with the sour cream. Spread the batter evenly into the prepared pan.
6. Bake for 22 to 25 minutes, until a toothpick inserted in the center comes out clean.
7. Let the cake cool completely in the pan on a wire rack.
8. Meanwhile, make the Nutella frosting: In a stand mixer fitted with the paddle, beat the butter until fluffy, 2 to 3 minutes. Add the Nutella and beat lightly just until incorporated.
9. On low speed, beat in the cocoa powder and then the powdered sugar 1 cup at a time.
10. Add the vanilla, salt, and milk and beat until creamy and combined. If it is too thick for your liking, add a splash more milk at a time until you reach your desired consistency. You want it creamy and spreadable.
11. Frost the top of the cooled cake while it's still in the pan. If desired, top with nonpareil sprinkles.

STORAGE: **Store in a sealed cake saver or cover the top of the pan tightly with plastic wrap being careful not to touch the frosting for up to 5 days.**

NUTELLA FROSTING

8 tablespoons (4 ounces/1 stick) unsalted butter, at room temperature

⅓ cup Nutella

⅓ cup dark Dutch-process cocoa powder, preferably Hershey's Special Dark, sifted to remove lumps

2 cups powdered sugar

2 teaspoons pure vanilla extract

Dash of fine table salt

2 tablespoons milk or half-and-half, or more as needed

Garnish: Nonpareil sprinkles (optional)

SCONE QUEEN TIP

If you prefer the frosting firmer, refrigerate the cake before enjoying.

craig's cake (chocolate snacking cake with peanut butter ganache)

This Chocolate Peanut Butter Cake quickly became a family favorite, especially for my Uncle Craig's birthday. Moist, rich, and finished with a thick, chewy ganache, it's as easy as it is crowd-pleasing. The sheet pan format is perfect for gatherings filled with the kind of laughter Craig always inspires—especially when he cuts his birthday slice with a self-whittled knife while wearing a cowboy hat.

MAKES ONE 15 × 10-INCH SHEET CAKE

CAKE

Softened butter and flour, for the pan

8 ounces (2 sticks) unsalted butter

½ cup dark Dutch-process cocoa powder, preferably Hershey's Special Dark, sifted to remove lumps

1 teaspoon instant espresso powder (optional)

1½ cups granulated sugar

½ cup packed dark brown sugar

1¾ cups all-purpose flour

1 teaspoon baking soda

½ teaspoon fine table salt

3 large eggs, at room temperature

2 teaspoons pure vanilla extract

¾ cup sour cream

PEANUT BUTTER GANACHE

10 tablespoons plus 2 teaspoons unsalted butter

⅔ cup whole milk

2 (10-ounce) packages peanut butter chips (I like Reese's)

2 teaspoons pure vanilla extract

⅛ teaspoon fine table salt

2 cups powdered sugar

GARNISH

½ cup semisweet chocolate chips

1 teaspoon vegetable shortening, such as Crisco

1 Preheat the oven to 375°F (or 350°F on the convection setting). Butter and lightly flour a 15 × 10-inch jelly-roll pan.

2 Make the cake: In a medium saucepan, combine 1 cup water, the butter, cocoa powder, and espresso powder (if desired). Heat over medium heat, stirring occasionally, until the butter melts and the mixture begins to boil. Remove from the heat to cool slightly.

3 In a stand mixer fitted with the whisk, stir together the granulated sugar, brown sugar, flour, baking soda, and salt.

4 Add the eggs, vanilla, and sour cream and mix until blended. Add the cocoa mixture on low speed and mix just until blended. Pour the batter into the prepared pan and transfer to the oven.

5 Bake for 20 to 25 minutes, until a toothpick inserted in the center comes out clean.

6 Let the cake cool in the pan on a wire rack.

7 Meanwhile, make the peanut butter ganache: In a small saucepan, combine the butter, milk, and peanut butter chips and cook over low heat, stirring gently yet constantly, until melted and smooth. Remove from the heat and stir in the vanilla and salt.

8 In a stand mixer fitted with the whisk (or in a bowl using a hand mixer), on low speed, beat together the powdered sugar and peanut butter mixture until blended and smooth.

9 Spread the ganache evenly over the cake with an offset spatula. Let the ganache set while you make the garnish.

10 To garnish: In a small microwave-safe bowl, combine the chocolate chips and shortening. Microwave for 30 seconds, stir and then again microwave for another 20 to 30 seconds or until melted and smooth.

11 Pour the chocolate into a pastry bag with a small round tip or use a spoon, to drizzle the top of the cake in any pattern you like! A checker pattern, swirls, zig-zags whatever you prefer! Allow the chocolate to set before eating.

STORAGE: **Cover the pan with plastic wrap and store at room temperature for up to 5 days.**

fudge iced golden cake

Like its counterpart the Chocolate Chip Crumb Loaf (page 232), this frill-free snacking cake is inspired by a grocery store packaged cake that typically lived on my grandma's countertop. This classic, American-style yellow cake has a moist, buttery texture and the ganache topping is only two simple ingredients but has the perfect fudgy chew. This is one of those desserts that you keep the knife in so you can keep coming back to it, all day, cutting off little squares, bit by bit.

MAKES ONE 9-INCH SQUARE CAKE

CAKE

- Cooking spray
- 2 cups cake flour (not self-rising)
- 1 tablespoon baking powder
- 1 teaspoon fine table salt
- 8 ounces (2 sticks) unsalted butter, at room temperature
- 2 cups sugar
- 1 tablespoon pure vanilla extract
- 4 large eggs, separated
- ½ cup sour cream
- ⅔ cup whole buttermilk

GANACHE

- ⅔ cup semisweet chocolate chips
- ½ cup heavy cream

1. Preheat the oven to 350°F (or 325°F on the convection setting). Spray an 9 × 9-inch pan with cooking spray.
2. Make the cake: In a medium bowl, stir together the cake flour, baking powder, and salt. Set aside.
3. In a stand mixer fitted with the paddle (or in a bowl using a hand mixer), beat the butter, sugar, and vanilla on medium speed until light and fluffy, 3 to 5 minutes.
4. Beat in the egg yolks and sour cream until fully incorporated.
5. On low speed, add the flour mixture in two additions, alternating with the buttermilk, and beat until just combined. Do not overmix.
6. In a separate bowl, beat together the egg whites in a bowl using a hand mixer or by hand with a little elbow grease, until stiff peaks form.
7. Fold the stiff egg whites into the batter gently. It is best to start with one-third of the egg whites first to loosen the batter up and then add the remaining two-thirds, placing the stiff egg whites on top of the batter and then using a rubber spatula to turn the egg whites into the batter until no large chunks of egg white remain, but you still may see some streaks.
8. Spread the batter into the prepared pan and transfer to the oven.
9. Bake for 20 to 25 minutes, until a toothpick inserted in the center comes out clean.
10. Let the cake cool in the pan on a wire rack.
11. Meanwhile, make the ganache: Put the chocolate chips in a heatproof bowl. In a microwave-safe bowl, microwave the heavy cream for about 1 minute, or until piping hot. Pour the hot cream over the chocolate chips and let it sit for 2 to 3 minutes, or until melted.
12. Whisk the chocolate together until smooth and then spread the ganache evenly over the top of the cooled cake.
13. Pop the cake in the fridge for about 15 minutes, or until it is just set, do not leave it in the fridge too long or the ganache will harden too much (unless you prefer that!). Serve and enjoy!

STORAGE: **Cover the pan with plastic wrap and store at room temperature for up to 3 days.**

great-grandma lena's applesauce cake

Great-Grandma Lena was my Grandpa Carmine's mother. She looked like the quintessential Italian nonna. She was tiny and hunched and always sporting a muumuu, knit sweater, and slip-on shoes. She cared so much about me and my sisters and I can still picture her frail, wrinkled hands crawling up my arms to tickle me. As sweet as she was with us, she was not afraid to tell my dad and grandfather what was bothering her, which was a lot, might I add. Let's just say she was as spicy as this cake! I can still hear her voice in my head, a unique American Southern accent mixed with Sicilian, as her family had immigrated to Louisiana in the early 1900s.

Like most Italian immigrant females, she spent the majority of her days in the kitchen hovered over a tiny stove. Grandma Lena always hosted holidays like Saint Joseph's Day, where she would create an altar adorned with homemade breads, cookies, and confections that her parish priest would come and bless before we indulged. When my Grandma Rosemarie married into the family, she began helping with all the holiday preparations and cooking, and in all honesty she was a bit more skilled, so the baked goods got better and better. I'll never forget Lena's "sawdust" cookies (as we called them), so dry but nostalgically delicious.

This applesauce cake was one of Lena's recipes that Grandma Rosemarie zhuzhed up and then made every fall season. Great for breakfast, dessert, or an afternoon snack and totally customizable! Perhaps you want to top it with whipped cream or a brown butter frosting? Find your inner Rosemarie and get creative!

MAKES ONE 10-CUP BUNDT CAKE

- Softened butter and flour, for the Bundt pan
- 8 ounces (2 sticks) unsalted butter, at room temperature
- 1 cup granulated sugar
- 1 cup packed dark brown sugar
- 2 teaspoons pure vanilla extract
- 2 large eggs, at room temperature
- 2 cups applesauce
- 3 cups cake flour (not self-rising)
- 1 teaspoon fine table salt
- 2 teaspoons baking soda
- 1 tablespoon ground cinnamon
- 1¼ teaspoons ground nutmeg
- 1 teaspoon ground allspice
- Garnish: Powdered sugar, for dusting

1. Preheat the oven to 375°F (or 350°F on the convection setting). Grease and flour a 10-cup Bundt pan.
2. In a stand mixer fitted with the paddle, beat together the butter, granulated sugar, brown sugar, and vanilla until light and fluffy, about 3 minutes.
3. Add the eggs to the butter/sugar mixture one at a time, beating to just combine after each addition. Beat in the applesauce.
4. In a separate bowl, sift together the cake flour, salt, baking soda, cinnamon, nutmeg, and allspice.
5. On low speed, gradually add the flour mixture to the butter/sugar mixture in two additions, scraping the bowl down after each addition. Mix until just combined. Do not overmix. Note, the batter will appear "broken" or "curdled," but don't fear, this is due to the applesauce and it will still result in a beautiful cake.
6. Bake for about 45 minutes, or until a toothpick inserted in the center comes out clean.
7. Let the cake cool in the pan for 10 minutes before turning it out onto a wire rack. Before serving, dust the cake with powdered sugar, then slice and serve!

STORAGE: **Store in an airtight cake container or wrapped in parchment paper and then aluminum foil at room temperature for up to 3 days.**

cookie butter swirled pumpkin bread

Pumpkin and Biscoff are a match made in fall heaven. The warm spice notes in the cookie butter spread complement the pumpkin so perfectly you may never want plain pumpkin bread again. I launched this bread as a one-time "drop" on The Hungry Gnome website and we sold one hundred loaves in minutes, so we decided to add it to our permanent fall menu. You'll see why! Enjoy it when it's still slightly warm for the social media post-worthy "goo" factor.

MAKES ONE 9 × 5-INCH LOAF

Cooking spray, for the loaf pan

8 tablespoons (4 ounces/1 stick) unsalted butter, at room temperature

¼ cup canola or vegetable oil

1 cup granulated sugar

½ cup packed dark brown sugar

1½ teaspoons pure vanilla extract

2 large eggs, at room temperature

1½ cups canned pumpkin puree (I like Libby's)

2 cups all-purpose flour

¾ teaspoon baking soda

½ teaspoon baking powder

¾ teaspoon fine table salt

2 teaspoons ground cinnamon

¼ teaspoon ground nutmeg

¼ teaspoon ground ginger

⅛ teaspoon ground cloves

½ cup sour cream

1 cup Biscoff cookie butter spread or Speculoos spread

Optional: any of your favorite mix-ins, such as chocolate chips or nuts

GARNISH

2 tablespoons Biscoff cookie butter spread, for drizzling

3 Biscoff cookies, crumbled up into fine crumbs

1. Preheat the oven to 350°F (or 325°F on the convection setting). Spray a 9 × 5-inch loaf pan with cooking spray and line it with a strip of parchment paper, letting the paper hang over the pan at least 1 inch on the long sides, then lightly spray the top of the paper.
2. In a stand mixer fitted with the paddle (or in a bowl using a hand mixer), beat the butter, canola oil, granulated sugar, brown sugar, and vanilla until light and fluffy, about 3 minutes.
3. Add the eggs one at a time, beating to just combine after each addition.
4. Add the pumpkin puree and beat well until incorporated, about 2 minutes. Scrape down the sides of the bowl and mix again for a few seconds to ensure it is properly mixed.
5. In a separate bowl, stir together the flour, baking soda, baking powder, salt, cinnamon, nutmeg, ginger, and cloves.
6. On low speed, add the flour mixture to the pumpkin mixture in two additions, alternating with the sour cream. Scrape down the bowl after each addition and then add your favorite optional mix-ins (if using). Mix just until everything is incorporated. Do not overmix.
7. Spread one-third of the batter into the prepared pan, then dollop half of the cookie butter spread on top. Use a wooden skewer or knife to gently swirl it into the batter just slightly. Repeat with another one-third of the batter and the remaining cookie butter spread. Top with the remaining batter and transfer to the oven.
8. Bake for about 1 hour 15 minutes, or until a toothpick inserted in the center comes out clean.
9. Meanwhile, prepare the garnish: In a small microwave-safe bowl, melt the cookie butter spread for 20 to 30 seconds, until it's loose enough to drizzle.
10. Let the cake cool in the pan for 15 minutes and then carefully lift the parchment paper to remove the cake from the pan and place it onto a wire rack. Let it cool slightly, then garnish the top of the loaf with a heavy drizzle of the melted cookie butter spread and the crushed Biscoff cookies. Let the cookie butter set (about 15 minutes) and then slice and enjoy.

STORAGE: **To store, wrap it in parchment paper and then aluminum foil tightly and leave it on the counter at room temperature or in a sealed container for up to 5 days. This bread also freezes well.**

dad's date nut bread

When I was growing up, my parents often had boxes of muesli cereal in the pantry. I was surprised to find sweet, chewy, caramel-like chunks hiding among the nuts and grains. They were dates—nature's candy! This cake takes everything that is delicious about dates and combines them into a cake inspired by a date-nut bread my dad loved, crossed with a spice cake and an English sticky toffee pudding. We like it with a little cream cheese and a cup of coffee, but you can eat it all day long or griddle it in a pan with butter and top with vanilla ice cream for a decadent dessert!

MAKES ONE 9 × 5-INCH LOAF

- Cooking spray
- 1½ cups chopped pitted dates, preferably Medjool
- 8 tablespoons (4 ounces/1 stick) unsalted butter, at room temperature
- ¾ cup granulated sugar
- ¾ cup packed dark brown sugar
- ¼ cup canola or vegetable oil
- 1½ teaspoons pure vanilla extract
- 2 large eggs
- ½ cup applesauce (I used plain Mott's)
- 2 cups all-purpose flour
- 1¼ teaspoons fine table salt
- 1 teaspoon baking soda
- ½ teaspoon baking powder
- 1 teaspoon ground cinnamon, plus more for dusting
- ⅛ teaspoon ground nutmeg
- ¼ teaspoon ground cloves
- 1 cup chopped walnuts
- 1 to 2 tablespoons raw or turbinado sugar, for sprinkling

STORAGE: **Store in an airtight container or covered with parchment paper and then plastic wrap at room temperature for up to 4 days.**

1. Preheat the oven to 375°F (or 350°F on the convection setting). Spray a 9 × 5-inch loaf pan with cooking spray and if you'd like, line it with a strip of parchment paper to make for an easy bread removal later.
2. In a small saucepan, combine ¾ cup of the chopped dates and ¾ cup water. Cover and bring to a simmer over medium heat. Let it cook and simmer for 10 to 12 minutes, until the dates are nice and soft. Transfer the dates and their liquid to a food processor and blend until smooth. If it's too thick add a splash of water and blend again until it is a thick, smooth puree. Set aside.
3. In a stand mixer fitted with the paddle (or in a bowl using a hand mixer), beat the butter, granulated sugar, brown sugar, and canola oil until light and fluffy, 3 to 5 minutes.
4. Beat in the vanilla. Add the eggs one at a time, beating to just combine after each addition. Scrape down the sides of the bowl to make sure everything is incorporated. Beat in the applesauce until combined, then beat in the date puree.
5. In a separate bowl, stir together the flour, salt, baking soda, baking powder, cinnamon, nutmeg, and cloves.
6. On low speed, gradually add the flour mixture to the butter/sugar mixture until just combined. Don't overbeat it or it can make for a gummy cake.
7. Use a rubber spatula to fold in the chopped walnuts and the remaining ¾ cup of chopped dates.
8. Pour the batter into the prepared pan and dust the top with a little cinnamon and sprinkle with the raw sugar. Transfer to the oven.
9. Bake for 30 minutes. Rotate the pan front to back and reduce the oven temperature to 350°F (or 325°F on the convection setting). Continue to bake for 20 to 35 minutes, until a toothpick inserted in the center comes out clean. If the top of the cake gets too dark during the baking process, feel free to loosely cover the top with foil.
10. Let the loaf cool in the pan on a wire rack for 15 to 20 minutes. Carefully remove the bread from the pan and let cool completely on the rack.

zucchini bread

When my husband and I left the Big City and moved to the suburbs of Long Island, we were so excited to finally tend our own vegetable garden. I believe witnessing a plant grow from seed, and then picking a ripe, juicy tomato to enjoy on a slice of griddled sourdough with olive oil and flaky sea salt, is one of life's greatest pleasures. Dan and I treat our garden like it's our baby. Each evening after work we go out back hand in hand and check on its progress. By July the garden is typically spitting out more zucchini than we care to cook, so zucchini bread is always the answer! It's a sweet yet earthy treat with subtle warmth from the spices and I love nothing more than a thick slice slathered with whipped cream cheese.

When I was creating this recipe I knew I wanted this loaf to be a few things: moist, plush on the inside, crisp on the outside, sweet but not too sweet, and a little bit spiced but not too much to overpower the zucchini. My recipe has butter, oil, and applesauce in it, which makes it super moist and fluffy and very flavorful. An important step is to allow this bread to cool completely in the pan, uncovered, even overnight or at least for 8 to 10 hours. This lets all the flavors really meld together and the texture become just right. I'm pretty confident this will be the best zucchini bread you've ever had.

MAKES ONE 9 × 5-INCH LOAF

Cooking spray

8 tablespoons (4 ounces/1 stick) unsalted butter, at room temperature

¼ cup canola or vegetable oil

1 cup granulated sugar

½ cup packed dark brown sugar

½ cup plain applesauce

1 teaspoon pure vanilla extract

2 large eggs, at room temperature

2¼ cups grated unpeeled zucchini (see Tip)

2 cups all-purpose flour

1½ teaspoons fine table salt

¾ teaspoon baking soda

¾ teaspoon baking powder

1¾ teaspoons ground cinnamon, plus more for dusting

⅛ teaspoon ground nutmeg

Small dash of ground cloves

1½ cups chopped walnuts

2 to 3 tablespoons raw or turbinado sugar, for sprinkling

1. Preheat the oven to 375°F (or 350°F on the convection setting). Spray a 9 × 5-inch loaf pan with cooking spray.
2. In a stand mixer fitted with the paddle (or in a bowl using a hand mixer), beat together the butter, canola oil, granulated sugar, and brown sugar until light and fluffy, about 3 minutes.
3. Add the applesauce and vanilla and beat until combined. Beat in the eggs, one at a time, beating to just combine after each addition.
4. On low speed, add the grated zucchini and mix until just combined.
5. In a separate bowl, stir together the flour, salt, baking soda, baking powder, cinnamon, nutmeg, and cloves.
6. On low speed, gradually add the flour mixture to the wet ingredients and just mix until combined. Do not overmix or the bread can get tough and chewy. Mix in the chopped walnuts or fold them in with a spoon.
7. Spread the batter evenly into the prepared pan. Generously sprinkle the top with the raw sugar and an extra dusting of cinnamon. Transfer to the oven.
8. Bake for 50 to 55 minutes, until a toothpick inserted in the center comes out clean.
9. Let cool completely in the pan. Leave in the pan, unwrapped, overnight or for 24 hours, until removing it carefully from the pan and serving in slices.

STORAGE: **Zucchini bread keeps for 4 to 5 days at room temperature. I wrap only the cut end of the cake in foil and return it to the baking pan, leaving the top exposed so that it stays crunchy.**

SCONE QUEEN TIP
Grate the zucchini on the large holes of a box grater and pack it into the measuring cup. But do not wring it out—it contributes to a moist cake.

chocolate chip crumb loaf

When I was growing up on Long Island we always had Entenmann's cakes, cookies, and donuts and still to this day I can't walk by them in the grocery store without contemplating buying every single one. It's the epitome of nostalgia! In fact, one of my favorite comedians Sebastian Maniscalco even does a bit about these cakes. It's that cake every mom or grandma purchased and stored on top of the microwave or hid in the corner of the kitchen "in case company comes over." My family's favorite flavor was always the Chocolate Chip Crumb Loaf, so I had to re-create it. It's moist and fluffy, you get the perfect amount of chocolate chips in every bite, and the crumb topping has a hint of dark cocoa powder and the perfect amount of buttery crunch.

MAKES ONE 8 × 4-INCH LOAF

CRUMB TOPPING

- ¾ cup plus 2 tablespoons cake flour (not self-rising)
- 3 tablespoons granulated sugar
- 3 tablespoons dark brown sugar
- 1 tablespoon dark Dutch-process cocoa powder, preferably Hershey's Special Dark, sifted to remove lumps
- Dash of ground cinnamon
- Pinch of fine table salt
- 2 to 4 tablespoons unsalted butter, melted

CAKE

- Cooking spray
- 4 tablespoons (2 ounces/ ½ stick) unsalted butter, at room temperature
- 2 tablespoons plus 2 teaspoons canola or vegetable oil
- ⅔ cup granulated sugar
- 1 cup cake flour (not self-rising), plus 1 tablespoon for the chocolate chips
- ¼ teaspoon baking soda
- ¼ teaspoon baking powder
- Scant teaspoon fine table salt
- 1 large egg, at room temperature
- 1 teaspoon pure vanilla extract
- ½ cup sour cream
- ¾ cup semisweet chocolate chips (or use mini chips)

1. Make the crumb topping: In a medium bowl, whisk together the cake flour, granulated sugar, brown sugar, cocoa powder, cinnamon, and salt. Add 2 tablespoons melted butter to combine using a fork. If the crumbs appear too dry and floury, add another tablespoon or two of melted butter until you have small, moist crumbs. Set aside while you make the batter.
2. Make the cake: Preheat the oven to 350°F (or 325°F on the convection setting). Spray an 8 × 4-inch loaf pan with cooking spray and line with parchment paper; allow excess to overhang the two long sides of the pan. (You can also just butter and flour the loaf pan, however sometimes you lose some crumbs this way when you remove the cake from the pan.)
3. In a stand mixer fitted with the paddle (or in a bowl using a hand mixer), beat the butter, canola oil, and granulated sugar on medium-low speed until light and creamy, 3 to 4 minutes.
4. In a separate bowl, stir together the cake flour, baking soda, baking powder, and salt to combine. Set aside.
5. On low speed, add the egg, beating until light and fluffier. Add the vanilla.
6. Add the flour mixture in three additions, alternating with the sour cream, mixing on low speed until just combined. Scrape down the bowl in between the additions to ensure everything mixes properly. Do not overbeat, just mix until fully incorporated.
7. In a small bowl, toss the chocolate chips with the flour just to coat, as this prevents them from sinking to the bottom of the cake. By hand, fold the chocolate chips into the batter.
8. Pour the batter into the prepared loaf pan and spread into an even layer. You only want the batter to go three-quarters the way up the sides of the pan as it needs room to rise properly.
9. Break apart the crumb topping into large pea-size pieces and spread in an even layer over the batter, beginning with the perimeter and then working toward the center. Gently press the crumbs into the batter to adhere them without sinking them.
10. Bake for 45 to 50 minutes, until a wooden skewer inserted into center of cake comes out clean.

GARNISH

2 to 3 tablespoons mini semisweet chocolate chips

Powdered sugar, for dusting

11 To garnish: As soon as you take the cake out of the oven, sprinkle with the mini chocolate chips.

12 Let cool in the pan on a wire rack at least 30 minutes. Remove the cake from the pan by lifting the parchment overhang. Dust with powdered sugar before serving.

STORAGE: **Store in an airtight container or wrapped in parchment paper and then plastic wrap at room temperature for up to 4 days.**

madeleine loaf

In the summer of 2023, I went on my dream vacation to Paris and the South of France, something I fantasized about for many years. My first madeleine of the trip was at a Michelin-starred restaurant in Paris and it was especially memorable because it had a cornbread quality that was unique and pleasant. Many pastries in France also had a subtly floral essence, sometimes orange blossom and other times elderflower. As soon as I got home from the trip I began to test this cake. I wanted it to be in loaf form because most people do not own a madeleine pan, and there would be a higher ratio of plush cake center. I use an elderflower syrup that is less potent than the liqueur, which results in a more subtle flavor: however, if you want to amplify the floral notes, add in a touch of elderflower extract or liqueur, too!

MAKES ONE 9 × 5-INCH LOAF

CAKE

- Cooking spray
- 8 ounces (2 sticks) unsalted butter, at room temperature
- ¼ cup vegetable oil or canola oil
- 1 cup granulated sugar
- ½ cup packed light brown sugar
- ⅓ cup elderflower syrup
- 1½ teaspoons pure vanilla extract
- ½ teaspoon finely grated orange zest
- 3 large eggs, at room temperature
- 1 large egg yolk
- 1¼ cups cake flour (not self-rising)
- 1 cup fine cornmeal
- ¼ teaspoon baking soda
- 1 teaspoon baking powder
- ¾ teaspoon fine table salt
- ½ cup sour cream
- ⅓ cup freshly squeezed orange juice

GLAZE

- 2 to 3 tablespoons elderflower syrup

1. Preheat the oven to 350°F (or 325°F on the convection setting). Spray a 9 × 5-inch loaf pan with cooking spray. Line the pan with a strip of parchment paper that overhangs the long sides and then lightly spray again. Place the pan on top of a sheet pan in case of any spillage while baking.
2. In a stand mixer fitted with the paddle, beat together the butter, vegetable oil, granulated sugar, brown sugar, elderflower syrup, vanilla, and orange zest until light and fluffy, about 3 minutes.
3. Add the whole eggs and egg yolk one at a time, beating to just combine after each addition.
4. In a separate bowl, whisk together the cake flour, cornmeal, baking soda, baking powder, and salt.
5. On low speed, add the flour mixture to the butter/sugar mixture in two additions, alternating with the sour cream until just combined, scraping down the sides of the bowl in after each addition.
6. Add the orange juice and mix on low speed until incorporated. Spread the batter into the pan and transfer to the oven.
7. Bake for 45 to 50 minutes, until a toothpick inserted in the center comes out clean.
8. Let cool in the pan on a wire rack for about 15 minutes before carefully lifting the parchment paper to release it from the pan. Gently place the loaf onto the rack. While it is still warm, heavily baste the top and sides with the elderflower syrup and then let it cool completely. If you have any extra syrup, drizzle a little in your tea!
9. Slice and enjoy on its own or served with a dollop of Easy Clotted Cream (page 36).

STORAGE: **Cover the pan with plastic wrap and store at room temperature for up to 5 days.**

spumoni loaf

If you're not from the New York tristate area, you may be saying, what the heck is spumoni?! Spumoni is an Italian-inspired ice cream swirled with three flavors: chocolate, pistachio, and almond (or sometimes cherry). I was first introduced to the stuff at the Brooklyn institution L&B Spumoni Gardens, a casual Italian eatery known for their pizza and, you guessed it, spumoni. While perusing the bakery aisle of my local supermarket, the classic marble pound cake caught my eye, and I began to ponder what other famous flavor combos may fare well in a delicious loaf cake. Aha! The spumoni loaf was born! I mean how cute is this thing, if I do say so myself?! The crowd goes wild when you cut the first slice and reveal the beautiful brown, cream, and green swirls of cake. I put the pistachio and almond cake batters in the pan in two stripes side by side and then top them with the chocolate batter to get the perfect marbling. The cake is not overly decadent, which makes this a great breakfast or afternoon snack accompanied by a cup of hot tea or coffee.

MAKES ONE 8 × 4-INCH LOAF

Softened butter and flour, for the loaf pan

1½ cups all-purpose flour

1 teaspoon baking powder

½ teaspoon fine table salt

12 tablespoons (6 ounces/ 1½ sticks) unsalted butter, at room temperature

⅓ cup canola or vegetable oil

1¼ cups granulated sugar

2 teaspoons pure vanilla extract

4 large eggs, at room temperature

CHOCOLATE (BROWN) SECTION

¼ cup bittersweet chocolate (chopped or in chips)

1 tablespoon dark Dutch-process cocoa powder, preferably Hershey's Special Dark, sifted to remove lumps

¼ teaspoon instant espresso powder

ALMOND CAKE (WHITE) SECTION

¼ teaspoon pure almond extract

1. Preheat the oven to 350°F (or 325°F on the convection setting). Butter and lightly flour an 8 × 4-inch loaf pan.
2. In a bowl, whisk together the flour, baking powder, and salt. Set aside.
3. In a stand mixer fitted with the paddle (or in a bowl using a hand mixer), beat together the butter, canola oil, granulated sugar, and vanilla until light and fluffy, 3 to 4 minutes.
4. Add the eggs one at a time, beating to just combine after each addition. Scrape down the sides of the bowl after each addition.
5. On low speed, add the flour mixture to the butter/sugar mixture, mixing just until incorporated. Do not overmix!
6. Use a kitchen scale to weigh out the batter or use a large liquid measuring cup to figure out the weight or volume of the batter. Divide the batter into 3 equal portions, placing each in a separate bowl.
7. For the chocolate section: In a microwave-safe bowl, microwave the bittersweet chocolate in 30-second increments until melted. Add the melted chocolate, cocoa powder, and espresso powder into one of the bowls of batter and stir until just combined. Set aside.
8. For the almond section: Stir the almond extract into the second bowl of batter. Set aside.
9. For the pistachio section: Stir the almond extract, ground pistachios, and green food coloring into the third bowl of batter until combined.
10. Pour the batters into the prepared pan in this order: Pour the almond batter (white) in a lengthwise strip covering half of the pan. Pour the pistachio batter (green) beside the almond batter so there is now a green and white stripe of batter side by side. Pour the chocolate batter on top of everything and carefully spread it over the pistachio and almond batter covering them in a flat layer. Transfer to the oven.

PISTACHIO CAKE (GREEN) SECTION

⅛ teaspoon pure almond extract

¼ cup finely ground lightly salted roasted pistachios (grind in a food processor)

4 to 5 drops green food coloring

GLAZE

1 cup powdered sugar

¼ teaspoon vanilla bean paste or pure vanilla extract

Pinch of fine table salt

11 Bake for 45 to 50 minutes, until a toothpick inserted in the center of the cake comes out clean.

12 Let the cake cool in the pan on a rack for 10 minutes. While the cake is cooling for the first 10 minutes, make the glaze.

13 Make the glaze: In a small bowl, whisk together the powdered sugar, vanilla bean paste, salt, and 1 tablespoon water. You want the glaze smooth and pourable. If it's too thick add a few drops of water at a time until it loosens.

14 Turn the cake out of the pan onto the rack and drizzle the glaze all over the top and sides with a spoon. When the cake cools, the glaze will leave a nice sugary crust on the outside.

15 Slice when the cake is cooled and the glaze is set and expose the beautiful, colorful sections of the cake.

STORAGE: **Store in an airtight container or wrapped in parchment paper and then plastic wrap at room temperature for up to 4 days.**

pumpkin yogurt loaf

When we were kids, my mom always gave us pumpkin bread slathered with a thick layer of tangy, smooth cream cheese. Whether you make this in October or May, it is craveable year-round and the addition of Greek yogurt makes for a moist and tender crumb and rich flavor without too many added calories. I add lots of warm spices and maple syrup, which make the flavor reminiscent of pumpkin pie.

MAKES ONE 9 × 5-INCH LOAF

Cooking spray

8 tablespoons (4 ounces/1 stick) unsalted butter, at room temperature

¼ cup vegetable or canola oil

1¼ cups sugar

¼ cup pure maple syrup

2 large eggs

1½ cups canned pumpkin puree (I like Libby's)

½ cup whole-milk Greek yogurt (I prefer Fage 5%)

¾ teaspoon pure vanilla extract

2 cups all-purpose flour

1 teaspoon baking soda

½ teaspoon fine table salt

1½ teaspoons ground cinnamon

¾ teaspoon ground nutmeg

½ teaspoon ground ginger

Pinch of ground cloves

1. Preheat the oven to 350°F (or 325°F on the convection setting). Spray a 9 × 5-inch loaf pan with cooking spray and line it with a strip of parchment paper letting the paper hang over the pan at least 1 inch on the long sides. Lightly spray the paper as well once it is in the pan.
2. In a stand mixer fitted with the paddle (or in a bowl using a hand mixer), beat together the butter, vegetable oil, sugar, and maple syrup until light and fluffy, about 5 minutes.
3. Add the eggs one at a time, beating to just combine after each addition.
4. Add the pumpkin puree, Greek yogurt, and vanilla and beat well until incorporated. Scrape down the sides of the bowl and mix again to make sure it is properly mixed.
5. In a separate bowl, stir together the flour, baking soda, salt, cinnamon, nutmeg, ginger, and cloves.
6. On low speed, add the flour mixture to the pumpkin mixture in three additions. Scrape down the bowl after each addition. Mix just until everything is incorporated. Do not overmix. Pour into the prepared loaf pan and transfer to the oven.
7. Bake for 55 to 60 minutes, until a toothpick inserted in the center comes out clean.
8. Let the bread cool in the pan for about 20 minutes. Run a sharp knife around the edges and use the parchment paper to carefully lift the bread from the pan. You can enjoy this warm or at room temperature.

STORAGE: **To store it, wrap it in parchment paper and then aluminum foil tightly and leave it on the counter at room temperature or in a sealed container for up to 5 days. This bread also freezes well.**

matcha almond loaf

This loaf cake has all the flavors of your favorite morning matcha latte, including pleasantly earthy green tea and sweet almond and vanilla. The addition of the cream cheese in the batter gives this cake both moisture and structure, resulting in the perfect crumb.

MAKES ONE 8 × 4-INCH LOAF

Softened butter and flour, for the loaf pan

1 cup all-purpose flour

1½ teaspoons baking powder

¼ teaspoon fine table salt

8 tablespoons (4 ounces/1 stick) unsalted butter, at room temperature

5 ounces cream cheese (I prefer Philadelphia), at room temperature

¾ cup granulated sugar

2 large eggs, at room temperature

2½ teaspoons matcha green tea powder

½ teaspoon pure vanilla extract

¾ teaspoon pure almond extract

GLAZE

½ cup powdered sugar

2 teaspoons fresh lemon juice

⅛ teaspoon pure almond extract

Garnish: ⅓ cup sliced almonds, lightly toasted

1. Preheat the oven to 350°F (or 325°F on the convection setting). Butter and flour an 8 × 4-inch loaf pan.
2. In a bowl, whisk together the flour, baking powder, and salt. Set aside.
3. In a stand mixer fitted with the paddle, cream together the butter, cream cheese, and granulated sugar until light and fluffy, 3 to 4 minutes.
4. Add the eggs one at a time, beating to just combine after each addition. Beat in the matcha powder, vanilla, and almond extract.
5. On low speed, beat in the flour mixture, mixing just until incorporated. Do not overmix! Spread the batter in the prepared pan and transfer to the oven.
6. Bake for 40 to 55 minutes, until a toothpick inserted into the center comes out clean.
7. Let the cake cool in the pan on a rack for 10 minutes. While the cake is cooling, make the glaze.
8. Make the glaze: In a small bowl, whisk together the powdered sugar, lemon juice, and almond extract. You want the glaze smooth and pourable. If it's too thick add a few drops of water at a time until it loosens.
9. Turn the cake out of the pan onto the rack and drizzle the glaze over the top with a spoon and brush the sides of the cake with the glaze using a pastry brush. While the glaze is still wet, sprinkle the top with the toasted sliced almonds. Allow the glaze to set and then slice and enjoy!

STORAGE: **Store in an airtight container or wrapped in parchment paper and then plastic wrap at room temperature for up to 4 days.**

ACKNOWLEDGMENTS

Publishing this cookbook with Knopf is more than a dream come true; it's a full-circle moment. When I was growing up, my Grandma Rosemarie and I had a weekend tradition: We'd watch Julia Child together every Sunday while a pot of tomato sauce simmered on the stove. To now be published by the same house that brought Julia to the world feels like a sign from above. I know Grandma was smiling down on me when I signed on the dotted line.

To my wonderful editor, Lexy Bloom, and my incredible agent, Rica Allannic, thank you for believing in me and this project and for guiding it with such care, patience, and heart. To Deb Wood and Kelly Blair—thank you for designing the book I saw in my head and making it even better in real life. And to Mary Dodd—thank you for testing the recipes with such love and attention and for putting me at ease even with the ones I've made thousands of times in the bakery.

To my amazing Hungry Gnome Bakery team: Thank you for your tireless work, creativity, and belief in our mission. You "Gnomies" are my family, and I am so beyond lucky to have you by my side each day. To our incredible managers, Angelina and Nancy—thank you for always going with the flow and buying into this dream. You've adapted to my organized chaos with grace, and knowing that the business is in your capable hands gives me a peace I can't even describe. To all our wholesale partners and loyal customers—thank you for keeping our business going and growing and for showing us so much love and support along the way. I wouldn't be here if it wasn't for you.

To my incredible social media community, thank you for your constant excitement, encouragement, and love in the lead-up to this book. Your enthusiasm keeps me inspired and energized to create new recipes every single week. To my social media manager, friend, and emotional support "pet" Chris Russo, and the entire Russo Strategic Partners team—thank you for helping me build this community and for bringing my (sometimes wacky) ideas to life on-screen with such creativity, enthusiasm, and care.

To Nico Schinco, my gifted photographer; Katie Wayne, my brilliant food stylist; and Maeve Sheridan, prop styling extraordinaire—thank you for understanding my vision from the very first meeting. You made the photos not only beautiful but deeply personal, capturing the essence of who I am and what this book represents. I wish I could work with you every day; those two weeks were some of the best of my life.

To Audree Kate López, my fashion stylist—thank you for dressing me with such care and intention, and thanks for April Anguiano, my "glam girl." You both helped me feel confident, radiant, and truly myself throughout the book shoot.

To my husband, Dan—thank you for letting me take over every inch of our tiny New York City apartment in the early days of The Hungry Gnome, just so I could fill orders. Thank you for sticking by me even when I was waking you up at 3 a.m. begging you to go out and find more eggs (*during a pandemic,* no less). Thank you for allowing me to stretch your waistline while I tested all one hundred recipes, and for loving me through it all. Your support grounds me, lifts me, and keeps me going.

To my family—Dad, thank you for doing countless hours of free legal work and for always, *always* having the answers to my questions, no matter the subject. You are a walking encyclopedia of wisdom. Mom, thank you for your endless love and for letting your three daughters unload all their "stuff" onto you, emotionally, verbally, you name it. You are our rock. Christiana and Julia, thank you for your brutal honesty, your brilliant minds, and the kind of friendship only sisters can understand. Maybe it's a Long Island Italian thing, but does anyone else have a minimum of five calls a day with their family? Some say it's too much . . . but I wouldn't have it any other way.

To my beautiful friends—thank you. I am so blessed to have friendships that span more than twenty-eight years, as well as friendships that are greener but just as deep. You come from every stage of my life—from fifth-grade classrooms to sorority sisters, past workplaces to mutual best-friend matchmakings—and my cup is so full because of you all.

And to my nieces and nephew—Vivienne, Violette, and Millet, you make me so excited to teach a new generation of bakers. You keep me laughing, humble, and deeply grounded in what matters most.

Thank you all for helping me bring *The Scone Queen Bakes* to life. It's a dream baked into reality.

With love and butter,

Danielle

INDEX

(Page references in*italics* refer to illustrations.)

A

accompaniments. *See* spreads & accompaniments
almond:
- Frangipane Filling, 144
- Matcha Loaf, 240, *241*
- Peach Upside-Down Cake, *210*, 211
- Spumoni Loaf, 236-7, *237*
- Toffee Brittle, Mom's, *101*, 102, *102*

almond flour, in Breakfast Bars, 130, *131*
almond paste:
- Almond Peach Scones, 24, *25*
- Better Bakery Sprinkle Cookies, 68, *69*
- Italian Rainbow Cookies, 84-6, *85*, *87*
- Pignoli Cookies, *112*, 113

Anisette Toast, *106*, 107
apple:
- Cheesecake Biscoff Bars, *128*, 129
- Walnut Scones, *26*, 27

Applesauce Cake, Great-Grandma Lena's, 224, *225*
apricot:
- Glaze, 144
- jam, in Italian Rainbow Cookies, 84-6, *85*, *87*

B

Babka, Coco Loco, 158-61, *159*, *160*
Baci Buns, 148-50, *149*
Baklava, Chocolate, 92, *93*
banana:
- Chip Crumb Cake, 202-3, *203*
- Coco Loco Babka, 158-61, *159*, *160*
- Cream Icebox Cake, 204, *205*
- Hummingbird Muffins, *60*, 61
- Nutella Snacking Cake, 218-19, *219*

bars, 129-37
- Biscoff Apple Cheesecake, *128*, 129
- Breakfast, 130, *131*
- Lemon Icebox, *132*, 133
- Muddy Buddy, 134, *135*
- S'mores Blondies, *136*, 137
- *see also* brownies

Bastianich, Lidia, xi
BBB (Bada$$ Baking B*tch) Cookies, 88, *89*
Better Bakery Sprinkle Cookies, 68, *69*
Big Brunch, The, xix-xx, 155, 258
Birthday Confetti Scones, Danielle's, 14, *15*
Biscoff (cookie butter spread):
- Apple Cheesecake Bars, *128*, 129
- Cookie Butter Swirled Pumpkin Bread, *226*, 227
- as substitute for peanut butter, 95
- Vegan Cookie Butter Chip Cookies, *94*, 95

Biscotti, Chocolate-Dipped Pistachio Cherry, *106*, 108
Biscuits, Raisin Tea, 166-7, *167*
Blondies, S'mores, *136*, 137
blueberry:
- Crumb Muffins, *42*, 43
- White Chocolate Scones, *22*, 23

braided loaf: Mom's Snow Day Bread, 170, *170*
breads, 139-91
- Brioche with Pearl Sugar, 165
- Chocolate Chunk Brioche with Pearl Sugar, 162-5, *163*, *164*
- Cinnamon Raisin Loaf with Cinnamon Sugar Crust, 182-3, *183*
- Cinnamon Sugar Popovers with Maple Pecan Butter, 189, *190*, *191*
- Coco Loco Babka, 158-61, *159*, *160*
- Easter, Italian, 186-8
- French Toast Monkey, 174-8, *175-7*
- Irish Soda, 184, *185*
- Snow Day, Mom's, 170, *170*
- *see also* buns; quick breads; rolls

Breakfast Bars, 130, *131*
breakfast or brunch:
- Anisette Toast, *106*, 107
- Applesauce Cake, Great-Grandma Lena's, 224, *225*
- Apple Walnut Scones, *26*, 27
- Breakfast Bars, 130, *131*
- Chocolate Chip Pancake Muffins, 54-5, *55*
- Chocolate Chunk Brioche with Pearl Sugar, 162-5, *163*, *164*
- Chocolate Date Cinnamon Buns with Tahini Frosting, 140-2, *141*
- Chocolate-Dipped Pistachio Cherry Biscotti, *106*, 108
- Coco Loco Babka, 158-61, *159*, *160*
- Cranberry Orange Scones, *30*, 31
- French Toast Monkey Bread, 174-8, *175-7*
- Honey Butter, 35, *35*
- Nutella Pound Cake, 194, *195*
- PB&J Cinnamon Buns with Fluff Frosting, *154*, 155-7, *157*
- Pistachio Chocolate Chip Crumb Cake, 198-9, *199*
- Raisin Tea Biscuits, 166-7, *167*
- Spumoni Loaf, 236-7, *237*
- *see also* muffins

brioche:
- Chocolate Chunk, with Pearl Sugar, 162-5, *163*, *164*
- with Pearl Sugar, 165

Brittle, Toffee Almond, Mom's, *101*, 102, *102*
brownies, 121-7
- Condensed Milk, *124*, 125
- Galactic, 126, *127*
- Unboxed, 122, *123*

Brown Sugar Streusel, 47
brunch. *See* breakfast or brunch; muffins
Bundt cakes:
- Applesauce, Great-Grandma Lena's, 224, *225*
- Coconut Crunch, 212, *213*

buns, 139-57
- Baci, 148-50, *149*
- Cinnamon, Chocolate Date, with Tahini Frosting, 140-2, *141*
- Hot Cross, 172-3, *173*
- PB&J Cinnamon with Fluff Frosting, *154*, 155-7, *157*
- Poppyseed Danish, 151-2, *153*
- Rainbow, Italian, *143*, 143-4, *145-7*

butter:
- Cookies, Chocolate-Dipped, *101*, 103
- Glaze, Maple, 28, *29*
- Honey, 35, *35*
- Maple Pecan, 189
- Pecan Scones, 28, *29*

C

cakes. *See* crumb cakes; icebox cakes; snacking cakes
Cannoli Icebox Cake, 208, *209*
Caramel Sauce, Maple, 178
"cereal, cookie," 74
Cheesecake Bars, Biscoff Apple, *128*, 129
cherries, dried and freeze-dried:
- Breakfast Bars, 130, *131*
- Chocolate-Dipped Pistachio Cherry Biscotti, *106*, 108
- Julia Gulia Cookies, 78, *79*

Child, Julia, xx
Chinese flavors, in Red Bean Scones with a Sesame Crust, 12-13, *13*
chocolate, xxiii
- Baklava, 92, *93*
- BBB (Bada$$ Baking B*tch) Cookies, 88, *89*
- Brownies, Unboxed, 122, *123*
- Chip Banana Crumb Cake, 202-3, *203*
- chip cookies, in "cookie cereal," 74
- Chip Cookies, Lunch Box, 74, *75*
- Chip Cookies, Soft & Chewy, 64, *65*
- Chip Crumb Loaf, 232-3, *233*
- Chip Pancake Muffins, 54-5, *55*
- Chip Pistachio Crumb Cake, 198-9, *199*
- chips, in Cannoli Icebox Cake, 208, *209*
- chips, in Muddy Buddy Bars, 134, *135*
- chips, in The Dans' Cookies, *116*, 117
- chips, mini, in Breakfast Bars, 130, *131*
- chips, mini, in Chocolate Baklava, 92, *93*
- Chip Scones, THE, 32-3, *33*
- Chunk Brioche with Pearl Sugar, 162-5, *163*, *164*
- Chunk Coconut Scones, *16*, 17
- chunks, dairy-free, in Vegan Cookie Butter Chip Cookies, *94*, 95
- chunks, in S'mores Blondies, *136*, 137
- Cocoa-Swirled Coffee Cake Muffins, 48-9, *49*
- Coco Loco Babka, 158-61, *159*, *160*
- Condensed Milk Brownies, *124*, 125
- Craig's Cake (Chocolate Snacking Cake with Peanut Butter Ganache), 220, *221*
- Crinkle Cookies, Jumbo, 110, *111*
- Crumb Topping, 198, 200
- Date Cinnamon Buns with Tahini Frosting, 140-2, *141*
- Dip, 108
- -Dipped Butter Cookies, *101*, 103
- -Dipped Pistachio Cherry Biscotti, *106*, 108
- Double-, Cream Cheese Muffins, 51
- Double-, Espresso Nut Cookies, 100, *101*
- Double-, Muffins, *50*, 51
- Double-, Sheet Cake, *214*, 215-16, *217*
- Frosting, *214*, 216, *217*
- Fudge Iced Golden Cake, *222*, 223
- Galactic Brownies, 126, *127*
- Ganache, *85*, 86, *87*, *222*, 223
- Glaze, 144, *146*
- Gnommies (M&M Oatmeal Chip) Cookies, 118, *119*
- Hazelnut Filling, 148-50
- Julia Gulia Cookies, 78, *79*
- Molasses Cookies, *98*, 99
- Nutella Pound Cake, 194, *195*
- One Toff Cookies, 90-1, *91*
- Peanut Butter Pudding Cookies, *66*, 67
- Pear Strudel, Easy, 168, *169*

  - Spumoni Loaf, 236–7, *237*
  - Toffee Almond Brittle, Mom's, *101*, 102, *102*
  - Topping, 126, *127*
  - *see also* Nutella; white chocolate
- cinnamon:
  - Buns, Chocolate Date, with Tahini Frosting, 140–2, *141*
  - Buns, PB&J, with Fluff Frosting, *154*, 155–7, *157*
  - Crumb Topping, 203
  - Raisin Loaf with Cinnamon Sugar Crust, 182–3, *183*
  - & Sugar Mall Pretzels, 179–81, *180*
  - Sugar Popovers with Maple Pecan Butter, 189, *190*, *191*
- citron, candied, in Italian Fig Cookies, *80*, 81, *82–3*
- Classic Top-Heavy Deli Crumb Cake, *196*, 197
- Clotted Cream, Easy, 36, *37*
- Cocoa-Swirled Coffee Cake Muffins, 48–9, *49*
- Coco Loco Babka, 158–61, *159*, *160*
- coconut:
  - BBB (Bada$$ Baking B*tch) Cookies, 88, *89*
  - Chocolate Chunk Scones, *16*, 17
  - Coco Loco Babka, 158–61, *159*, *160*
  - Crunch Bundt Cake, 212, *213*
  - Crunch Glaze, 212, *213*
  - Hummingbird Muffins, *60*, 61
  - Snowball Icebox Cake, *206*, 207
  - sugar, in Breakfast Bars, 130, *131*
  - toasting, 16
  - Topping, *206*, 207
- Coffee Cake Muffins, Cocoa-Swirled, 48–9, *49*
- Condensed Milk Brownies, *124*, 125
- Confetti Scones, Danielle's Birthday, 14, *15*
- cookie butter spread. *See* Biscoff (cookie butter spread)
- Cookie Butter Swirled Pumpkin Bread, *226*, 227
- "cookie cereal," 74
- cookies, 62–119
  - Anisette Toast, *106*, 107
  - BBB (Bada$$ Baking B*tch), 88, *89*
  - Chocolate Baklava, 92, *93*
  - Chocolate Chip, Lunch Box, 74, *75*
  - Chocolate Chip, Soft & Chewy, 64, *65*
  - Chocolate-Dipped Butter, *101*, 103
  - Chocolate-Dipped Pistachio Cherry Biscotti, *106*, 108
  - Chocolate Molasses, *98*, 99
  - Chocolate Peanut Butter Pudding, *66*, 67
  - Cream Cheese Thumbprint, Grandma's, *70*, 72
  - & Cream Crumb Cake, 200–1, *201*
  - The Dans' Cookies, *116*, 117
  - Double-Chocolate Espresso Nut, 100, *101*
  - Fig, Italian, *80*, 81, *82–3*
  - Gingerbread, Grandma's, 104–5, *105*
  - Ginger Molasses Chews, *76*, 77
  - Gnommies (M&M Oatmeal Chip), 118, *119*
  - Julia Gulia, 78, *79*
  - Jumbo Chocolate Crinkle Cookies, 110, *111*
  - Maple Pecan Sandwich, 114–15, *115*
  - Nut Cups, Grandma's, *70*, 71
  - One Toff, 90–1, *91*
  - Pignoli, *112*, 113
  - Rainbow, Italian, 84–6, *85*, *87*
  - Sprinkle, Better Bakery, 68, *69*
  - Strawberries & Cream, 96, *97*
  - Toffee Almond Brittle, Mom's, *101*, 102, *102*
  - Vegan Cookie Butter Chip, *94*, 95
- Cookies & Cream Crumb Cake, 200–1, *201*
- Cornmeal Strawberry Scones, 20, *21*
- Corn Muffins, Honey, 58, *59*
- COVID-19 pandemic, xv, xvi
- Craig's Cake (Chocolate Snacking Cake with Peanut Butter Ganache), 220, *221*
- cranberry(ies) (dried):
  - Breakfast Bars, 130, *131*
  - Orange Scones, *30*, 31
- cream:
  - Cannoli, 208
  - Cookies &, Crumb Cake, 200–1, *201*
  - Whipped, Topping, 204, *205*
- cream cheese:
  - Biscoff Apple Cheesecake Bars, *128*, 129
  - Double-Chocolate Muffins, 51
  - dough, in Grandma's Nut Cups, *70*, 71
  - Fluff Frosting, 156, *157*
  - Frosting, 152
  - Maple Pecan Creme Filling, 115
  - Thumbprint Cookies, Grandma's, *70*, 72
- Crinkle Cookies, Jumbo Chocolate, 110, *111*
- crumb cakes:
  - Banana Chip Crumb, 202–3, *203*
  - Classic Top-Heavy Deli, *196*, 197
  - Cookies & Cream, 200–1, *201*
  - Pistachio Chocolate Chip, 198–9, *199*
- Crumb Loaf, Chocolate Chip, 232–3, *233*
- Crumb Muffins, Blueberry, *42*, 43
- Crumb Topping, 57, 197, 232
  - Chocolate, 198
  - Cinnamon, 203
- crusts:
  - Biscoff cookie crumb, *128*, 129
  - graham cracker, *132*, 133
- Curd, Lemon, 36, *37*
- Currant Scones (variation), 8, *8*, 9, *10–11*

D

- Dad's Date Nut Bread, 228, *229*
- dairy-free baking:
  - Breakfast Bars, 130, *131*
  - Vegan Cookie Butter Chip Cookies, *94*, 95
- Danielle's Birthday Confetti Scones, 14, *15*
- Danish Buns, Poppyseed, 151–2, *153*
- The Dans' Cookies, *116*, 117
- date:
  - Chocolate Cinnamon Buns with Tahini Frosting, 140–2, *141*
  - Nut Bread, Dad's, 228, *229*
- Dip, Chocolate, 108
- double-chocolate:
  - Cream Cheese Muffins, 51
  - Espresso Nut Cookies, 100, *101*
  - Muffins, *50*, 51
  - Sheet Cake, *214*, 215–16, *217*
- *Drew Barrymore Show, The,* 78
- dunking, cookies good for:
  - Anisette Toast, *106*, 107
  - Chocolate-Dipped Pistachio Cherry Biscotti, *106*, 108
  - Lunch Box Chocolate Chip Cookies, 74, *75*

E

- Easter Breads, Italian, 186–8
- Easy Chocolate Pear Strudel, 168, *169*
- egg(s):
  - flaxseed meal and water as substitute for, 95
  - hard-boiled and dyed, in Italian Easter Breads, 186–8
  - Wash, 20
- elderflower syrup, in Madeleine Loaf, *234*, 235
- El-Waylly, Sohla, xix, 155
- Entenmann's, 232
- Epiphany, Baci Buns and, 148–50, *149*
- Esposito, Mary Ann, xi
- Espresso Double-Chocolate Nut Cookies, 100, *101*
- extracts (pantry), xxiii

F

- fats & oils (pantry), xxiii
- Fig Cookies, Italian, *80*, 81, *82–3*
- fillings:
  - Almond Frangipane, 144
  - Chocolate Hazelnut, 148–50
  - Maple Pecan Creme, 115
  - Poppyseed, 151
- flaxseed meal:
  - Vegan Cookie Butter Chip Cookies, *94*, 95
  - water and, as egg substitute, 95
- flaxseeds, in Breakfast Bars, 130, *131*
- flours & powders (pantry), xxii
- Fluff. *See* Marshmallow Fluff
- Frangipane Filling, Almond, 144
- French toast:
  - Cinnamon Raisin Loaf with Cinnamon Sugar Crust good for, 182–3, *183*
  - Monkey Bread, 174–8, *175–7*
- frostings:
  - Chocolate, *214*, 216, *217*
  - Chocolate Ganache, *85*, 86, *87*, *222*, 223
  - Cream Cheese, 152
  - Fluff, 156, *157*
  - Hazelnut Topping, 150
  - Nutella, 219, *219*
  - Peanut Butter Ganache, 220, *221*
  - Tahini, *141*, 142
- Fudge Iced Golden Cake, *222*, 223

G

- Galactic Brownies, 126, *127*
- ganache:
  - Chocolate, *85*, 86, *87*, *222*, 223
  - Peanut Butter, 220, *221*
- gingerbread:
  - Cookies, Grandma's, 104–5, *105*
  - Muffins, 52, *53*
- Ginger Molasses Chews, *76*, 77
- glazes:
  - Apricot, 144
  - Chocolate, 144, *146*
  - Coconut Crunch, 212, *213*
  - Confetti, 14, *15*
  - Lemon, 19
  - Maple, 55
  - Maple Butter, 28, *29*
  - Strawberry Jam, 20, *21*
  - Vanilla, 45, 52, 56, *76*, 77, 166–7
  - Vanilla Bean, 9, *9*
- gluten-free baking: Breakfast Bars, 130, *131*
- Gnommies (M&M Oatmeal Chip) Cookies, 118, *119*
- Golden Cake, Fudge Iced, *222*, 223
- graham cracker(s):
  - Cannoli Icebox Cake, 208, *209*
  - Crust, *132*, 133
  - S'mores Blondies, *136*, 137
- Grandma's Cream Cheese Thumbprint Cookies, *70*, 72
- Grandma's Gingerbread Cookies, 104–5, *105*
- Grandma's Nut Cups, *70*, 71
- Great-Grandma Lena's Applesauce Cake, 224, *225*
- Greek flavors, in Chocolate Baklava, 92, *93*
- Guidara, Will, xix

H

hazelnut:
- Chocolate Filling, 148–50
- Topping, 150
- *see also* Nutella

honey:
- Butter, 35, *35*
- Corn Muffins, 58, *59*

Hot Cross Buns, 172–3, *173*
Hummingbird Muffins, *60*, 61
Hungry Gnome, origins of, xv–xx

I

Icebox Bars, Lemon, *132*, 133
icebox cakes:
- Banana Cream, 204, *205*
- Cannoli, 208, *209*
- Snowball, *206*, 207

Icing, Royal, 105, *105*
Irish Soda Bread, 184, *185*
Italian (flavors):
- Anisette Toast, *106*, 107
- Baci Buns, 148–50, *149*
- Chocolate-Dipped Pistachio Cherry Biscotti, *106*, 108
- Easter Breads, 186–8
- Fig Cookies, *80*, 81, *82–3*
- Pignoli Cookies, *112*, 113
- Rainbow Buns, *143*, 143–4, *145–7*
- Rainbow Cookies, 84–6, *85*, *87*
- Spumoni Loaf, 236–7, *237*

J

jam:
- apricot and raspberry, in Italian Rainbow Cookies, 84–6, *85*, *87*
- Grandma's Cream Cheese Thumbprint Cookies, *70*, 72
- Raspberry Rose, 36, *37*

jelly, in PB&J Cinnamon Buns with Fluff Frosting, *154*, 155–7, *157*
Joe Coffee, xv–xvi
Julia Gulia Cookies, 78, *79*
Jumbo Chocolate Crinkle Cookies, 110, *111*

L

L&B Spumoni Gardens, Brooklyn, 236
Lavender Lemon Scones, 18–19
Lebanese flavors: Chocolate Date Cinnamon Buns with Tahini Frosting, 140–2, *141*
lemon:
- Curd, 36, *37*
- Honey Butter, 35
- Icebox Bars, *132*, 133
- Lavender Scones, 18–19
- Poppyseed Muffins, 56, *57*

Levy, Dan, xix, 155
Lunch Box Chocolate Chip Cookies, 74, *75*

M

Madeleine Loaf, *234*, 235
M&M's, in Gnommies (M&M Oatmeal Chip) Cookies, 118, *119*
maple (syrup):
- Butter Glaze, 28, *29*
- Caramel Sauce, 178
- Glaze, 55
- Pecan Butter, 189
- Pecan Creme Filling, 115
- Pecan Sandwich Cookies, 114–15, *115*
- S'mores Blondies, *136*, 137

marshmallow(s):
- cutting into pieces, *136*, 137
- Muddy Buddy Bars, 134, *135*
- pieces, in S'mores Blondies, *136*, 137

Marshmallow Fluff:
- Coconut Topping, *206*, 207
- Frosting, 156, *157*
- Homemade, 157
- uses for, 157

mascarpone, in Cannoli Icebox Cake, 208, *209*
Massih, Edy, 140
Matcha Almond Loaf, 240, *241*
Maureen's Kitchen, Smithtown, NY, 198–9
mix-ins (pantry), xxiii
molasses:
- Chocolate Cookies, *98*, 99
- Ginger, Chews, *76*, 77

Mom's Snow Day Bread, 170, *170*
Mom's Toffee Almond Brittle, *101*, 102, *102*
Monkey Bread, French Toast, 174–8, *175–7*
Muddy Buddy Bars, 134, *135*
muffins, 41–61
- Blueberry Crumb, *42*, 43
- Chocolate Chip Pancake, 54–5, *55*
- Cocoa-Swirled Coffee Cake, 48–9, *49*
- Double-Chocolate, *50*, 51
- Double-Chocolate Cream Cheese, 51
- Gingerbread, 52, *53*
- Honey Corn, 58, *59*
- Hummingbird, *60*, 61
- Lemon Poppyseed, 56, *57*
- Pumpkin Spice, 44–5, *45*
- Raspberry Ricotta, *46*, 47

N

nut(s):
- Cups, Grandma's, *70*, 71
- Date Bread, Dad's, 228, *229*
- Double-Chocolate Espresso Cookies, 100, *101*
- *see also* almond; hazelnut; peanut butter; pecan(s); pistachio(s); walnut(s)

Nutella:
- Banana Snacking Cake, 218–19, *219*
- Frosting, 219, *219*
- Pound Cake, 194, *195*

O

oat(meal)(s):
- Breakfast Bars, 130, *131*
- Gnommies (M&M Oatmeal Chip) Cookies, 118, *119*

oils & fats (pantry), xxiii
One Toff Cookies, 90–1, *91*
orange:
- candied, in Italian Fig Cookies, *80*, 81, *82–3*
- Cranberry Scones, *30*, 31
- Honey Butter, 35
- Hot Cross Buns, 172–3, *173*

Oreo thins, in Snowball Icebox Cake, *206*, 207

P

Pancake Muffins, Chocolate Chip, 54–5, *55*
pantry, xxii–xxiii
- chocolate & mix-ins, xxiii
- extracts & spices, xxiii
- flours & powders, xxii
- oils & fats, xxiii
- refrigerated ingredients, xxiii
- spreads & preserves, xxiii
- sugars & sweeteners, xxii

pastry, puff, in Chocolate Pear Strudel, Easy, 168, *169*
PB&J Cinnamon Buns with Fluff Frosting, *154*, 155–7, *157*
peach:
- Almond Scones, 24, *25*
- Almond Upside-Down Cake, *210*, 211

peanut butter:
- Biscoff spread or vegan cookie butter as substitute for, 95
- Chocolate Pudding Cookies, *66*, 67
- The Dans' Cookies, *116*, 117
- Ganache, 220, *221*
- Muddy Buddy Bars, 134, *135*
- PB&J Cinnamon Buns with Fluff Frosting, *154*, 155–7, *157*

Pear Chocolate Strudel, Easy, 168, *169*
pearl sugar:
- Brioche with, 165
- Chocolate Chunk Brioche with, 162–5, *163*, *164*

pecan(s):
- Butter, Scones, 28, *29*
- Double-Chocolate Espresso Nut Cookies, 100, *101*
- Hummingbird Muffins, *60*, 61
- Italian Fig Cookies, *80*, 81, *82–3*
- Maple, Butter, 189
- Maple Creme Filling, 115
- Maple Sandwich Cookies, 114–15, *115*
- Nut Cups, Grandma's, *70*, 71

phyllo dough, in Chocolate Baklava, 92, *93*
Pignoli Cookies, *112*, 113
pineapple, in Hummingbird Muffins, *60*, 61
pine nuts, in Pignoli Cookies, *112*, 113
pistachio(s):
- Cherry Biscotti, Chocolate-Dipped, *106*, 108
- Chocolate Baklava, 92, *93*
- Chocolate Chip Crumb Cake, 198–9, *199*
- Spumoni Loaf, 236–7, *237*

Popovers, Cinnamon Sugar, with Maple Pecan Butter, 189, *190*, *191*
poppyseed:
- Danish Buns, 151–2, *153*
- Lemon Muffins, 56, *57*

potato chips, in BBB (Bada$$ Baking B*tch) Cookies, 88, *89*
Pound Cake, Nutella, 194, *195*
powders & flours (pantry), xxii
preserves (pantry), xxiii
pretzels:
- Cinnamon & Sugar Mall, 179–81, *180*
- The Dans' Cookies, *116*, 117
- salty/savory coatings for, 181

pudding mix, for soft, chewy cookies, 64, 67
puff pastry, in Chocolate Pear Strudel, Easy, 168, *169*
pumpkin:
- Bread, Cookie Butter Swirled, *226*, 227
- seeds, in Breakfast Bars, 130, *131*
- Spice Muffins, 44–5, *45*
- Yogurt Loaf, *238*, 239

Puppy Scones, *38*, 39

Q

quick breads, 227–41
- Chocolate Chip Crumb Loaf, 232–3, *233*
- Cookie Butter Swirled Pumpkin, *226*, 227
- Date Nut, Dad's, 228, *229*
- Madeleine Loaf, *234*, 235
- Matcha Almond Loaf, 240, *241*
- Pumpkin Yogurt Loaf, *238*, 239
- Spumoni Loaf, 236–7, *237*
- Zucchini, 230, *231*

R

Rainbow Buns, Italian, *143*, 143–4, *145–7*
raisin:
  Cinnamon Loaf with Cinnamon Sugar Crust, 182–3, *183*
  Tea Biscuits, 166–7, *167*
raspberry:
  jam, in Italian Rainbow Cookies, 84–6, *85*, *87*
  Ricotta Muffins, *46*, 47
  Rose Jam, 36, *37*
Red Bean Scones with a Sesame Crust, 12–13, *13*
refrigerated pantry staples, xxiii
Rice Chex cereal, in Muddy Buddy Bars, 134, *135*
ricotta:
  Cannoli Icebox Cake, 208, *209*
  Raspberry Muffins, *46*, 47
Rose Raspberry Jam, 36, *37*
Royal Icing, 105, *105*
Rubinstein, Jonathan, xv

S

Sandwich Cookies, Maple Pecan, 114–15, *115*
Scone Calendar, 6, *7*
scones, 1–39
  Apple Walnut, *26*, 27
  bake temperatures for, 4
  Blueberry White Chocolate, *22*, 23
  Butter Pecan, 28, *29*
  THE Chocolate Chip, 32–3, *33*
  Coconut Chocolate Chunk, *16*, 17
  Confetti, Danielle's Birthday, 14, *15*
  Cranberry Orange, *30*, 31
  Currant (variation), 8, *8*, 9, *10–11*
  5 tips to mastering the art of, 3
  Lavender Lemon, 18–19
  Peach Almond, 24, *25*
  prepping in advance, 4
  Puppy, *38*, 39
  Red Bean, with a Sesame Crust, 12–13, *13*
  spreads & accompaniments for, 34–6
  storing and reheating, 4
  Strawberry Cornmeal, 20, *21*
  tea biscuits compared to, 166
  Vanilla Bean, Classic, 8–9, *9*
Sesame Crust, Red Bean Scones with, 12–13, *13*
Sheet Cake, Double-Chocolate, *214*, 215–16, *217*
Sicilian (flavors):
  Anisette Toast, *106*, 107
  Cannoli Icebox Cake, 208, *209*
  Italian Easter Breads, 186–8
  Italian Fig Cookies, *80*, 81, *82–3*
S'mores Blondies, *136*, 137
snacking cakes, 192–225
  Applesauce, Great-Grandma Lena's, 224, *225*
  Banana Chip Crumb, 202–3, *203*
  Banana Cream Icebox, 204, *205*
  Banana Nutella, 218–19, *219*
  Cannoli Icebox, 208, *209*
  Coconut Crunch Bundt, 212, *213*
  Cookies & Cream Crumb, 200–1, *201*
  Craig's (Chocolate Snacking Cake with Peanut Butter Ganache), 220, *221*
  Crumb, Classic Top-Heavy Deli, *196*, 197
  Double-Chocolate Sheet, *214*, 215–16, *217*
  Fudge Iced Golden, *222*, 223
  Nutella Pound, 194, *195*
  Peach Almond Upside-Down, *210*, 211
  Pistachio Chocolate Chip Crumb, 198–9, *199*
  Snowball Icebox, *206*, 207
Snowball Icebox Cake, *206*, 207
Snow Day Bread, Mom's, 170, *170*
Soda Bread, Irish, 184, *185*
Soft & Chewy Chocolate Chip Cookies, 64, *65*
Speculoos spread. *See* Biscoff (cookie butter spread)
spice(d)(s), xxiii
  Date Nut Bread, Dad's, 228, *229*
  Gingerbread Cookies, Grandma's, 104–5, *105*
  Gingerbread Muffins, 52, *53*
  Ginger Molasses Chews, *76*, 77
  Italian Fig Cookies, *80*, 81, *82–3*
  Maple Pecan Sandwich Cookies, 114–15, *115*
  Pumpkin Muffins, 44–5, *45*
  Zucchini Bread, 230, *231*
spreads (pantry), xxiii
spreads & accompaniments, 34–6
  Clotted Cream, Easy, 36, *37*
  Honey Butter, 35, *35*
  Lemon Curd, 36, *37*
  Raspberry Rose Jam, 36, *37*
sprinkle(s):
  Birthday Confetti Scones, Danielle's, 14, *15*
  Cookies, Better Bakery, 68, *69*
Spumoni Loaf, 236–7, *237*
Stewart, Martha, xi, xii
strawberry(ies):
  Cornmeal Scones, 20, *21*
  & Cream Cookies, 96, *97*
  freeze-dried, grinding into powder, 96
Streusel Topping, 48–9, *49*
  Brown Sugar, 47
Strudel, Chocolate Pear, Easy, 168, *169*
sugar(s), xxii
  Cinnamon &, Mall Pretzels, 179–81, *180*
  Pearl, Chocolate Chunk Brioche with, 162–5, *163*, *164*
sunflower seeds, in Breakfast Bars, 130, *131*
sweeteners (pantry), xxii
Syrup, Vanilla Bean-Infused Honey, 92, *93*

T

Tahini Frosting, *141*, 142
Tea Biscuits, Raisin, 166–7, *167*
Thumbprint Cookies, Cream Cheese, Grandma's, *70*, 72
toffee:
  Almond Brittle, Mom's, *101*, 102, *102*
  bits, in BBB (Bada$$ Baking B*tch) Cookies, 88, *89*
  bits, in One Toff Cookies, 90–1, *91*
  Chunks, Homemade, 91
toppings:
  Brown Sugar Streusel, 47
  Chocolate, 126, *127*
  Chocolate Crumb, 198
  Cinnamon Crumb, 203
  Coconut, *206*, 207
  Crumb, 57, 197
  Crumbs, 45
  Whipped Cream, 204, *205*
  see also glazes

U

Unboxed Brownies, 122, *123*
Upside-Down Cake, Peach Almond, *210*, 211

V

vanilla bean:
  Glaze, 9, *9*
  Scones, Classic, 8–9, *9*
vanilla bean paste, 9
vanilla extract, 9
Vanilla Glaze, *76*, 77, 166–7
vegan baking:
  Cookie Butter Chip Cookies, *94*, 95
  flaxseed meal and water as egg substitute in, 95

W

walnut(s):
  Apple Scones, *26*, 27
  Breakfast Bars, 130, *131*
  Chocolate Baklava, 92, *93*
  Date Nut Bread, Dad's, 228, *229*
  Double-Chocolate Espresso Nut Cookies, 100, *101*
  Grandma's Cream Cheese Thumbprint Cookies, *70*, 72
  grinding into meal, 72
  Italian Fig Cookies, *80*, 81, *82–3*
Whipped Cream Topping, 204, *205*
white chocolate:
  BBB (Bada$$ Baking B*tch) Cookies, 88, *89*
  Blueberry Scones, *22*, 23
  Cookies & Cream Crumb Cake, 200–1, *201*
  Julia Gulia Cookies, 78, *79*
  One Toff Cookies, 90–1, *91*
  Strawberries & Cream Cookies, 96, *97*

Y

yeast, xxiii
yeasted breads:
  Baci Buns, 148–50, *149*
  Chocolate Chunk Brioche with Pearl Sugar, 162–5, *163*, *164*
  Chocolate Date Cinnamon Buns with Tahini Frosting, 140–2, *141*
  Cinnamon Raisin Loaf with Cinnamon Sugar Crust, 182–3, *183*
  Coco Loco Babka, 158–61, *159*, *160*
  French Toast Monkey Bread, 174–8, *175–7*
  Italian Easter Breads, 186–8
  Italian Rainbow Buns, *143*, 143–4, *145–7*
  Mom's Snow Day Bread, 170, *170*
  PB&J Cinnamon Buns with Fluff Frosting, *154*, 155–7, *157*
  Poppyseed Danish Buns, 151–2, *153*
Yogurt Pumpkin Loaf, *238*, 239

Z

Zucchini Bread, 230, *231*